Critical Muslim 8
Men in Islam

Critical Muslim is published quarterly by C. Hurst & Co (Publishers) Ltd on behalf of and in conjunction with Critical Muslim Ltd and the Muslim Institute, London.

All correspondence to Muslim Institute, CAN Mezzanine, 49–51 East Road, London N1 6AH, United Kingdom
e-mail for editorial: editorial@criticalmuslim.com

C. Hurst & Co (Publishers) Ltd.,
41 Great Russell Street, London WC1B 3PL

Printed in Great Britain by TJ International Ltd, Padstow, Cornwall

ISBN: 978-1-84904-317-5
ISSN: 2048-8475

To subscribe or place an order by credit/debit card or cheque (pounds sterling only) please contact Kathleen May at the Hurst address above or email kathleen@hurstpub.co.uk Tel: 020 7255 2201

A one year subscription, inclusive of postage (four issues), costs £50 (UK), £65 (Europe) and £75 (rest of the world).

The British
Museum

Discover
the Islamic
World

From early scientific
instruments to
contemporary art,
explore how Islam
has shaped our
world through objects
for centuries

Great Russell Street,
London WC1B 3DG
⊖ Tottenham Court Road,
Holborn, Russell Square
britishmuseum.org

Mosque lamp. Enamelled glass.
Syria, c. AD 1330–1345.

Wider Concerns of Halal

You think you know what is *halal*?

It's not just about '*halal* meat' and '*halal* food'.

In fact, *halal* is one of the most sophisticated concepts of Islam. It is best translated as 'praiseworthy' and has a direct relationship to public interest, environment, business ethics and moral behaviour. During the 'Golden Age of Islam', the concept of *halal* was used to generate policy and legislation for city planning, protection of flora and fauna, trade and commerce and was a driving force behind social and cultural productions of Muslim civilisation.

We aim to advance a more holistic understanding of what is *halal* and what it means to lead an ethical, socially responsible life in the twenty-first century.

Look out for our workshops, seminars and school visits.

Halal Food Foundation is a charitable arm of Halal Food Authority.

Halal Food Foundation
109 Fulham Palace Road, London W6 8JA, UK
Registered Charity Number: 1139457
Website: www.halalfoodauthority.com
E-mail: info@halalfoodauthority.com

CM8

October–December 2013

CONTENTS

A miniature by the Pakistan artist, Imran Qureshi; from *Moderate Enlightenment* 2006-9, exhibited at the Venice Biennale 2013

Subscribe to Critical Muslim

Now in its second year, *Critical Muslim* is the only publication of its kind, giving voice to the diversity and plurality of Muslim reporting, creative writing, poetry and scholarship.

Subscribe now to receive each issue of Critical Muslim direct to your door and save money on the cover price of each issue.

Subscriptions are available at the following prices, inclusive of postage. Subscribe for two years and save 10%!

	ONE YEAR (4 Issues)	TWO YEARS (8 Issues)
UK	£50	£90
Europe	£65	£117
Rest of World	£75	£135

TO SUBSCRIBE:

CRITICALMUSLIM.HURSTPUBLISHERS.COM

41 GREAT RUSSELL ST, LONDON WC1B 3PL
WWW.HURSTPUBLISHERS.COM
WWW.FBOOK.COM/HURSTPUBLISHERS
020 7255 2201

MEN IN ISLAM

THE SHADOWS OF MUSLIM MEN

Ziauddin Sardar

A confession. In case you did not know I am a man. A generic, universal entity about which the seventeenth century French aristocrat Madame de Sevigne knew a thing or two. 'The more I see of men', she declared, 'the more I admire dogs'. Knowing myself as well as I do, I appreciate her preference.

My gender has moulded the world in its own image. Everything from politics to finance, law to science, art and architecture, sports and entertainment are shaped, structured and led by men – and contain the fingerprints of masculinity. History is almost exclusively made by men; and it is always His story. Men hold a virtual monopoly in the corridors of power: whether in political institutions or banks, the judiciary or the media, universities or research laboratories, businesses or corporate organisations – anywhere where policies are made, decisions are announced, and all life on Earth is regulated. Not surprisingly, statistically men also perpetuate more crime than women, conventional as well as white-collar, from murders and killings, to football hooliganism, to nasty and greedy bankers ripping off the rest of society. The favourite pastime of men is, of course, war, perpetuated in the name of religion and ideologies but always focused on power and territory. And war imagery is integral to the sports that real men — that is 'men with added man', as an advertisement for chocolate milk playfully suggests — play: rugby, boxing, ice hockey and American football, which function as endlessly renewed symbols of war and masculinity. 'Machismo' is the foundation of most national narratives. Violence and men go together; and a great deal of violence, in this truncated half-human world that men have fashioned, is directed against women.

Worse: I am a Muslim man. So it can be taken for granted that I am a power hungry, frustrated misogynist, the archetype and ideal contemporary representative of what sociologists and geographers call 'hegemonic masculinity'. Everything that Muslim men have produced, from scriptural interpretations to Shari'a Law to even our mysticism, is designed to keep women subjugated and isolated in a confined space. And our historic gift, patriarchy, ensures that things remain as they should. Even those who do not consciously enact their God-given right to hegemony (such as more liberal minded Muslims and enlightened scholars) receive the benefits of patriarchy.

From the women's perspective, the history of Islam is not unlike the story of Dave, the protagonist of Stephen Collins' wonderful graphic novel, *The Gigantic Beard That Was Evil*. Dave lives in a rather clean and sensible land, where not everything makes sense but people struggle to discover the meaning of life, called the island of Here. Then one day, he wakes up to feel a 'roaring black fire climbing up through his face' as his beard appears from nowhere. It is an extraordinary beard from a place far, far beyond the tidy and reasonably rational abode of Dave. And it grips Dave in a suffocating embrace. A bit like how Shari'a Law, based on the misogynist interpretation of the Qur'an and the life of Prophet Muhammad, is suddenly canonised in the ninth century and acquires a stranglehold on the Muslim imagination. Dave trims his beard all night, hoping to bring it down to manageable proportion, but at sunrise it is back to its mammoth and monolithic self. Soon it spreads everywhere and becomes a petrifying spectacle. The hairdressers of Here, working on scaffolding around the beard, are defeated. The police and the army try to contain it but to no avail. Soon the beard takes over the whole of the island Here. Other citizens start to experiment with their own beards, hairstyles and clothes. And an island that was once a neat and tidy place comes to resemble a bearded jungle. It becomes obvious that the gigantic, evil beard will kill its host. Like Dave's beard, the hegemonic masculinity of Muslim thought, exegesis, law, history, and piety is threatening to turn Islam into a wasteland.

To appreciate what Muslim men are up to consider the events of a single day: Saturday 6 July 2013. Apart from the front page story, 'Death toll grows as Egyptian factions fight in street', my copy of *The Guardian* brought other important news. In Cairo's Tahrir Square, where the anti-President Morsi protestors were gathered, there were 169 cases of assaults on women within a week: 'we are talking about mob sexual assaults, from stripping women naked and dragging them on the floor – to rape', explained a women's right advocate. 'In a typical attack, lines of men push their way through the square, surround alone women, and start ripping at their clothes until they are naked', reports *The Guardian*. Some women were violated by men using their hands, others with sharp objects. The place where men were gathered to fight for 'freedom' is described by women as 'the circle of hell'. One woman writes of her experience: 'suddenly, I was in the middle, surrounded by hundreds of men in a circle that was getting smaller and smaller around me. At the same time, they were touching and groping me everywhere and there were so many hands under my shirt and inside my pants'. A few pages on we read the story of an Iranian woman, Elham Asghari, who, on a chilly winter's morning, swam the Caspian sea in a ground-breaking nine hour feat. Surely an achievement to be celebrated! But even though she was covered from head to toe in 'full Islamic dress code', the authorities refused to recognise her record because, 'the feminine features of my body were showing as I came out of the water'. And she lamented: 'my record has been held hostage in the hands of people who cannot swim 20 metres'. Underneath this story, we have another one from Saudi Arabia, surely the most Islamic place in this best of all possible worlds. Under the heading 'Saudi women activists fight jail threat', *The Guardian* reports that two women are facing ten months in prison 'for delivering a food parcel to a woman who told them she was imprisoned in her house with her children and unable to get food'. While I was reading through these stories, another story popped up around lunchtime: Boko Haram, a Nigerian brand of Islamists, had killed twenty-nine pupils and a teacher in a pre-dawn attack on a school in Mamudo town, Yobe state. The bearded and pious men of Boko Haram arrived with containers full of fuel and set fire to the school. Some children were burned alive, others were shot as they tried to flee.

Let's beat around the bush a little. There are Muslim men who would argue that this is yet another example of the bias of the western media, which is hell-bent on demonising Islam and Muslims. Some other Muslim men would suggest that these are extreme examples, only fanatics and such sorts engage in these types of nefarious activities. Still others would point out, and rightly so, that not all Muslim men are like this. But I am not of these men. For me this is clear evidence of a culture gone pathological. Being an infinitesimally small part of the 'western media' myself – and I suspect just as biased – and reading these stories day after day, and having travelled extensively around the Muslim world, I am forced to conclude that the lunatics have taken over the asylum. And as a fully paid up member of the asylum I am obliged to put up my hand and declare: it is all my fault.

Lest you think I am being brave and original, I should add that I am simply following the example of a woman. The woman in question appears in Merryl Wyn Davies' discussion on 'The Problem of Men'. Some years ago, Davies addressed a meeting on 'women in Islam', a topic upon which she is often called to pontificate. 'My presentation', she writes, 'attempted to get beyond the standard repertoire of the status, role and rights of women as idealised from Islamic sources and focus on what those ideals might mean and imply for living today in a globalised world, not Mecca in the seventh century or somewhere else long ago and far away in some imaginary Muslim society. A lively discussion ensued during which one lady who had been thoughtfully quiet for some time interjected. "It's my fault I think", she said. This seemed a rather large claim and onerous responsibility to take on. She went on to explain that she had raised sons and daughters and it was clear to her she had encouraged and enabled different standards for the boys as opposed to the girls. If there is a problem with Muslim men, and she was quite clear there was, then how she raised her sons, the kind of behaviour, expectations and attitudes she inculcated, permitted and tolerated were part and parcel of the problem. It was a brave statement to make, one that contains much truth to reason with. Mutual expectations are not conjured from thin air. How we interpret and apply our moral vision of society is what we can expect to see replicated.'

But what if 'our moral vision' itself is perverted? It is not just that the Qur'an has been largely interpreted by men. Nor that the Shari'a, which serves as both morality and law, has been socially constructed in history by men. Rather, many of the doctrines, institutions, and cultures of Islam are intrinsically masculine. Or to put it another way: the ideology of hegemonic masculinity has been the guiding principle of Islam in history and contemporary times. It is embedded in the thoughts, actions and practices of Muslims; and permits and continues Muslim men's domination over Muslim women.

The problem starts not with men, but with God Himself, the deity invoked every moment of the day by every pious Muslim. It seems to me that Muslims have turned their God into a tribal leader – more specifically, a leader of the Quraysh, the tribe of the Prophet Muhammad. The Quraysh already have a mythical status in Islamic folklore. The Prophet, it is claimed, declared that 'the leaders are from the Quraysh. The righteous among them are the leaders of the righteous, and the wicked among them are the leaders of the wicked'. So, if we accept this hadith as authentic, then Muslims are lumbered with the Quraysh for all eternity. A rather improbable task given that there are not enough of them to go around the globe. Since the Quraysh personify the best qualities of leadership, it is not surprising that the Ultimate Leader, the Creator of the Universe itself, is portrayed as though he was from the Quraysh. 'This is a deity', writes Abdennur Prado, 'who judges, who is severe in punishment', a vengeful, autocratic God who rules by fear and is without any attributes 'except those that service goals of brute power'.

Given that fear, vengeance, and brute power are seen as the prime attributes of God, it is not surprising that they have become the dominant themes of Muslim societies. Without fear, Yusuf al-Qaradawi — seen by many as one of the most influential Sunni clerics in the Middle East — told his television audience: 'if they had gotten rid of the punishment for apostasy, Islam would not exist today'. There is no moral qualm here; indeed, there is no notion of morality at all. To kill apostates is the most natural thing to do. It is after all part of God's design and law. Al-Qaradawi's sentiments would be echoed by conservative Muslim scholars from Saudi Arabia to Iran, Pakistan to Indonesia. And it is the same fear that is used to keep women in their prescribed positions.

Of course, God has no gender; and His attributes reflect both masculine and feminine characteristics. As Prado notes, Muslim scholars have divided the Names of God into two categories: Names of Majesty, which reflect the masculine attributes; and Names of Beauty, which reflect the feminine attributes. Patriarchy has been entrenched, suggests Prado, by giving prominence to the masculine over the feminine attributes of God. And it has been further enhanced by the masculinisation of both the biography (*Sira*) and the examples (*Sunnah*) of the Prophet Muhammad. 'The Prophet is presented as a political and patriarchal leader', with 'emphasis on military elements, conquests, and dominion'. The *ulama*, or the religious scholars, the historical counterparts of Al-Qaradawi such as al-Tabari (838-923) and ibn Kathir (1301-1373) and his contemporary colleagues, systematically read the Qur'an in patriarchal ways to establish 'the primacy of the normative over the ethical, the judicial above the spiritual'.

One particular tactic in masculine readings of the Qur'an involved imposing Biblical mythology on the Sacred Text. As Saleck Mohamed Val shows,
male interpreters have systematically shrouded the Qur'anic text with Jewish and Christian traditions, known in Islamic terminology as *Israiliyyat*. So,
for al-Tabari, Eve was to blame for the fall of Adam from Paradise; and for
ibn Kathir, Eve was from Adam's 'left rib while he was asleep'. Of course,
this alien imposition requires some local justification. So a host of truly
misogynist manufactured hadith are cited to support this position, such as:
'the woman was created from man, so that her desire would always be to
him, while man was created from earth so that his desire would always be
to it; you have then to incarcerate your women'. The end product is a doctrine that makes women innately inferior.

To ensure that the container of confinement is properly sealed, an entire
body of law was developed to regulate and manage women. It was constructed almost as a confidence trick on behalf of men. In her contribution,
'Out of This Dead-End', Ziba Mir Hosseini provides a good example from
the fourteenth century jurist Ibn Qayyim Jawziyya. While acknowledging
that the Shari'a 'embraces Justice, Kindness, the Common Good and Wisdom', he nevertheless suggests that 'the wife is her husband's prisoner, a
prisoner being akin to a slave. The Prophet directed men to support their
wives by feeding them with their own food and clothing them with their
own clothes; he said the same about maintaining a slave'. There is no connection between the premise and the conclusion; it seems the Shari'a is only
kind and just to men.

In some cases, the jurists and the *ulama* resort to even more questionable
tactics. Take the case of the prominent Syrian scholar Sheikh Wahba az-
Zuhaili, who has written over a dozen books on Islamic jurisprudence and
legal philosophy. The good Sheikh cites the following hadith: 'Ibn Umar
said: I saw a woman who came to the Prophet and said: "O Messenger of
Allah, what is a wife's obligation towards her husband?" Muhammad said:
"Her obligation is that she does not go out of her house except by permission, and if she does, God, the Angels of Mercy, and the Angel of Anger will
curse her until she repents or until she comes back". She said: "And if he
oppresses her?" Muhammad said: "Even if he oppresses her". On the basis of
this hadith, which provides a perfect justification for both misogyny and
oppression, the 'Dr Prof' declares that 'the woman is not to go out of her

house even to perform the Hajj, except with the permission of her husband. And he (the husband) has the right to prevent her from going to the mosque and other places'. But there is no such hadith, or anything resembling it, in the six authentic collections, as Anne Sofie Roald, the Swedish Muslim feminist scholar, discovered after a long search. Az-Zuhaili also cites another hadith: 'Verily the woman is *awra* (here: deficient). If she goes out, Satan will raise a glance at her. She will be closest to her Lord's mercy inside the house'. Roald discovered that classical Muslim scholars did not accept this as an authentic hadith, as it has only one narrator and the chain of narrators is missing. Moreover, even in its original rejected form the hadith only contains the first part; there is nothing about staying at home.

Once the doctrine has been made manifest, a hadith has been cited for its justification, and the law canonised, there is nothing for women to do but obey a remote God who dictates His laws, and who has authorised the *ulama* as sole interpreters of His will and enforcers of His commands. The women themselves are constructed as a binary opposite of a mythological manhood: 'hence the dominant idea of female sexuality in Muslim societies', notes Prado, 'as uncontrollable, a potential source of *fitna* (strife, sedition, rebellion) that must be tamed and appeased in some way'. This process consolidated 'a specific type of masculinity: man as head of household, responsible for preserving the body and the honour of the women and providing for them; women, seen as weak and a source of conflict, are locked up indoors for protection and domestic chores'. This hegemonic masculinity is enforced in different ways by state institutions, such as constitutions, family law, gender relations, educational policies, dress codes, and even who can and cannot drive a car. 'The end product', writes Prado, 'is the pre-eminence of a legal system focused on repression and the imposition of a perverted morality'.

The logical conclusion of this process is men who are perpetually ready to defend their honour (by killing women if necessary), always keen to impose their version of Islam on all Others (by violence if necessary), and to keep the main source of *fitna* – women – in chains. At the apex of this hegemonic masculinity, according to Prado, are the Taliban: 'The masculinity embodied by the Taliban is one in which the feminine has completely disappeared. All is determined by the reality of war and its necessities. There is no need for attentive and kind people, only ruthless warriors able to kill the enemy without flinching. For greater effectiveness, the enemy and everything associated with him is turned into a demon. It is a lifestyle with no notion of compassion'. I would also put Boko Haram, the Shabab of Somalia, and the jihadis of various ilks in the same category.

This lifestyle, which sees religion and politics as one and the same thing, has no place for 'love, beauty, joy and pleasure', which, writes Ziba Mir-Hosseini, 'were all banished from public space' after the Iranian revolution, 'and anyone expressing them risked punishment'. It was all justified, as always, in 'the name of Islam: it was God's law, the Shari'a'. This combination of patriarchy and theological despotism has not only drained Islam of all sense of ethics and morality but also all notions of humanity.

One suspects that the recent cases of sexual grooming, abuse and exploitation of vulnerable teenage girls by Pakistani men in England is a product of the same lifestyle. During the last few years, eight different groups of Muslim Pakistani men have been convicted of sexual grooming in Oldham, Rotherham, Derby, Nelson, Telford, Rochdale and Oxford. Details in some of these cases are truly horrific, involving gang rapes, beatings, threats and passing girls from men to men. As Shamim Miah notes, 'most of the perpetrators involved are married with children. Some are regular mosque goers; one was even a religious teacher in his local mosque'. Of course, these men are criminals, and criminals are to be found in all cultures and societies. They are paedophiles; and, it seems, paedophiles are crawling out of the woodwork like dreaded beetles throughout inhabited lands. So we cannot see this in terms of a specific race, religion or culture. We have to resist, as Miah warns, 'the notion of the "Muslim sexual predator", creating a new folk-devil' that has been perpetuated by the British tabloid press. But two things cannot go unnoticed. These are all specifically Muslim Pakistani Men. Their religious and cultural context, which encouraged them to see young white women as 'fair game' who could be legitimately exploited, must have played some part in their nefarious behaviour. The way that some Muslims have justified this behaviour, blaming the women themselves and describing them as 'uncovered meat', hints that religion and culture are active players. Miah admits that 'part of the answers lie in how women are perceived in certain Muslim circles'.

There is ample research to suggest that the notion of men's honour and the shame that is supposedly associated with women's very existence often lead to brutalisation of women in Muslim societies. For example, in *Spaces of Masculinities*, B van Hoven and K Horschelmann describe how men in Lebanon, challenged by the civil war, blamed the misery of war and urban life on women. Whether Shia or Sunni, the only way they knew of redeeming their war-torn honour was by exercising their rights as 'protectors' of women and thus ruthlessly repressing them. When you lose control in society, it is only natural that you should turn to the one place where you have the God given right to be 'in control of your women'. A discourse was created that blamed a hated Other for their miseries, and the Other that became a punch bag for their frustrations was within their own families. When masculinity is defined both in terms of identity and ideology, humanity evaporates and all Others become fair game – including vulnerable white girls.

Of course, we should avoid the trap of essentialising Muslim men and their character, or imposing a false unity on a fluid ideology. Masculinity is not a fixed entity embodied in the personality trait of an individual man. Masculinities work as a configuration of practices that are accomplished in social actions and can differ according to particular social settings. Even 'the Muslim man everyone is trying to describe as "the Islamist", Tanjil Rashid points out, 'is not made of Islam', but is 'a more complex composite of ideas and influences'. The particular Islamist in question is Sayyid Qutb, the ideologue of the Muslim Brotherhood, and surely the most influential 'Islamist' of our time. Qutb is credited with developing the *takfiri* ideology, the tendency to call other Muslims who disagree with you apostates, or *kuffar* (infidels). He had significant influence on al-Qaida, the Egyptian Islamic Jihad, and 'the shrine-smashing Shabab today terrorising Somalia'.

But Qutb is a paradoxical character. During the 1930s, he was a progressive poet who saw constant recall to religion as 'the battle-cry of the feeble-minded'. He went on to have a shining literary career as romantic poet, noted novelist, and respected literary critic who envisioned the present and the future 'pregnant with possibilities outside the pale of the past'. He was first to spot the literary genius of the Nobel Laureate Naguib Mahfouz, who in turn gave glowing reviews to Qutb's novels. He did more than anyone, writes Rashid, 'to lend literary legitimacy to Mahfouz, but also did more than anyone to legitimise the insurgence that so menaced Mahfouz'. Mahfouz himself described Qutb as 'a superb poet, story-teller and writer,' who also 'inspired the Islamic groups from whose ranks emerged the person who attempted to kill me. It's a paradox'.

His most influential work is *Milestones*, published in 1964, 'a screed every bit as influential as Marx's *Manifesto*, decreeing that "attacking the non-believers in their territories is a collective and individual duty"'. *Milestones* presents Qutb as a fully-fledged radical. However, his misogyny is evident even in a much earlier and neglected work: *Social Justice in Islam*, which appeared in 1945. It was translated in 1970 by the American Council of Learned Societies to create a 'better understanding among American readers of the thinking and problems of Near Eastern people'. Here, Qutb presents Islam as a 'universal theory' of salvation based on 'freedom of conscience', 'human equality' and 'mutual responsibility in society'. While 'Islam has guaranteed to women a complete equality with women', Qutb tells us, it is necessary for man to be 'overseers of women', to receive double the share of inheritance, and be the leaders and thinkers of society. The reason for this 'discrimination lies in the physical endowment' of a woman, who is 'restricted for most of her life to family cares'. As 'a man is free from the cares of the family, he can attend to the affairs of society' and thus 'apply to these affairs all his intellectual powers'. Women should concentrate on 'emotions and passions', while men devote their time 'in the direction of reflection and thought'. Qutb's character may be paradoxical but in matters of religion he was always unconventional.

Another man who commands almost as much influence as Qutb is the Turkish creationist Adnan Oktar, who writes under the rubric of 'Haroon Yahya'. As Stefano Bigliardi points out, Yahya is a one-man mega industry devoted to promoting creationism, or what Val will describe as *Israiliyyat*, the Biblical account of creation. Ostensibly, Yahya aims to 'demonstrate that Muslim faith is in harmony with science and compatible with a hyper-technological lifestyle', a goal that appeals to generations of Muslim men in need of serious psychotherapy. The astounding global success of Yahya is a product of this mentality. But Yahya, as Bigliardi shows, has nothing to do with science. His wrath is directed against evolution which he sees as 'the source of all the violent and repressive phenomena of the last centuries such as terrorism, totalitarianism, communism, fascism and racism as well as romanticism, capitalism, Buddhism, and Zionism (which to date he explicitly distinguishes from Judaism, after a flirt with Holocaust denial in the

1990s)'. They are all interconnected in Yahya's view, and hell-bent on destroying the moral gendered order of Islam: 'they all stem from and foster materialism, atheism, and pessimism'.

Like Qutb, Yahya is a paradoxical man. He is a great believer in science but knows nothing of how science works and devotes most of his efforts to disparaging one of its main theories – evolution. He promotes his creationism but dresses it as science. While dishing out some pernicious nonsense for the simple-minded to lap up, he remains as romantic at heart as Qutb. In fact, all Muslim men are paradoxical and contradictory. That's the nature of human beings. Masculinities are always complex in the way they are socially constructed, produced, consumed and performed.

The problem arises when masculinities are analysed by looking only at men (a bit like what I have done!) and women are not considered as part of the analysis – what Davies would call a 'faulty perspective'. All men are unique and diverse; and we can construct hegemonic masculinities that do not correspond to real lives of actual Muslim men. However, this does not mean that Muslim men do not, as a whole, contribute to hegemony and oppression of women in society. And it is not surprising those men who function as models of hegemony, such as Qutb or al-Qaradawi, or Mohammad Morsi, the former President of Egypt, exhibit contradictions.

The challenge is to move away from what Prado calls 'perverted morality' to 'an ethic, a moral code that values the contributions of both men and women in their uniqueness and diversity' that Davies argues for. But a new inclusive morality will only have meaning for Muslims if it emerges from within Islam and is based on Islamic sources. Our own sources, as Mir Hosseini argues, provide us all we need to challenge patriarchal interpretations of the Qur'an and Shari'a, and pull the carpet from underneath hegemonic notions of masculinity. Mir Hosseini, who has devoted all her adult life to fighting patriarchy, seeks 'to engage with juristic constructs and theories, and to unveil the theological and logical arguments and legal theories that underpin them'. She narrates how her personal struggle led to the formation of, and her involvement in, Musawah, a movement that links 'scholarship with activism to develop a holistic framework integrating Islamic teachings, universal human rights law, national constitutional guarantees of equality, and the lived realities of women and men'.

The journey must begin by returning to God and His Names of Beauty. Notions of masculinity in Muslim societies derived from the Names of Beauty have existed beside hegemonic ideals of masculinity. Prado shows how in the life of the Prophet Muhammad, or the ideas of ibn Arabi and ibn Rushd, we can find an alternative vision. Ibn Arabi, for example, argued that a man is not complete unless he has internalised the feminine; only then is he capable of actually receiving the Grace of God. A true believing man incorporates and inculcates the primary qualities of women such as compassion, nurturing, receptivity, and unconditional love. In advertising terms, we would call such men: 'men with added woman'.

It would help if we had a better understanding and appreciation of the original and immense contribution made by women in Islamic history. Asma Afsaruddin suggests early Islamic history was shaped as much by women as men. Not only did women play an active part in society, they even influenced revelation itself. Afsaruddin recalls Umm 'Umara, who observed that, up to that point, the Qur'an did not mention women. She told the Prophet: 'I see that everything pertains to men; I do not see the mention of women'. As a result 33:35 was revealed, which 'maintains the absolute religious and spiritual equality of women and men - no ifs or buts'. The verse states: 'Those who have surrendered to God among males and females; those who believe among males and females; those who are sincere among males and females; those who are truthful among males and females; those who are patient among males and females; those who fear God among males and females; those who give in charity among males and females; those who fast among males and females; those who remember God often among males and females – God has prepared for them forgiveness and great reward'. Women also played political roles and had full citizenship rights in the early Islamic community. By making a personal pledge to the Prophet, they entered the Muslim polity as equals, and went on to be appointed as public inspectors and judges, and many, such as A'isha and Umm Salama, widows of the Prophet, transmitted prophetic traditions and were regarded as fountains of religious knowledge.

Much of this history is invisible because it has been written off by later historians – a process that continues to this day. In her razor sharp dissection of some recent contributions to Islamic studies, Kacia Ali shows how the process works. It is argued that the bar 'of the super tradition of Islam' is

too high for women to reach, that women have to be 'recognised' as legitimate participants in discourse before their work can be considered, that
women do not have large enough followings to be considered as influential
thinkers, and by insisting that 'the topic of women is too important to be
dealt with briefly' thereby deferring it perpetually. Eager to acknowledge
the contributions of kindred spirits in history, 'the omnipotent male scholar'
is able to produce a plethora of excuses to ignore and marginalise women.
'Not only do people writing about Muslim reformers generally fail to take
women seriously', writes Ali, 'so do reformers themselves'.

Ali is surely right to suggest that the right question that will take us forward is an epistemological one. Theological issues – deliberate misinterpretation, use of dubious hadiths, imposition of alien, aggressive masculinities
on Islamic sources, and obscurantist arguments – have received 'quite short
shrift in Muslim feminist thinking'. But underlying these theological matters, and issues of legal and practical aspects of Muslim life, are epistemological questions: how do we determine what constitutes valid knowledge,
what ways of knowing are possible, are there gendered dimensions to epistemology? 'Does women's personal experience play a role, and if so, what
sort of role? How can experience be communicated and verified? How and
when can one generalise from one's own experience to say something
broader about Islam, about humanity, about the world we inhabit?'

As I argued several decades ago in *Islamic Futures: The Shape of Ideas to Come*,
the central challenge for Muslims is to rediscover a contemporary epistemology that emphasises the diversity and plurality of Islam, 'the totality of
experience and reality, and promotes not one but a number of diverse
forms of knowledge from pure observation to the highest metaphysics'. We
need to move away from a notion of masculinity that essentialises male-
female difference and makes the subject invisible to a new, more inclusive
idea of what it means to be a Muslim in the twenty-first century.

The formidable challenge to orthodoxy and traditional authority from
Muslim feminists, such as Mir Hosseini, Kecia Ali and Asma Afsaruddin, has
already taken the vital first steps towards a new ethics and morality in Islam.
But it is not just the feminist scholars, largely located in the West, who are
making original and ground-breaking contributions. Traditional female
scholars in the Muslim world are also pushing the boundaries. The four
scholars examined by Val - Aicha Abd al-Rahman (who wrote as Bint al-

Shati), Zainab al-Ghazali, Fawkiyah Sherbini, and Kariman Hamzah – have done sterling work in an exceptionally difficult traditionalist environment. Indeed, just the fact that they are standing up to an oppressive tradition under repressive conditions to offer new readings of the Qur'an is worthy of awe and respect. Moreover, as Val notes, they cannot be dismissed for 'flirting with patriarchy' or labelled as 'conspirators to their own subjugation'. And Val raises some important questions: 'why have feminist scholars neglected these women?' Why are certain feminist scholars, such as Amina Wadud, lionised, while the work of traditional female scholars looked down upon and dismissed 'as a product of a patriarchal tradition'? It is not unusual for reformers, even women reformers, to end up constructing monolithic and exclusive enclaves.

To be inclusive we need to include all women in our discourse: traditional, modern, feminist, and those who do not subscribe to feminism – including women who were men. In her moving account of 'not being a man', Leyla Jagiella relates how she overcame bigotry and 'conflicts surrounding my gender variant behaviour'. Jagiella was born a boy in a Protestant German family. Even as an infant, she felt like a girl with a male body. She had strong spiritual leanings from an early age, and embraced Islam as a teenager. As a result of her gender issues and conversion, she faced prejudice at school and at the mosque as well as problems at home. 'My teenage years were spent in fighting simultaneously on different fronts', she writes. Not surprisingly, she had 'suicidal thoughts'. Then on her 21st birthday, during a visit to the shrine of Sufi saint Khwaja Gharib Nawaz in Ajmer, India, she decided 'to start life as a woman'. Eventually she found solace not with the mainstream Muslim community, 'not the most welcoming place' for people who do not live up to 'gender expectations', but within the *hijra* (transsexual) community of India and Pakistan.

Change can be external or internal. In Jagiella's case it came from the inside; her 'real self' rebelled against the construction and restrictions of sex roles. If we wish to restructure gender roles in Islam, and dismantle hegemonic masculinities, we need to change Muslim men more than anything else. This is a task that requires us to stand up to our history. The trajectory of Islamic history shows that, with few notable exceptions, men in Islam have tended to exhibit a rather unsavoury variety of masculinity. Right at the formative phase of Islam, we find the famous 'Story of Umm Zar'. It is said to be a hadith, narrated by Aisha, but is in fact more like a parable. A group of eleven women get together to talk about their husbands. The first one describes her husband as 'a sort of the meat of a lean camel placed on the top of a mountain, which is difficult to climb up, and the meat is not good enough that one finds in oneself the urge to fetch it from the top of that mountain'. The second declares, 'my husband is so bad that I am afraid I will not be able to describe his defects both visible and invisible completely'. The third one says, 'my husband is a tall fellow. If he learns that I describe him, he will divorce me, and if I keep quiet I will be made to live in a state of suspense neither completely abandoned by him nor entertained as a wife'. And so it goes on in this fashion. One husband is foul mouthed and 'suffering from all kinds of conceivable diseases'; another 'eats so much that nothing is left back and when he drinks he drinks so that no drop is left behind, and when he lies down he wraps his body and does not touch me so that he may know my grief'. There are one or two decent men in this parable, but the one who comes out on top is Umma Zar's husband, a wealthy individual who showers his wife with expensive gifts. But even he divorces her after meeting 'a woman, having two children like leopards playing with her pomegranates under her vest'.

Given this line-up, the burden of history is indeed arduous. Men in Islam, including the folks like me who think of themselves as liberals, cast a long and unhealthy shadow over the Muslim community. But cracks have begun to appear in this formidable façade. We all — men, women and those in-between — need to continue chipping away at the edifice of hegemonic masculinity until it collapses, in the hope that we can move forward to the warm, life-enhancing and generous sunshine of the liberating spirit of the Qur'an.

THE PROBLEM OF MEN

Merryl Wyn Davies

To paraphrase the classic pop song: men — what are they good for? Currently a consensus appears to be forming around the song's repost — absolutely nothing! In which case it may be necessary to issue the time-honoured alert to ground control: Houston, humanity has a problem.

Our age it seems, at least in western societies, has little use for men; it is the era in which anything men can do women can and should do. Old ideas of manual labour conjuring visions of heads of households who are strong horny-handed sons of toil venturing forth as breadwinners is passé. Women have been liberated from the drudgery of housework and released into the wild open spaces of employment. They have been uncoupled from reliance on men for financial support while contraception has given them control of their reproductive options making them even more independent. Indeed, advances in the technology of reproduction have created so many options – donor sperm, *in vitro* fertilisation, surrogate pregnancy, with anonymity at each stage along the way, that a newborn can be delivered to a mother without any of the messy transitional stages requiring the forming of human relationships. When mother and child become the basic unit of society supported by a system of entitlements to state benefits – who needs fathers? The consequence of these immense social changes is a crisis of masculinity, a problem of men.

Muslim discourse is so mired in the intractable conventions of debate on the problem of women that it hardly knows how to address the reality of the lives of real women or men. Yet Muslims are not immune to the predicaments of the society or the planet on which they live. There are growing numbers of single Muslim mothers in all our states and nations; family breakdown, domestic violence, inter-generational tensions are the norm everywhere. The perverse self-image foisted on Muslim men and women that incarnates female temptresses and requires exclusionary avoidance as the only answer demonstrates the inability of traditionalist strictures to fit young people facing such problems. These are the kind of issues nice Muslim gatherings and organisations sidestep with diplomatic silence while they concentrate on broadcasting idealised abstractions. The abstractions insist we have all the answers while they are patently failing to materialise in the lives lived in our communities.

There are, of course, caveats to all aspects of these discussions. Those who raise the problem of men are not without a political agenda. When, for example, Labour MP Diane Abbott raised the issue of 'Britain's Crisis of Masculinity' in a speech to the Demos think tank (16 May 2013), one could be forgiven for remembering that the Labour Party is conscious of its problems with white working class male voters. Those sons of toil that once were the bedrock of its support have been evaporating as a secure voting block since the days of Margaret Thatcher. Such considerations, however, do not obviate the issue of widespread underachievement, poverty of ambition, hopelessness, frustration and all its consequent social ills which a recent report by the Office for Standards in Education, Children's Services and Skills (Ofsted) has now shown is more severe among white boys than any other section of British society.

Also in Britain, the Centre for Social Justice has reported that the rise in single parenting, predominantly featuring single mother heads of households, is the greatest engine of child poverty and a signal of social dysfunction. Advocates for single mothers responded defiantly that poverty was the issue, not the lack of fathers. Society has become more complex and the idea that only the presence of a father could set children on a secure path to becoming well adjusted and successful adults, despite statistics, was no causative factor, demeaning to single mothers as a class and blind to the diversity of human ingenuity and ability to survive. The lack, or otherwise, of male role models is a matter of individual personal circumstance, not a matter for social engineering by a nanny state.

When the Muslim Institute decided to reverse the usual terms of address and debate 'Men in Islam' at its Winter Gathering in December 2012, there was much trepidation on the part of the male participants: it would merely be an excuse for another onslaught of demonisation from monstrous regiments of women. While female participants rightly and righteously objected to the way being women is debated as the eternal existential problem of

Muslim society, in the end the discussion fell back on familiar ground, bemoaning of the fate of women. Male participants ended up pleading for understanding of the social dilemmas faced by Muslim men: stereotyped, demeaned, undervalued, regarded with fear as a potential global threat, they were now being told they could not even look for reassurance and status in their own homes. How could we raise generations of men able to withstand the pressures wider society placed upon them if they had no bastion of strength to rely upon? By general consensus the Gathering became convinced we had a subject category – 'men in Islam' – but no way to refine or describe the issues or debate the nature of its problems let alone consider solutions.

Men in society: discuss. The subject is pertinent, timely and necessary. Everyone has problems, in different dimensions and aspects; there are no get-out clauses or let-offs for any section of society. Nor can there be any question that a problem of men, with men or about men implicates, affects and reflects on the question of women. We all have a humanity problem. We have reached a point where on all fronts we are unable to debate human relationships with any consensus of equity, mutuality and reciprocity. Community has become the congregation of individuals and no individual circumstance in life choices or chances can be made to bear the burden of reasoned argument as either cause or inevitable outcome in any particular aspect of problems of human relationships.

We face a morass of complexities and it would be worthwhile considering not so much how we got to this point as interrogating the terms and ideas through which we view the problems. Are we looking at the questions with a faulty perspective? Are our terms of reference part of the problem? Is it the idealised abstractions taken as the basis of 'normality' that are at the root of our inability to talk through our issues?

To begin at the beginning, let us consider the ideal of patriarchy. Is man the hunter the original model and base of all social reality? There was a time in the nineteenth century when armchair speculators in thought flirted with the idea of primal matriarchy. The origins of humanity were so bereft of moral discipline and institutional formation that only women could know with certainty the identity of their own offspring while having only the vaguest notion of which man might have impregnated them. This flirtatious moment of free thinking, which would return in different guise in more modern discourse, stood in contrast to the uniformitarian idea that men have always been bigger, stronger, more gregarious, less burdened by the impediments of child rearing and therefore naturally, socially and morally empowered to take charge. This vision of patriarchal power has been interpreted into the plurality of religious texts and their moral ideals of how society works: patriarchy rules and that's that.

The trouble with patriarchy is that human diversity simply does not support such a simplistic uniformitarian reading of history and society. In hunting and gathering societies, whose history is as long and therefore has been as subject to adaptation as any other kind, the majority of the food intake is provided by women whose work is essential to the survival of the group. The idea that hunting invests men with superior status is an assumption foisted upon such societies by outside observers. It was a view of human organisation taken for granted rather than interrogated to explore questions of mutuality and parallel dispensations of power and authority.

What can be read into the origins of human social organisation is most often to be found in the predilections and prejudices of modern academics and the way they utilise information from societies they regard as less developed than their own. But no archaeologist can identify the gender of the maker of a cave painting, or pot, or the originator of an idea whose identity is buried in time. Facts such as these are suspended in a speculative domain, which often tells us more about the observer than that which is observed. Considering the actual lives of living societies markedly different from modern western mores has eventually disgorged, with much intellectual effort and difficulty, just how wrong are so many of the foundational premises of the concept of patriarchy. Take the debacle of agriculture in Africa. How many decades of development investment were misspent and ineffectual because dispensers of western aid worked on the premise of patriarchy? Quite simply men clear fields, and the farmers are women. Therefore unless women were involved in education, in the development schemes and recipients of the proffered technical and financial resources, farming could not and cannot enjoy the expected benefits. In the 1950s the British colonial administrators of the Bamenda region of Cameroon in West Africa were affronted by the way Bamenda men seemed to live lives of lazy dissipation while they oppressed their over-burdened womenfolk. They employed an anthropologist, the remarkable Phyllis Kaberry, to investigate this unconscionable situation. The answers she found offered an alternate view of supposedly repressive patriarchy, though it took decades before her findings permeated the wider discourse where they belonged. The answer to lazy men was simple. The roles that men had traditionally fulfilled had been usurped by the colonial administration itself. Agriculture had always been the province of women and Bamenda men acknowledged the superior skill and authority of women in this sphere of activity. There was in fact a parallel hierarchy of authority among women which exercised social importance for Bamenda society in general. Because colonial administrators who were men had no access to the world of women they were blithely ignorant of how the Bamenda thought about themselves, their society and the facts of life.

It has been the role of female anthropologists, or more generally anthropological wives, to bring such insights out of the shadows. The world of women around the world has been closed, occluded or simply ignored by the majority of observers and commentators, males that is, who constructed what have been taken as the 'normal' order of things. And one does not have to look only to far flung and markedly different societies, nor exclusively to male observers to find such blind spots and oversights. I vividly recall watching a television dramatisation of Vera Britten's classic of female emancipation *Testament of Youth*. The narrative concerns the vexations of an intelligent, articulate middle class Edwardian woman frustrated by the limitations placed upon her life chances because she was born woman. The scene that sticks in my mind has the heroine stand front and centre bemoaning that she is prevented from applying for a place at university just as her contemporary male friends will and thus how the world of useful gainful employment is closed to her. All that awaits her is a vapid existence of being a lady. Meanwhile in the background a young tweenie, a serving maid, is hard at work cleaning out the grates in fully engaged gainful employment. I did not see this as subversive comment so much as social blindness. When we learn in school about the passing of factory acts, the implementation of social consciousness to the awful working conditions of the industrial revolution, how often do we stop to reflect on the obvious point? If you had to pass laws to stop women working down the coal mines and in other hazardous places such as iron and steel foundries it was because they actually did do such work. The legislation engineered by male legislators curtailed the option for the kind of employment women are now demanding. The simple fact is working class and peasant women have always worked. Their work was often hard graft and their families depended on their labour for survival. Until the mid-twentieth century domestic labourers, people like that maid in *Testament of Youth*, were always among the top five categories of employment and their ranks were composed of men and women. Think of all the dramas that nowadays depict the upstairs downstairs world of this bygone time and how many strong working women, some in significant positions of authority, are part of the dramatis personae.

The world of male and female roles is a social construct which challenges blinkered imagination. What it is possible to know from history and beyond the gaze of western scholarship suggests that Patriarchy, with a capital P and full unquestioned male authority and dominance, may be more imagined than actually demonstrable. This is not to say that gender tensions do not exist, that male dominance of recording what is taken as fact has not predominated. It is merely to question whether this has ever been the whole story, the only way of looking at things. How many questions should we ask of past times and different societies about parallel hierarchies and the compatibility of female work, education, scholarship and spheres of authority? Is there not a plurality of ways of organising society that we have as yet failed to consider? If plurality and diversity have been lurking in the background all the while are there not alternative terms in which to think about, discuss and seek solutions to the predicaments of our time?

One thing we can be sure of: the uniformitarian assumptions that underpin the dominant ideas about gender roles and relations are not helping society face the transitions affecting daily life. The men are from Mars women from Venus formula of sexual dimorphism has been extended so far that the education system as a whole has been charged with complicity in undermining male self-esteem. Learning and exam culture favour female proclivities we are told; they are better at engaging and developing female minds. Boys need different kinds of education, more practicality and applied routes to learning. Technical education that once was available for boys that could lead on to apprenticeships and a world of manly trades and work has all but disappeared and is having to be reconstructed, ineffectually, in the teeth of adverse economic circumstance. We can produce educated women but their advancement in the economy at large is a matter of glass ceilings unshattered and enduring inequalities in pay. Disparities in the workplace, low pay and the proliferation of part-time work of the most disadvantageous kind means single mothers are most susceptible to poverty for themselves and their children. The breakdown of wider family networks and the astronomical costs of child care along with the stalling of policy to address the problems mean child poverty is inevitably destined to increase. Dissatisfactions abound and the numbers of young people not in education or training swell into ranks of lost generations. Equality is the watchword in deeply inequitable conditions where young people are more demanding, more isolated, more frustrated and bombarded from all sides with images that tell them that if they do not have it all they are essentially failures.

It is hard not to conclude that society has boxed itself into a corner which can be marked 'advanced individualism'. It is an ideal that is now biting back. The ranks of young people disadvantaged in education and employment are fitted with the idea that teenage rebellion is the norm, that life means one should become independent and set off to make one's own nuclear network of relationships. However, relationships are a risk since they exist to compromise one's independence, to constrain the freedom of one's choices and actions; they are fraught with perils and pitfalls and therefore are best considered temporary arrangements. Individualism, however, has to confront economic realities. More and more young people are priced out of the independence they have been taught to value and have to fall back on living with their parents, who emerge on the social stage as put-upon providers of economic support of the last resort. Middle-aged parents are now constrained by their offspring and denied the economic security and freedom of leisure they anticipated and which society envisaged they were entitled to expect. Family as a nexus of social tension is reinforced the more it is demonstrated to be essential.

The times we live in assert that men should stop being domineering while women should have every choice possible. In all the permutations of these essential premises of debate, there is almost nothing we can discuss without being incorrect, without advancing demeaning stereotypes or offensive caricatures. In short we have no language to engage with very real problems. How can we talk realistically about men, women and family beyond the old familiar contours of irresolvable argument? We desperately need alternative terms of reference.

The problems we face are ones of human relationship and begin from the inescapable fact that humanity is composed of men and women. It is not political correctness to acknowledge that these are not simple and uniform categories. Societies beyond the west have, if only they would remember, acknowledged that male and female are diverse plural forms of being which admit numerous ways of social expression and inclusion. The fundamentalist strictures abroad in Muslim discourse today deny the flexibility and adaptability that some of our societies have demonstrated in history for both men and women. Male and female exist, and they exist with diversity of sexual orientation. The question is how should this basic human truth be incorporated in social organisation and understanding? Questions of equity, mutuality and reciprocity are about how we conceive of society with and including sexual diversity; they are about finding a balance between individuality, which can never be denied, and collective groupings, the living with others that cannot be eradicated from human existence. Each man and woman is a unique person, yet neither man nor woman is or can thrive as an island isolated from others. If this is all so self-evident why do we have any problem?

The problems, and they are numerous as has been mentioned, are all in the balance and the context of our times which are always transitional. Circumstances change, the ability of our ideas about self, society, individuality and social formations to be flexible and adapt usually lags far behind. What then is mutuality? We need an ethic, a moral code that values the contributions of both men and women in their uniqueness and diversity. We need to establish the ground rule that justice must be done to the contributions made by men and women and that they do not have to be the same to be equally valuable and necessary to society as a whole. These ground rules should be foundational to the very concept of society. Equally valuable, however, does not necessarily mean the same. Equitable rewards require adjustments to be made to the value of all work, for example work within the home with work in the open marketplace. A well-balanced society appreciates the reciprocal contributions all members of society make in their different ways. A balanced view of society would also keep in mind that not all choices are mutually compatible and attainable. In life we make choices and choices have consequences. We seem to have forgotten the constructive understanding of limits, that not everything is humanly possible, that the best of all possible worlds may not yet be attainable. The power of choice is an exercise of responsibility and free will. Its consequences in not delivering everything one could possibly wish for are not therefore a conspiracy of malign unjust social forces.

We have to live with other people and therefore we have to learn how to operate and manage social relations. The family is the place where this most basic learning curve begins. There are many forms of family that exist and have existed through time and across the globe. Can we not agree that the nuclear family is the most fragile, truncated and unstable idea humanity has experimented with? The nuclear family exists in a social setting where community and neighbourliness have been undermined by economic and social forces beyond the command of individuals, family groups or particular communities. There are few stable settled communities that offer the prospects of work and advancement for all. The most stable old-fashioned communities tend to be remote places, often failing to offer affordable housing that enables new families to live near their parents and close relatives, or the prospect of gainful employment. We simply do not create the kind of housing opportunities for multi-generational families, or the easy opportunities for networks of close kin to live near each other. Wealth and life chances determine the kind of community we can have which often means people have little option but to struggle to survive in isolation whatever fate brings. Society has to make different choices in our current circumstances to nurture and value the idea of extended families. Families have to value mutuality and reciprocity to make society take note of the kind of changes that are necessary to ensure the collective needs of their members are met. It is not a question of idealising or demonising family life. What society needs is serious thinking that places the infrastructure of family life, its potential and possibilities at the centre of thinking, planning and organising. Instead of constantly invoking the idea of family and eulogising family values it is the practicalities that make them possible that we should be debating.

Social mobility employing a mobile and adaptable workforce is the determining social norm demanded by the economic forces of our time. How can we negotiate these forces to accommodate and include the needs of mutuality and reciprocity in human relations? Are we only functions of economic forces or moral agents shaping society to get answers to our human requirements? There is no virtue in harking back to an idyllic former age when things were different. The challenge society faces today is to make a mature transition that adapts all aspects of existence. We require flexibility that is humane, that enables the kind of change in economic and social life that enhances the quality and worth of human lives. Debating transition, charting the future course of how we live together in society as men and women and families needs a more plural vision of where we have come from and where we might aim to arrive. We need a broader vision of what constitutes wealth and self-worth if we are to define the terms of the kind of debate we actually need. Our need is to develop new kinds of debates that reassert that mutuality — mutual responsibility and reciprocal obligations are basic to social health. Only such debates can get us out of the increasing tendency to see society as increasingly riven by irreconcilable sectional interests. We know when politicians say we are all in it together that we are being sold a bill of goods. But what alternatives can be found to make collective exertion, common endeavour, a pragmatic option. There is little to hope for in this or any future time by opting to think we are all in it for ourselves alone.

It seems to me the problem of men is much the same as the problem of women. Men and women are moral social agents, people who make choices. It is the options available that often prejudge the choices we can make. There is no answer to the problem of men unless they can acknowledge and live up to their moral obligations in mutuality, reciprocity and justice to women. The self-same obligations are incumbent upon women. We desperately need to get beyond the impasse of the stereotypes and caricatures that produce mutual demonisation. Male and female self-respect are not separate entities; they are the same coinage, not different sides of the same coin, however equitably distributed. What is most morally reprehensible is to assume or assert that men are the problem of women and women the problem of men. This was brought home to me some years ago when addressing a gathering of Muslim women on the hoary chestnut of women in Islam. My presentation attempted to get beyond the standard repertoire of the status, role and rights of women as idealised from Islamic sources and focus on what those ideals might mean and imply for living today in a globalised world, not Mecca in the seventh century or somewhere else long ago and far away in some imaginary Muslim society. A lively discussion ensued during which one lady who had been thoughtfully quiet for some time interjected. 'It's my fault I think', she said. This seemed a rather large claim and onerous responsibility to take on. She went on to explain that she had raised sons and daughters and it was clear to her she had encouraged and enabled different standards for the boys as opposed to the girls. If there is a problem with Muslim men, and she was quite clear there was, then how she raised her sons, the kind of behaviour, expectations and attitudes she inculcated, permitted and tolerated were part and parcel of the problem. It was a brave statement to make, one that contains much truth to reason with. Mutual expectations are not conjured from thin air. How we interpret and apply our moral vision of society is what we can expect to see replicated.

What it is to be a good man is forged not only by men. What it means to be a good woman is determined not solely by the female of the species. We live in a mutual world. We are influenced and affected by the ideas and actions that surround us. We are framed by the social conditions in which we live. And yet we can never exonerate ourselves from being moral agents, people with responsibility for the way the world works whether we like it or not, whether it works to our benefit and advantage or not. Being effective moral agents, people who enhance and adapt the world around us to better ends begins with finding a more plural vision of our mutual responsibility and need for each other as collaborating human beings in all the diversity of our maleness and femaleness. If we cannot find more imaginative and constructive ways to talk about ourselves in reciprocal relations there is very little hope for improving the fate of humanity.

MUSLIM MASCULINITIES

Abdennur Prado

There is no lack of books, pamphlets, scholarly tomes and polemical works on 'Women in Islam'. Every genre is covered: classical, traditional, modernist and reformist. And we must not forget the digital media: a quick search on YouTube alone will generate over two million hits. Works on gender issues are, almost exclusively, about women. Yet any discussion of gender is incomplete without a consideration of masculinity. Despite this, there are hardly any studies that, as Limousine Ouzga notes, 'render Muslim men visible as gendered subjects and that show that masculinities have a history and are part of gender relations in Muslim cultures'.

This may be due to the fact that we cannot define a unique and univocal Islamic concept of masculinity. The concept of masculinity dominant in a precise historical moment, in Islam as in any other religion or culture, is conditioned by economics, society, class, age, ethnicity, membership, history and political situation. Denying this would contradict the very nature of the gender studies that have led to the emergence of the category of 'masculinity'. Moreover, highlighting the historicity of the concept of masculinity keeps us from falling into the trap of essentialism. It helps us avoid a Eurocentric reading, projecting the myths of Western culture on Islam.

We know a great deal about western stereotypes of Muslim women. But the image of 'Muslim men' in the West is also monolithic. Think of the billionaire Sheikh, the obscurantist Mullah, the vociferous young Muslim, the violent terrorist. Interestingly, these current images contrast with the Middle Age image of Muslim men as effeminate. The accounts of Western travellers in the Muslim world conveyed an image of sensuality and delicacy, of a refined and mannered civilisation. The history of Islam also offers a variety of models of masculinity. Some of them present us with a warrior conception of manhood, while others offer a model that incorporates aspects considered 'feminine': the use of perfumes, grooming, affection, the culture of the bathrooms, even crying as an expression of masculinity. In Persian and Ottoman miniatures, men are often portrayed as sensitive and sensual, rather than tough and uncompromising.

Theoretically, we can say that there is no single model of Muslim masculinity. Practically, we are aware of a dominant model that has existed in Muslim history and is prevalent today. It is the product of a patriarchal mentality that we can trace to the early phase of Islam during which man is constructed as the One and the woman as the Other. The man is considered as the paradigm of the human, and the woman is subordinated. And it is precisely to preserve this concept of 'ideal masculinity' that it is necessary to seclude women, segregate them in a differentiated mental and social space. We can argue that this ideal masculinity subjugates men, just as the concept of weak and untrustworthy women subdues women. Both models are instruments of pressure that society exerts over its members to maintain a cohesive social structure. This pressure becomes a repressive morality that is virtually impossible to escape; in the hands of patriarchal religious elites, it becomes an orthodoxy that has to be preserved at all costs.

The patriarchal model of manhood has always been in tension with another, less known, model of Islamic masculinity. In this model, both the feminine and the masculine are seen as an integral part of being human. One cannot be separated from the other. Both models have their origins in traditional Islam — and both have existed throughout history.

To understand the origins of these models we must first situate ourselves within the traditional paradigm. By 'traditional Islam' I mean the characteristics of Muslim society that are based, or are perceived to be based, on an unbroken chain of knowledge that can be traced to the Qur'an. Traditional thinking is constituted as a set of symbols deeply rooted in the collective psyche. A religion cannot be understood simply by analysing its doctrines and practices or by appealing only to a sociological perspective. There is a symbolic dimension that gives meaning to such practices and doctrines. A traditional society sees itself as an organic society in which each individual naturally takes his place as a part of a whole that is designed to fully develop the individual's spiritual capacities.

For a traditional society, masculine and feminine are attributes that are beyond men and women; they are archetypal features of creation as a whole. The Qur'an teaches that Allah created everything in pairs, and that

Creation is supported on a Balance, in a perfect equilibrium. In the world of forms, everything is dual: male-female, wet-dry, high-low, dark-light. Every quality has another that opposes it, and with which it seeks to be in harmony. The male-female duality is related to other dualities, between active and passive, action and contemplation, Heaven and Earth, spirit and body, the transcendent and the immanent. In traditional thinking, the male is described as active, rational, regulatory, courageous and austere. The female is receptive, emotive, intuitive, sensitive and sensual.

This duality has cosmological implications. In the traditional symbolic universe, everything that exists in the world of creatures is a manifestation of a higher plane. The sun and moon correspond, in a certain sense, to man and woman, although I must say that in Arabic sun and moon are feminine words. Beyond the easy identification, the most important relationship is that the pair sun-moon has an equivalent in the male-female pair. Not because the sun can be compared with the man and the moon with the woman, but because as with sun and moon, man and woman form an inseparable pair. It is the harmony between these two principles that makes possible the development of life, understood as an endless cosmic cycle. At the same time, the male-female and sun-moon polarities are manifestations of the creative power of Allah, who is beyond all dualities. This balance between masculine and feminine can be seen as a synthesis between the solar and lunar cults, in which the moon represents the Mother Goddess, the feminine creative power.

Masculine and Feminine in Allah

The masculine-feminine duality also has an application in the conception of Divinity. At the heart of the Islamic worldview is the idea of *tawhid*, the Oneness of all that is the created, the idea that all is united by its origin in Allah. Although Allah is One, there are inside Allah some dualities which are also manifested in His creation: Allah is the Giver of Life and the Giver of Death, the Manifest and the Hidden, the First and the Last. Allah is one, and the Creation is the manifestation of the Attributes or Names of Allah. Muslim theologians have divided the Names of Allah into two categories: Names of Majesty (*Asma al-Jalal*) and Names of Beauty (*Asma al-Jamal*). Those of Majesty are the majority: *al-Malik* (the King), *al-'Azîz* (the Powerful), *al-Jabbar* (the Dominator), *al-Mutakabbir* (the Haughty), *al-Qahhâr* (the Subjugator), *al-'Alî* (the Almighty), *al-Kabir* (the Greatest), *al-Ÿalil* (the Majestic), and so on. These are Names that generate fear because they speak of His greatness and the insignificance of man, a creature constantly exposed to pain and joy, a dependent creature, in need of food and affection. This is a deity who judges, who is severe in punishment, and on whom the humans are totally dependent.

Names of Beauty include *al-Rahman* (the Merciful), *al-Rahim* (the Compassionate), *al-Halim* (The Meek), *al-Salam* (the Peace) and *al-Wadud* (The Loving), among others. These Names are inviting us to trust and love Allah, because through them Allah is shown as Compassionate, Close, Loving. He is a protective deity, radiating mercy and compassion, Who relates to His creatures with tenderness and cosmic love.

All the chapters of the Qur'an (except one) begin with the Bismillah: *bismil-lâhi ar-Rahmani ar-Rahim*, which is generally translated as 'In the Name of God, the Most Compassionate, the Most Merciful'. In the Qur'an Allah says 'My mercy overspreads everything' (7:156) and that Allah 'has willed upon Himself the law of grace and mercy' (6:12). There is also an authentic tradition of the Prophet Muhammad (Hadith *qudsi*) in which Allah declares: 'My mercy prevails over My wrath'. The word usually translated as Mercy is *Rahma*. The names Rahman and Rahim originated in the Arabic triliteral r-h-m. The Arab word *rahâm*, from the same root, means uterus or womb. We can thus conclude that in the Islamic concept of the divine, the feminine element takes precedence over the masculine.

Patriarchy signifies, on theological and symbolic levels, the predominance of the masculine attributes of Allah over the feminine attributes. That is, it puts the emphasis on the attributes of majesty, dominion and power, over the feminine attributes of compassion and tenderness. The result, to use the words of Ouzgane, is 'a terrifying and monolithic idea of "God", *sans* all attributes except those that service goals of brute power and are disconnected from the feminine'. This imbalance can be partially explained by the facts that the Qur'an was revealed in a predominantly patriarchal society and that Islam developed as a world civilisation during a period when patriarchy was the norm.

Patriarchy as an historical process

Let us see how this imbalance manifested on different levels to entrench the concept of patriarchy. As a historical process, patriarchal Islam takes us progressively away from the worldview of the Qur'an. We can see the process working in the interpretation of the Qur'an, how the biography of the Prophet was written and the characteristics of the Prophet it emphasised, as well as in jurisprudence, the theory of government, Sufism and sexuality. Of course, these areas are not watertight compartments; they influenced each other in the unstoppable process of the masculinisation of Islam.

The values proposed in the Qur'an cannot be considered either masculine or feminine, or maybe they constitute a perfect balance of active and passive qualities that must occur within each human being. Values such as humility, courage, compassion, generosity, patience, flexibility, fairness, kindness, tolerance, and knowledge are not specific to any gender. But the Qur'an has been systematically read in patriarchal ways as can be seen from the works of classical authors like al-Tabari (838-923), ibn Kathir (1301-1373) and others. In some cases the Qur'anic commentators, classical and modern, openly display their misogyny. As a result, a masculinised Islamic ethics has been constructed that highlights those virtues that fall under the category of *Muruwwa* or virility. Bravery, courage, honour, excellence in fighting – a range of values that came from the pre-Islamic era, and are linked to men's role as guarantor of tribal and family honour. The Qur'anic values that are not specific to men and women are relegated to the background. While the Qur'an addresses men and women without distinction, and asks both to use their reason and intellect, men have claimed the exclusive right of knowledge and exegesis for themselves. Amongst the hundreds of classic commentaries, not a single commentary by a woman has survived. The absence of the feminine perspective on the Qur'an has had a devastating effect on Muslim societies; it is another factor in the entrenchment of patriarchy. It can be argued that classical commentators paganised Qur'anic ethics by imposing pre-Islamic concepts and totalitarian domination of men on the worldview of Islam.

Similarly, both the biography (*Sira*) and the examples (*Sunnah*) of the Prophet Muhammad have been masculinised. The Prophet is presented as a political and patriarchal leader and not as a spiritual master. The religious is subordinated to the political. The life of Muhammad has been explained as a story of salvation, as the foundational political myth of the caliphate. The public space is presented as characteristic of the prophetic mission, a domain which excludes women. Thus both the religious and the political end up being dominated by men. As women cannot produce religious knowledge, they are considered to be persons deficient in their religion. As they do not display real virtues of courage, honour and fighting skills, they cannot take up leadership roles, even in a mosque.

The biography of the Prophet firmly places emphasis on military elements, conquests, and dominion. The 'feminine' aspects of the Prophet's life have been completely expunged. The fact that Prophet Muhammad had an intimate relationship with nature, to the extent that there are traditions in which he speaks to animals and caresses the mountains, is overlooked. The fact that the Prophet was an exceptionally tender person, who was moved by the plight of others, and who cried at the injustices he saw around him, is ignored. He praised the use of perfumes, encouraged grooming, displayed affection, washed his clothes, cooked, and cleaned his house. I am not saying that grooming, washing and cooking are women's issues. What I mean is that the clear separation of roles established by tradition does not originate from the behaviour of the Prophet. Rather, it emerges from the selection of certain aspects of his character and life that resonate with the patriarchal gaze of the interpreters.

The superhuman virility attributed to the Prophet is best illustrated by the emphasis we find in his supposed prodigious sexual capacity as related, for example, in the hadith collected by Ibn Sa'd (784-845). One of these states that the Prophet visited nine wives in a single night. Several other so-called hadith, attributed to the Prophet, state that women should always be ready to satisfy their husbands: 'If a man calls his wife to cohabit with her, she should go immediately, even if she is busy in making bread.' And : 'when a man calls his wife to bed and she is opposed so that the man spends all night angry, the angels curse her until she wakes up in the morning'. This is an expression of a powerful manhood that is able to dominate and control the sexuality of several women. Relations between the sexes are presented as an issue of power; the power of the male to placate the female libido.

When you construct an exceptional, almost mythological manhood, an ideal of an all-powerful man, always in control, always seeking conquest, its binary opposite has to be dangerous, wild and uncontrollable. Hence the dominant idea of female sexuality in Muslim societies as uncontrollable, a potential source of *fitna* (strife) that must be tamed and appeased in some way. As Fatima Mernissi notes, in the West sexism is based in the belief that women are biologically inferior. In the Muslim world, subjugation of women derives from the idea that women are incredibly powerful and dangerous. That is why all sexual institutions (polygamy, seclusion, segregation of the sexes) are used as strategies to contain this power. There is a hadith attributed to Imam Ali that provides justification for this: 'Allah the Almighty, created sexual desire in ten parts, then gave nine parts to women and one to men'. The classic fifteenth century Arabic sex manual, *The Perfumed Garden* by Muhammad Nefzawi, states that a woman is 'never satiated or tired to copulate... Her thirst for sex is never exhausted'. Since most Muslim men do not have the imagined prodigious sexual capacity of the Prophet, the best way they can keep female libido at bay is by isolating and secluding women.

The classical sources also offer us an alternative, somewhat contradictory, portrait of the Prophet. There are several hadith that present an opposite image of the Prophet as a loving, caring and warm man, attentive and respectful to his wives. His love of women is confirmed by a well-known hadith: 'I was made to love three things in this world: women, perfume and the brightness of the eyes in prayer'. The paradigm case is the marriage between the Prophet and Khadija. Here the Prophet is presented as a faithful husband and loving father, which in fact drives from the Qur'anic image of marriage: 'He created you from one living entity (a single soul), and out of it brought into being its partner, that he might take rest in her' (7:189); '[Allah] created for you mates from yourselves that you might find rest in them, and He ordained between you love and mercy' (30:21); and 'Allah has given you mates of your own kind, and has given you, from your mates, sons and grandsons, and has made provision of good things for you' (16:72).

This dimension of manhood is illustrated in a number of traditions about sex. In one, the Prophet cites, as an example of one of the three types of cruelty, 'a man who makes love to his wife before stimulation'. Another hadith compares sex without previous stimulation with animal behaviour: 'When any of you make love with his wife, do not go to her as a bird. Instead, he should be slow and deliberate'. In yet another tradition, the Prophet said: 'There should be none among you who makes love to his wife like animals, but rather should be a messenger between (you and your wife)'. When asked about the meaning of the messenger, he said: 'It means kissing and talking'. Indeed, the Prophet totally undermines the super-masculinity that dominates Muslim society: 'the best of you is the one who best treats his wife'. Treating a woman with love and respect is equivalent to prayer: 'The man who goes to the mosque (for prayer) and the man who is next to his wife have the same reward'.

As we have seen, the life of the Prophet, the Qur'an, as well as the names of God, can be used to develop diametrically opposite notions of masculinity. Given its emphasis on the spirituality of the Qur'an, its high regard for the feminine, and the ontological equality it accords to both sexes, we should expect the alternative model to be dominant in Sufism. But patriarchy is institutionalised in Sufism too.

We know from biographies produced during the early centuries of Islam that there were hundreds of Sufi women. But as Sufism established itself as *tariqas* or institutionalised paths, it reached an accommodation with judicial Islam and developed as orders that excluded women. The Sheikh now becomes the patriarchal head of the order which is run and managed exclusively by men. Al-Ghazali, the twelfth century theologian, is often presented as the ideal jurist and mystic rolled into one. In his *The Alchemy of Happiness* we find a chapter titled 'Marriage as a help or hindrance to the religious life', with the following pearls:

A further advantage of marriage is that there should be someone to take care of the house; cook the food, wash the dishes, and sweep the floor, etc. If a man is busy in such work he cannot acquire learning, or carry on his business, or engage in his devotions properly...

A third disadvantage of marriage is that the cares of a family often prevent a man from concentrating his thoughts on God and on a future life...

Woman is created weak, and requiring concealment; she should therefore be borne with patiently...

Wise men have said, "Consult women, and act contrary to what they advise." In truth there is something perverse in women, and if they are allowed even a little licence, they get out of control altogether, and it is difficult to reduce them to order again.

It is quite evident that al-Ghazali was not a particularly wise man. At all times he speaks of marriage as a help or hindrance to the religious life — of the man. The possibility that the wife could also have a religious life totally escapes him. Moreover, the qualities that the wife should have are very different from the qualities that he attributes to the religious man. The wife's qualities are subordinate to man's desires, in this case to the pretension of a religious or spiritual life. She must be discreet and helpful, and not too annoying. Al-Ghazali's ideal man lives entirely for religion, he can go to the mosque, practise musical auditions, engage in lofty intellectual debates, and enter into mystical ecstasy by remembering Allah — while the wife waits locked up at home. In fact, al-Ghazali suggests that women should be confined so men can devote themselves to God. When you get to the next chapter, on the love of Allah, you read that the Prophet declared 'Allah created man in His image' forgetting all about woman. And when he speaks about love, it means love of God, the love of the Prophet, love of oneself, but there is not a single word on love of women or love within marriage. We are told that the most sublime spiritual claims are not at odds with the contempt and the acceptance of discrimination against women.

Clearly, the aggression and contempt that al-Ghazali shows toward women cannot be extended to Sufism as a whole. There are examples in Sufism of a radically different approach to manhood. For example, in ibn 'Arabi, the twelfth-century Andalusian mystic and philosopher, we find positions that are not only favourable to women, but a genuine gender awareness. According to ibn 'Arabi, masculinity and femininity are mere accidents of birth and do not belong to the essence of human nature which is one. He states that women can reach the highest spiritual levels, including the gift of prophecy, and become leaders of their time. Indeed, he tells us that his first spiritual teachers were women. And he argues that women can be Imams, or lead the prayers in a mosque:

Some maintain that the Imamate of a woman is fully legitimate, both before men and to women, and I share this view. Others consider that it is licit only in front of women, with no men present. The Prophet declared the perfection of certain women and some men, even if the number of men that reach this perfection was greater. You can consider this perfection as imamate. Consequently, the Imamate of a woman is valid and you should not be paying attention to those who oppose it without proof.

Ibn 'Arabi says that women can be creators of religious and legal precedent, as demonstrated by the example of Hajar, the wife of Prophet Ibrahim. Hajar ran desperately between the Meccan hills of Safa and Marwa in search of water for her thirsty son Ismail – an event that became the basis of one of the rites of hajj, the pilgrimage to Mecca. He uses a similar analogy to argue that in certain circumstances, for example in the case of the *idda*, the period a widowed or divorced woman has to wait before she can remarry, the testimony of a woman is worth that of two men. Only when we understand the role that the feminine plays in ibn 'Arabi's spirituality can we understand the complexity and sophistication of his thought, as expressed in this passage:

The disciple should not have women friends until he has become a woman in her own soul. When he becomes female, joins the lower world and sees how the upper world is in love with him, his soul will be constantly in all states, times and influence as a woman in the act of marriage. You should not see his soul in its formal unveiling, or his status as a man, nor consider it to be a man in any sense. It should be seen, however, entirely as a woman. From that marriage act he must become pregnant and raise children.

Masculinity that evokes this passage is that of a man who has internalised the feminine as part of its own essence. To convert oneself to a women means to reach the perfect stage of receptivity, which enables the disciple to receive Allah. That is to say that a true believer must have the ability to receive the Grace of God – an ability that is seen as the principal characteristic of the feminine. To receive the revelation, the soul of the Prophet had first to become a woman. And to become a true Muslim, a man must first embrace the feminine within him. As perfect receptivity is the specific feature of feminine attributes, ibn 'Arabi says, it should not surprise us to see that Allah is more evident in women.

This idea of masculinity could not be more different than the notions of masculinity we find in conventional Islamic jurisprudence or *fiqh*. Here the jurist, the 'man of knowledge', sits at the apex dispensing rulings to the masses. By definition the jurist is a male, trained because of his excellent mental faculties to extract from the Qur'an the norms and lists of dos and don'ts that the rest of the faithful must follow. The Truth is seen as an abstract principle that has an objective and measurable value only accessible to jurists and scholars. The structure is characterised by power, order, austerity, self-control, and uses authoritarianism as a means to legitimate forms of control. It is an oppressive culture that has repressed tenderness, feelings, femininity and abandoned all notions of justice. To a very large degree, the historic masculinisation of Islam parallels the evolution of Islamic jurisprudence and the emergence of jurists and clerics as the guardians of faith. Sufism has contributed to this trend in promoting unquestioning obedience to the Sheikh.

The mission of religious experts is to extract from the Qur'an and the Sunna of the Prophet an entire legal system to be imposed as a divine law on the whole society. This establishes the primacy of the normative over the ethical, the judicial above the spiritual. Being a Muslim amounts to nothing more than to obey a distant God who dictates His laws, laws that are in the hands of the *ulama*, who are authorised as the sole interpreters of God's Will. And this body of religious scholars excludes women, under the excuse that they are not trained to interpret the Qur'an objectively, because of their emotional nature and deficiencies in religion. The resulting jurisprudence is strongly patriarchal, sealing the fate of Muslim communities, corseting and cutting the liberating elements of the Qur'an. The end product is the pre-eminence of a legal system focused on repression and the imposition of a perverted morality.

All this consolidates a specific type of masculinity: man as head of household, responsible for preserving the body and the honour of the women and providing for them; women, seen as weak and a source of conflict, are locked up indoors for protection and domestic chores. Traditional patriarchal *fiqh* introduces a number of innovations, in clear violation of the Qur'an and the example of the Prophet, to keep women in their place:

1) Although the Qur'an says, literally, that men and women are *awliya* (protectors) of one another (9:71), the notion of male guardianship over women has been imposed. Every woman must have a *wali* or protector, who acts as a guardian and is responsible for validating transactions, mediating in the matrimonial negotiations, and so on. The women go from being supervised by parents and siblings to being controlled by husbands and their relatives.

2) The marriage, which in the Qur'an is presented as a free union of equals and a source of peace and tranquillity (30:21, 7:189), becomes a contract of sale: a

woman sells her sexual services exclusively to the husband in exchange for a dowry and maintenance. But the husband has all the prerogatives: the woman has the duty of obedience (*ta'a*), and the husband the unilateral right to divorce and beat his wife in case of rebellion.

3) Although polygamy in the Qur'an is an exception in a society without social security to ensure the protection of orphans and widows (4:3), traditional *fiqh* considers polygamy as a prerogative of men – and apart from four wives he may also have many concubines.

All the principles and rationales of traditional jurisprudence are designed to favour men and subjugate women. However, *fiqh* does recognise certain basic rights such as the right to work, to inheritance, to impose conditions in the marriage contract, to divorce and abortion, and to testify in court. No doubt, Muslim women have benefited from these rights throughout history. But once you establish the superiority of men over women, male guardianship, seclusion of women, and the obedience of the wife, these rights become meaningless.

In short, the rights that the Qur'an gave women are placed under a patri-archal and authoritarian control.

The curtailment and control of women is taken to an unthinkable extreme with the notion of *harim*, that is an entity that is forbidden and inviolable. We normally think of *harim* as the women's quarter in a Muslim household; hence the English word 'harem'. But the term actually applies to women themselves. As Gema Martín Muñoz, the noted Spanish scholar of Islam, points out:

The notion of *harim* is interpreted as characteristic of women, which makes them forbidden for all those men outside the traditional family. This concept defines the wife as *hurmat al-rajul* (the holy thing of man), and is directly related to the issue of safeguarding the family honour. The honour provides legitimacy to the man, making the virginity of the daughter, sister or bride as his best guarantee; thus his sacred-ness has to be placed in a private space out of the public gaze. In a conception of family in which the group or community are dominant over the individual, virtue inevitably serves the honour of the group. Therefore, in traditional society women acquire identity only through the male intermediary (belonging to a clan or lineage in which she is 'the daughter of', 'the wife of' or 'the mother of').

Way back in the twelfth century, the celebrated Andalusian philosopher Ibn Rushd predicted that the exclusion of women would lead to the ruin of Muslim cities. He was spot on. The subjugation and seclusion of women from public space not only played an important part in the decay and decline of Muslim civilisation but also reduced Muslim societies into, what Moroccan thinker Malik Bennabi (1905-1973) called a state of 'colonisibility'. That is to say that by the end of the eighteenth century Muslim societies were ripe for colonisation. And the arrival of colonialism added yet another layer of masculinity. The invasion of the motherland was perceived as a violation of the mother and a breach of honour. Western civilisation was equated with reason, strength, discipline and order, against a Muslim world that was seen as weak, chaotic and decadent. The West was the male that dominated a feminised Muslim world. The Muslim male was outraged. He discovered that in the eyes of 'Westerners' he was lazy, useless, passive, and effeminate. Under these conditions, everything favoured further enhancement of a model of aggressive masculinity.

The process was given an extra edge with the onslaught of modernity and the emergence of the 'Islamic movements', such as the Muslim Brotherhood of Egypt and Jamaat-e-Islami of Pakistan. Here every aspect of Islam is subjugated by the political. Islam is reinvented as an ideology of resistance in opposition to 'Western values'. The main objective is not just to resist modernity in all its forms but also to thwart the decline of the collective self. Thus, everything has to revolve around Islam, everything has to be 'Islamised', and all must come under the banner of 'Islamisation'. By reducing Islam to an ideology of the trench, its spiritual dimension is dismantled, the possibility of a non-sexist Islamic masculinity evaporates, and, aggressive notions of manhood become even more entrenched.

And so we come to the apex of patriarchal masculinity: the Taliban. The masculinity embodied by the Taliban is one in which the feminine has completely disappeared. All is determined by the reality of war and its necessities. There is no need for attentive and kind people, only ruthless warriors able to kill the enemy without flinching. For greater effectiveness, the enemy and everything associated with him is turned into a demon. It is a lifestyle with no notion of compassion.

The Pakistani feminist Durre S. Ahmed has explained how the Taliban were originally children of war, torn from their families at a young age, raised in madrasas, orphanages, and educated by warriors, in a context of war and for war. In many cases these are people who have reached adult-hood without ever having seen a woman or having had any intimacy with a woman, and are therefore devoid of any notion of the meaning of femininity and its values. We ought to feel pity for the Taliban, who are, after all, only the product of a geo-political struggle and western aggression. Their lives have been stolen and they are responding with the most basic instincts of survival. They have not had an opportunity to develop their humanity natu-rally. What can we expect of their behaviour towards women? This is, of course, largely true. But we cannot ignore the fact that the Taliban are also a product of a historic warrior culture where aggressive masculinity is prized above all else. The paradox is that Western invasions, often presented as defence of women, lead to the strengthening of an aggressive Islamic concept of manhood to the exclusion of alternative models of masculinity.

The Way Forward

To summarise: we find two basic models of masculinity in Muslim societies throughout history.

The first model is the dominant one, and can be described as 'normative', in the sense that it foregrounds the legal dimension and has a concrete manifestation in discriminatory laws and customs. Allah is conceived as a Sovereign who dictates laws to men through revelation, interpreted by a select male elite, and passed on to the masses who must obey and follow. This is justified by a patriarchal and legal reading of the Qur'an, and is endorsed by the presentation of the Prophet Muhammad as a warrior and political leader. Those virtues that come under the heading of *muruwwah*, or virility are emphasised and highlighted. As a consequence, men are pre-sented as superior in intellect, knowledge, piety and leadership capabilities. Thus, a social order that gives prominence to the collective over the indi-vidual, the public over the private, reason over instinct, the objective over the subjective, is created and established. Men are considered the head of household, the guardians of women, and protectors of honour. Manhood is defined as the ability to keep women under control. The woman is seen as an emotional and defective being, whose uncontrolled sexuality threatens the honour of men. This patriarchal masculinity has been settled and consolidated over time as the only possible Islamic model of masculinity.

In opposition, but coexisting with the previous model, is the notion of masculinity based on the Names of Beauty of Allah. We can describe it as 'spiritual' to the extent that it foregrounds the cosmology and ethics of the Qur'an, and is nourished by the Qur'anic symbolism of the divine. It is based on a dynamic conception of divinity, and seeks to integrate the masculine and feminine attributes to transcend them. It considers the Qur'an as a guide in the spiritual development of believers. The Prophet Muhammad is seen as a liberator with qualities we associate with the feminine. It sees revelation as an intimate event, which is aimed at everyone, to be understood and applied by each one according to his or her abilities and in his or her own context. It gives priority to intuition and inner search over legalistic and obscurantist notions. The relationships between men and women are based on affection, mutual support and spiritual equality. The biological characteristics are considered secondary; everyone has the equal ability to acquire religious knowledge and contribute to the intellectual, social and cultural development of society.

The tension between the two models of masculinity is part of a wider internal tension in Islam. It permeates our understanding of Islam; and is present in all Islamic discourses.

The traditionalist discourse negotiates patriarchy by arguing that Islam gave women their rights fourteen centuries ago. Far from subjugating women, Islam gives a 'high status' to women. However, just talking about 'the high status of women' implies a particular thought, in which women have a different status. All sorts of convoluted arguments are presented to suggest that the traditional Islamic model of family is not oppressive to women, or that it does perpetuate violence and injustice against women. Indeed, it is even pointed out that some women themselves accept this model as 'natural' and ordained by Allah.

This apologetic discourse is even embraced by many who are seen as reformists. The idea is to negotiate new areas of power and autonomy for women, without yielding the patriarchal structure that underpins these relationships. It has to be acknowledged that Muslim reformists have made significant improvements in the status of women. But these 'concession rights' are achieved in exchange for the acceptance of women in the traditional religious order, which involves not only the primacy of men over women in the family, but also the control of religious discourse by entirely male hierarchies. The patriarchal structure is unquestioned. It is precisely this persistence of the patriarchal structure that makes any legal reforms ineffective. Legal changes are important but as long as the prevalent concept of masculinity remains intact, the notion of honour and guardianship stays and women will continue to be subjected to physical and moral violence.

The way forward is to realise that masculine and feminine do not correspond to man and woman, but are internal to every human being. The feminine is in equilibrium with the masculine as much in a man as in a woman. To try to limit the feminine to women and subordinate it to the masculine as being the exclusive essence of men is to upset the internal equilibrium of men and women, a polarity which is present in all creatures.

Patriarchy upsets this equilibrium, fostering a society based on oppression and authority. In theological terms, this involves overemphasising the masculine attributes of Allah, presented as an absolute Sovereign who delegates the governance of society to men of knowledge. Male chauvinism is the destruction of Islam as a well-balanced worldview. It breaks with the very order of creation and imposes an artificial order which is justified on religious grounds. It has to be shunned.

We need to nurture a masculinity that recognises the full humanity of women, their moral agency and individual responsibility, as believing women. This alternative masculinity represents a return to non-institutionalised forms of spirituality. It involves dethroning the legalistic visions of Islam. It is not only about recognising Muslim women's rights as a category subject but also about overcoming male-female categories as the properties of men and women. It is about recognition of our status as *insan*, the whole human being. And it is mostly about giving priority to the creative mercy or *rahma* of Allah, as a feminine attribute that should guide the lives of Muslim men and women.

OUT OF THIS DEAD-END

Ziba Mir-Hosseini

In July 1979, six months into the Iranian Revolution that brought Islamists into power, Ahmad Shamloo wrote a poem, 'In This Dead-End', that proved to be prophetic and captured what was to come.

They smell your breath.
You better not have said, 'I love you.'
They smell your heart.
These are strange times, darling...
And they flog
love
at the roadblock.
We had better hide love in the closet...
In this crooked dead end and twisting chill,
they feed the fire
with the kindling of song and poetry.
Do not risk a thought.
These are strange times, darling...
He who knocks on the door at midnight
has come to kill the light.
We had better hide light in the closet...
Those there are butchers
stationed at the crossroads
with bloody clubs and cleavers.
These are strange times, darling...
And they excise smiles from lips
and songs from mouths.
We had better hide joy in the closet...
Canaries barbecued
on a fire of lilies and jasmine,
these are strange times, darling...

Satan drunk with victory
sits at our funeral feast.
We had better hide God in the closet.

Shamloo's poem spoke to me, as it did to many Iranians of my background and generation. With the merger of religion and politics in the
aftermath of the revolution, love, beauty, joy and pleasure were all banished
from the public space, and anyone expressing them risked punishment. The
new authorities justified this policy in the name of Islam: it was God's law,
the Shari'a. This was my first encounter with Shari'a, the core of the faith
into which I was born, but a vision of it that I had not experienced before
and now found unjust and frightening.

At the time of the revolution, which I strongly supported, I was in my late
twenties, finishing my doctorate at Cambridge University. In 1980 I
returned home, newly married and with my doctorate in hand. I was looking forward to becoming a university teacher and living happily with my
husband. But neither was to be fulfilled; I found myself in Shamloo's 'dead-
end'. Under the new regime's 'Islamisation' policy the universities were
closed, and when they reopened three years later, there was no place for
people like me. Not only was I not qualified to teach 'Islamic anthropology', I was not a 'good Muslim': the file on me contained a report that I had
never 'fully observed the rule of hijab'. My marriage also broke down, and
I was shocked to discover that the Shari'a contract I had signed left me at
my husband's mercy. We had entered the marriage as equals, and it had
never occurred to me that he, a highly educated and liberal man, could
behave as he did: he would neither agree to a divorce nor give me permission to leave the country. My only option was to negotiate my release in a
court presided over by a religious judge. I started to educate myself in
Shari'a family law, and learned it well enough to secure a divorce. In 1984
I returned to the UK, and to academic life in Cambridge, where I began a
research project on theory and practice in Shari'a family law.

In hindsight, my studies have all been a search for understanding why
Shamloo's 'dead-end' came about, and how to get out of it. Between 1985
and 1989, I did fieldwork in family courts in Iran and Morocco; I wanted to
know, as an anthropologist, what it means to be married and divorced
under a law whose advocates claim it to be sacred. Investigating the details

of marital disputes that came to court, I focused on the litigants' strategies, and how judges came to make their decisions. I went beyond the letter of the law to examine the complexity of human relations, how individuals understand and relate to the sacred in the law. What I learned during those years of sitting in courts and listening to litigants, observing and conversing with judges, was that there was nothing sacred about Shari'a family laws. By the time a marital dispute reached court, whatever was sacred and ethical in the law had evaporated; neither the judges nor the disputing couple were concerned with the sacred. What was left of the Shari'a was a strong patriarchal ethos that privileged men and placed women under male authority: it was an ideology that preserved unequal and unjust power relations in marriage and society, and denied women voice and choice. My research in the courts was the subject of my first book, *Marriage on Trial*.

In the 1990s, I began studying Islamic jurisprudence, seeking to comprehend how classical jurisprudential texts constructed their ideas of male and female nature and men's and women's roles in society, and how these gender notions are reproduced, modified and reconstructed by the contemporary custodians of the Shari'a – the religious scholars or *ulema*. In Iran, I worked with a cleric who facilitated my entry into the world of the seminaries in Qom – the centre of religious learning – and helped me to establish a dialogue with the clerics in charge of a woman's magazine financed by the seminaries. In the process of this research I came to realise the importance of engaging with the Islamic legal tradition, and the need to develop a language and framework to argue for justice and equality from within the tradition. The more I learned about Islamic legal texts and the way they used the Qur'an, the more adept I became at conducting critical discussions with the clerics and challenging their assumptions about gender and law. I spent much time with women visiting the shrines in Qom, and was enraged at how badly the shrine custodians treated them; I could see how the strict codes of gender segregation and hijab worked to marginalise women and their experiences, and then to exclude women from the production of religious knowledge.

It was also during my time in Qom, and my engagement with jurisprudential texts, that I came to realise that I no longer wanted to be just an observer. Then in 1996, while writing my second book, *Islam and Gender*, based on my research in Qom, I started working with Kim Longinotto, an experienced independent British filmmaker. I met Kim through a mutual friend and we discovered that we shared the same frustrations with British media stereotypes of the Muslim world. We decided to make a documentary film in Iran, inspired by the court cases in *Marriage on Trial*. The first step was to apply to British TV commissioning editors for funding, and to Iranian officials for access and permission to film. Kim focused on the first and I on the second. This, my first experience in filmmaking, involved me in a long series of negotiations, not only with the Iranian authorities for permission and access, but also with myself: I had to deal with personal ethical and professional dilemmas as well as with theoretical and methodological issues of representation. The film's subject matter – divorce – inevitably entailed both exposing individuals' private lives in the public domain, and tackling a major issue that divides Islamists and feminists: women's position in Muslim family law.

In the course of these negotiations I confronted my own multiple identities. I found myself in an uncannily familiar situation of shifting perspectives and self-redefinition. When I started the film project, I was fresh from fieldwork in Qom. In my discussions with the clerics, I had had to justify my feminist stance, while in making the film I wanted to honour the Muslim and Iranian aspects of my identity. I came to realise that the problem was also inside me. I could not integrate the multiple discourses and representations of women in Iran, nor could I synthesise my own identities and positions. I disagreed equally with Iranian and Western stereotypes of 'women in Islam', images that did not reflect a complex reality. As a feminist, an Iranian and a Muslim, I objected to how women were treated in Iranian law, and wanted to change it. But my objections were not the same as those implied in Western media discourses or those aired by feminists after the Revolution: I did not see women in Iran as victims, but as pioneers in a legal system caught between religious tradition and modern reality.

All these experiences gave a new edge to my research, which has since become more focused on laws regulating sexuality: family laws, rulings on hijab and *zina* (sex outside marriage). I examine these laws from a critical feminist perspective, engaging with their jurisprudential and social rationale. In this sense, my approach is rather different from that of other Muslim feminists, who go back to the sacred texts in order to 'unread patriarchy'. I am not concerned, nor indeed qualified, to offer yet another new reading of the sacred texts. This terrain is highly contested; both those who argue for gender equality and those who reject it can and do provide textual support for their arguments, though commonly, in both cases, they take the texts out of context. Rather, I seek to engage with juristic constructs and theories, and to unveil the theological and logical arguments and legal theories that under-pin them. I attempt a kind of 'ethnography' of the juristic constructs on which the whole edifice of gender inequality in Muslim legal tradition has been built. Clearly, my aim is to demystify this edifice, to show that there is nothing 'sacred' about it, and that consequently it is open to change.

In 2002, when I began collaborating with Zainah Anwar, founder of the Malaysia-based non-governmental organisation Sisters in Islam (SIS), I crossed the line between scholarship and activism. SIS, formed in 1988, remains one of the few Muslim women's groups that approach Islam from a rights perspective, with no qualms in identifying as both Islamic and femi-nist. Trips to conferences and meetings in Malaysia and Indonesia opened a new world to me, where I felt at ease. There was none of the tension between religious and secular feminists that I was used to in the forums in Europe and North America where I had been presenting my work. I did not have to deal with the scepticism and resistance of colleagues in the feminist and Islamic studies circles where I had operated previously. I now spoke and wrote, not just as an academic merely concerned to analyse and explain, but also as an activist in search of solutions. This I found liberating. It was, moreover, a welcome change from my experiences with secular-minded women's groups and organisations in other Muslim countries, who tended to shy away from addressing women's issues from within a religious frame-work; for them, religion itself was the main problem, holding back any struggle for equality, and they saw my approach and my work as futile and counter-productive. At the same time, most Muslim scholars I encountered were suspicious of my approach and my engagement with international human rights and feminism, both of which they saw as alien and western-inspired.

Working with SIS, I saw how this tension between advocates of 'Islam' and 'feminism' played out, and I became increasingly convinced that, as long as patriarchal interpretations of the Shari'a are not challenged from within, there can be no meaningful and sustainable change in family laws in Muslim contexts. I saw the main problem to be the antagonism between 'secularist' and 'Islamic' approaches to the issue of women's rights; partly a legacy of colonial polices, it blocked any fruitful debate and prevented women's groups from forging a viable strategy for Muslim family law reform. But I thought it was possible to overcome this antagonism, by building coalition and consensus among different groups of women's rights activists. The person who could do this, I felt, was Zainah Anwar; I was hugely impressed with her style of leadership, her commitment to her faith and to justice, and her sharp political analysis. Above all, as the founder of SIS, she was highly respected among women's groups. She shared my views and took the initiative to organise a workshop in Istanbul in February 2007 that brought together a diverse group of activists and scholars from a range of countries. Our aim then was to persuade secular feminists of the need to take religion seriously, since the vast majority of Muslims whose rights they were defending were believers and wanted to live according to the teachings of Islam, and effective change could only come through a meaningful and constructive dialogue with those teachings. We also wanted to convince Muslim scholars that feminist scholarship was not an alien force but an ally in the search for justice, and that there was common ground between Islamic and human rights principles.

The Istanbul meeting led to the formation of a planning committee, charged with the task of setting out the vision, principles and conceptual framework of a new movement to be called Musawah, with the aim of forging a new strategy for reform. We proposed to link scholarship with activism to develop a holistic framework integrating Islamic teachings, universal human rights law, national constitutional guarantees of equality, and the lived realities of women and men. We commissioned a number of concept papers by reformist thinkers such as Amina Wadud, Khaled Abou El Fadl and Muhammad Khalid Masud. We used them as a way of opening new horizons for thinking, to show how the wealth of resources within Islamic legal tradition, and in the Qur'anic verses on justice, compassion and equality, can support the promotion of human rights and a process of reform toward more egalitarian family relations. These papers came together as the book *Wanted: Equality and Justice in the Muslim Family*, and became the basis of a wider discussion over two years with a larger group of Muslim scholars and human rights and women's rights activists. This discussion, over the course of two other workshops in Cairo and London, followed by constant electronic communication among the members of the committee, shaped the Musawah *Framework for Action*.

In the *Framework for Action*, we grounded our claim to equality and arguments for reform simultaneously in Islamic and human rights frameworks. Taking a critical feminist perspective, but most importantly working within the tradition of Islamic legal thought, we invoked two of its main distinctions. The first distinction, between Shari'a and *fiqh*, underlies the emergence of various schools of Islamic law and within them a multiplicity of positions and opinions. Shari'a, literally 'the way', in Muslim belief is the totality of God's will as revealed to the Prophet Muhammad. *Fiqh*, jurisprudence, literally 'understanding', is the process of human endeavour to discern the Shari'a and to extract legal rules from the sacred sources of Islam: that is, the Qur'an and the Sunna (the practice of the Prophet, as contained in hadith, traditions). In other words, while the Shari'a is to be found in sacred sources, its understanding, *fiqh*, is human and, like any other system of jurisprudence, mundane, temporal and local.

The second distinction, which we also take from Islamic legal tradition, is that between the two main categories of legal rulings (*ahkam*): between *'ibadat* (ritual/spiritual acts) and *mu'amalat* (social/contractual acts). Rulings in the first category, *'ibadat*, regulate relations between God and the believer, where jurists contend there is limited scope for rationalisation, explanation and change, since they pertain to the spiritual realm and divine mysteries. This is not the case with *mu'amalat*, which regulate relations among humans and remain open to rational considerations and social forces, and to which most rulings concerning women and gender relations belong.

These distinctions gave us the language and conceptual tools to challenge patriarchy from within Muslim legal tradition. The genesis of the gender inequality inherent in Islamic legal tradition, we argued, lies in a contradiction between the ideals of the Shari'a and the patriarchal structures in which these ideals unfolded and were translated into legal norms. Islam's call for freedom, justice and equality was submerged in the norms and practices of Arab society and culture in the seventh century and the formative years of Islamic law. Patriarchal norms were assimilated into *fiqh* rulings through a set of theological, legal and social theories and assumptions that reflected the state of knowledge of the time, and were part of the fabric of society. This was done by the sanctification of existing marriage practices and gender ideologies and the exclusion of women from the production of religious knowledge.

The further we move from the era of the Prophet, we argued, the more we find that women are marginalised and lose their political clout; their voice in the production of religious knowledge is silenced; their presence in public space is curtailed; their critical faculties are so far denigrated as to make their concerns irrelevant to law-making processes. Women had been among the main transmitters of the hadith traditions, but by the time the *fiqh* schools were consolidated, over a century after the Prophet's death, they had reduced women to sexual beings and placed them under men's authority.

One central problem that confronts us is how to negotiate the wide gap that has opened between contemporary ideas of justice and those that informed the jurists' rulings and dominant interpretations of the Shari'a. This makes Muslim legal tradition and its textual sources appear hypocritical or at best self-contradictory, and it is most felt in the area of family law, where *fiqh* is still the main source. For instance, take the following two statements:

The fundamentals of the Shari'ah are rooted in wisdom and promotion of the welfare of human beings in this life and the Hereafter. Shari'ah embraces Justice, Kindness, the Common Good and Wisdom. Any rule that departs from justice to injustice, from kindness to harshness, from the common good to harm, or from rationality to absurdity cannot be part of Shari'ah.

The wife is her husband's prisoner, a prisoner being akin to a slave. The Prophet directed men to support their wives by feeding them with their own food and clothing them with their own clothes; he said the same about maintaining a slave.

Both statements are by Ibn Qayyim Jawziyya, a fourteenth century jurist, regarded as a great reformer of his time, who became the source of inspiration for many twentieth century Islamists. The first statement speaks to all contemporary Muslims, and both advocates of gender equality and their opponents often use it as an epigraph. It was on the Musawah website – as well as those of many conservative and reactionary Muslim organisations. But when it comes to marriage, Ibn Qayyim, in the same book, compares a wife to a prisoner or a slave: she must obey her husband, who has absolute power over her. So where is justice for women? In fact the Musawah planning committee had a long debate over whether to use the first quotation;

one member sent an email saying 'hey guys, be careful, as Ibn Qayyim also has misogynist views!'

We kept Ibn Qayyim's first statement on the website, as we agree with him regarding what Shari'a is about, but his second statement, which merely expresses the classical *fiqh* construction of marriage, we refuted by offering an alternative construction of marriage that is in line with contemporary notions of justice and the lived realities of Muslims.

In 2010, as part of the knowledge-building component of Musawah, we began a long-term, multi-faceted project to challenge and rethink key legal concepts in Muslim family laws that continue to legitimate and institutionalise a patriarchal model of the family. One of these concepts is *qiwama*, which the classical jurists derived from Qur'an verse 4:34. This verse continues to be the main textual evidence in support of men's authority over women. It is often the only verse that ordinary Muslims know in relation to family law:

Men are *qawwamun* (protectors/maintainers) in relation to women,
according to what God has favoured some over
others and according to what they spend from
their wealth. Righteous women are *qanitat* (obedient)
guarding the unseen according to what God
has guarded. Those [women] whose *nushuz* (rebellion)
you fear, admonish them, and abandon them in
bed, and *adribuhunna* (strike them) If they obey you, do not
pursue a strategy against them. Indeed, God is
Exalted, Great.

The italicised words are now the centre of debate among Muslims; any translation of each term amounts to an interpretation. The translations I have given approximate the consensus of classical Muslim jurists as reflected in a set of rulings that they devised to define marriage and marital relations. These rulings, as we shall see, are premised on one single postulate: God made men *qawwamun* of women, which places them under male authority. This is what I call the *qiwama* postulate — using postulate in the sense of 'a value system that simply exists in its own right'.

We see the working of this postulate in all areas of Muslim law relating to gender rights, but its impact is most evident in the laws that classical jurists devised for the regulation of marriage and divorce. For them, men's superiority and authority over women was a given, legally inviolable; it was in accordance with a conception of justice in which slavery and patriarchy were accepted, as long as slaves and women were treated fairly. They naturally understood the verse in this light. They used the four key terms to define relations between spouses, and notions of justice and equity; marriage was a contract of exchange, and patterned after the contract of sale (*bay'*), which served as model for most contracts in *fiqh*. The contract, called *'aqd al-nikah* (the contract of coitus), has three essential elements: *ijab*, the offer made by the woman or her guardian; *qabul*, acceptance by the husband; and *mahr*, a gift from the husband to the person of the bride.

The contract established a set of default rights and obligations for each party, some supported by legal force, others by moral sanction. Those with legal force revolved around the themes of sexual access and compensation, as expressed in two central legal concepts: *tamkin* and *nafaqa*. *Tamkin*, obedience or submission, specifically sexual access, became the husband's right and thus the wife's duty; whereas *nafaqa*, maintenance, specifically shelter, food and clothing, became the wife's right and the husband's duty. But if a wife was in a state of *nushuz* (disobedience), then she lost her claim to maintenance. While the husband was given the unilateral and extra-judicial right to terminate the contract by *talaq* or repudiation, a wife could only terminate the contract with her husband's consent or the intervention of the court – if she produced a valid reason.

Classical jurists made no attempt to restrict a man's right to *talaq*, although there are numerous moral injunctions that could have enabled them to do so. For instance, there are sayings of the Prophet to the effect that *talaq* is among the most detested of permitted acts, and that, when a man pronounces it, God's throne shakes. Yet in its legal structure *talaq*, unlike marriage, was defined as a unilateral act that needed neither grounds nor the consent of the wife.

There were, of course, differences between and within the classical schools over the meanings of the three interrelated concepts – *nafaqa*, *tamkin* and *nushuz* – but they all shared the same conception of marriage, and the large majority made a woman's right to maintenance dependent on her obedience to her husband. The reason for their disagreement, as Ibn Rushd, the great twelfth-century Andalusian philosopher tells us, was 'whether maintenance is a counter-value for (sexual) utilisation, or compensation for the fact that she is confined because of her husband, as the case of one absent or sick.' And it was within the parameters of this logic – men provide and women obey – that notions of gender rights and justice acquired their meanings.

Whether these rulings corresponded to actual practices of marriage and gender relations is another area of inquiry, one that recent scholarship in Islam has started to uncover. These studies give us a much more complex picture of marital relations and court practices. But the fact remains that *qiwama*, itself a juristic construct, became the rationale for other legal disparities, such as men's rights to polygamy and to unilateral repudiation, women's lesser share in inheritance, and the ban on women being judges or political leaders. That is to say, women were not qualified to occupy positions that entailed the exercise of authority in society, because they were under their husband's authority and thus not free agents, and they would be unable to deliver impartial justice. Similarly, since men provide for their wives, justice requires that they be entitled to a greater share in inheritance. These inequalities in rights were also rationalised and justified by other arguments, based on assumptions about innate, natural differences between the sexes, such as: women are by nature weaker and more emotional, qualities inappropriate in a leader; they are created for child bearing, a function that confines them to the home, which means that men must protect and provide for them.

The term *qiwama* does not occur in the Qur'an. In a brilliant study for Musawah, Omaima Abou Bakr, Professor of English and Comparative Literature at Cairo University, shows how it became a core element of gender relations by documenting the significant changes in exegetical (*tafsir*) understandings of Verse 4:34 in the past ten centuries. She shows how and through what processes the first sentence, 'men are *qawwamun* in relation to women according to what God has favoured some over others and according to what they spend from their wealth', was continually reinterpreted until it became a patriarchal construct. She identifies four stages in this reinterpretation. In the first, the sentence was isolated from the rest of the Qur'an and turned into 'an independent and separate (trans-contextual) patriarchal construct'. This, she shows, was done by taking the term *qawwamun* out of its immediate context and transforming it into a grammatical *masdar* (a verbal noun or infinitive) of *qiwama*. In the second stage, when the

concept was consolidated, rational arguments and justifications were provided for hierarchal relations between men and women. In the third stage,
qiwama was expanded by linking it to the idea that men have an advantage
over women, from the last phrase in Qur'anic verse 2:228: 'But men have
a daraja (degree) over them (women).' This phrase, part of a long passage
on the theme of divorce, was again taken out of its immediate context and
interpreted as further support for male superiority; and a selection of
hadith were also invoked to establish women's duty of obedience. The final
stage came in the late nineteenth century with the modernist thinkers when
qiwama was linked with the theory of the naturalness of 'Islamic law' and the
ideology of domesticity, using pseudo-psychological knowledge to argue for
men's and women's different natures (fitra).

The term qawwamun, on which the whole fiqh edifice of male authority is
constructed, only appears once in the Qur'an in reference to marital relations, in verse 4.34. As regards marriage and relations between spouses, two
other terms appear over twenty times: ma'ruf (good way, decent) and rahmah
wa muwada (compassion and love). The closely related term wilaya does occur
in the Qur'an, in the sense of friendship and mutual support, but never as
endorsing male authority over women, which is the interpretation of the
term that is enshrined, alongside qiwama, in juristic rulings on marriage.

Our project in Musawah is still unfolding. We are asking new questions,
such as why and how did verse 4:34, and not other verses in the Qur'an,
become the foundation for the legal construction of marriage? Why did the
jurists choose not to translate the two other terms, ma'ruf and rahmah wa
muwada into legal rulings? Why is qiwama still the basis of gender relations in
the imagination of modern-day jurists and Muslims who resist and denounce
equality in marriage as alien to Islam? How, and through what juristic processes, was men's authority over women legitimated and translated into laws?
What does male guardianship, as translated in the concepts qiwama and wilaya,
entail in practice? How can Muslim women rethink and reconstruct the concepts in ways that reflect our own notions of justice? Can Shari'a-based laws
accommodate gender equality? How can we argue for an egalitarian construction of Muslim family laws from within Muslim legal tradition?

Our aim is to insert women's concerns and voices into the processes of
production of religious knowledge and legal reform. In this sense what we
are doing is part of the larger struggle for the democratisation of knowledge

in Islam and for the authority to interpret its sacred texts. What is becoming more and more transparent is that the struggle for gender equality is as much political as it is theological, and it is hard and at times futile to decide when theology ends and politics begin. A growing popular understanding of the nature of this struggle has been one of many unintended consequences of the rise of political Islam. It was the Muslim intellectuals' failure to recognise these linkages in Iran in the 1970s that brought us to 'the dead-end' that Shamloo's prophetic poem describes.

THE INEVITABLE CALIPHATE?

A History of the Struggle for Global Islamic Union, 1924 to the Present

REZA PANKHURST

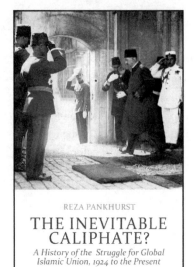

ISBN: 9781849042512

£18.99 / Paperback / 256pp

While in the West 'the Caliphate' evokes overwhelmingly negative images, throughout Islamic history it has been regarded as the ideal Islamic polity. In the wake of the 'Arab Spring' and the removal of long-standing dictators in the Middle East, in which the dominant discourse appears to be one of the compatibility of Islam and democracy, reviving the Caliphate has continued to exercise the minds of its opponents and advocates. Reza Pankhurst's book contributes to our understanding of Islam in politics, the path of Islamic revival across the last century and how the popularity of the Caliphate in Muslim discourse waned and later re-emerged. Beginning with the abolition of the Caliphate, the ideas and discourse of the Muslim Brotherhood, Hizb ut-Tahrir, al-Qaeda and other smaller groups are then examined. A comparative analysis highlights the core commonalities as well as differences between the various movements and individuals, and suggests that as movements struggle to re-establish a polity which expresses the unity of the ummah (or global Islamic community), the Caliphate has alternatively been ignored, had its significance minimised or denied, reclaimed and promoted as a theory and symbol in different ways, yet still serves as a political ideal for many.

'Reza Pankhurst provides a unique and probing examination of modern thinking on the caliphate. ... This detailed analysis of the ways in which the Muslim Brotherhood, Hizb ut-Tahrir, and al-Qaeda as well as smaller groups reformulate and use the concept today is both judicious and informed. It provides the most reliable guide available to an idea and political symbol that holds attraction for many Sunni Muslims while inciting anxiety, even fear, among others, including many non-Muslims and Shi'a.' — Professor James Piscatori, Durham University

WWW.HURSTPUBLISHERS.COM/BOOK/THE-INEVITABLE-CALIPHATE

41 GREAT RUSSELL ST, LONDON WC1B 3
WWW.HURSTPUBLISHERS.COM
WWW.FBOOK.COM/HURSTPUBLISHERS
020 7255 2201

THE OMNIPRESENT MALE SCHOLAR

Kecia Ali

Male scholars are everywhere. But where exactly are the women? The question leaps from the pages of yet another major study of the Islamic tradition. This one is by Muhammad Qasim Zaman, the highly regarded scholar and professor of Near Eastern Studies and Religion at Princeton University. *Modern Islamic Thought in a Radical Age* examines, the blurb tells us, 'some of the most important issues facing the Muslim world since the late nineteenth century'. It deals with major shifts in educational and political structures, transformed patterns of religious learning, and pervasive, endemic violence toward women, especially in the Indian subcontinent.

The index entry for 'women' has fifteen sub-headings; 'marriage' has ten. Yet in that same extensive index, actual women are virtually absent. Of nearly 250 named individuals, from formative-period scholars through medieval luminaries to contemporary pundits and academics, a scant three – barely more than one per cent – are women, all teaching in Western universities and none writing as a Muslim.

The index does contain one reference to a Muslim woman, an Indian divorcee whose rotten treatment by her ex-husband in 1985 provoked an uproar over Islamic law and spawned the misnamed Muslim Women Protection of Rights on Divorce Act; she lends her name to the 'Shah Bano controversy (India).' Other Muslim women, a few of them named, appear in the body of the book, especially in the chapter 'Women, Law, and Society,' as victims of honour crimes, harassment, and forced marriage. But there are no female scholars, thinkers, or leaders cited concerning either of topics in the book's subtitle, 'Religious Authority and Internal Criticism'. Even the thirty-page bibliography is light on contributions by women, with no more than two or three female authors per page. Leila Ahmed's canonical 1992 *Women and Gender in Islam* is missing; so is Samira Haj's *Reconfiguring Islamic*

Tradition: Reform, Rationality, and Modernity, published in 2010. Also absent are the numerous monographs by women on women in early twentieth century Egypt, a time and place Zaman discusses at some length.

Zaman is a careful scholar, and gender issues are clearly on his mind in this otherwise excellent book. So how is it that despite the centrality of women's issues to the story of ideas Zaman tells, one looks in vain for women's ideas on the issues?

Who is an authority?

Let me acknowledge that it's bad form to criticise someone for writing the book they actually wrote rather than the one you wish they had written. Zaman's 'dramatis personae' are the traditionally-educated *ulama*, or religious scholars. He draws on philosopher Alisdair MacIntyre's famous description of a tradition as 'an argument extended through time in which certain fundamental agreements are defined and redefined' through ongoing argument and debate with external and internal critics. Since the *ulama* include practically no women, it is no surprise that its internal critics are male.

Still, this cannot entirely explain women's striking absence from the book. There is no hermetic seal around the category of *ulama*. The key players in *Modern Islamic Thought* are Indian Deobandis and Egyptian Salafis along with Qatar-based mufti Yusuf al-Qaradawi but non-*'alim* men pop up throughout. The late Pakistani scholar Fazlur Rahman, who wrote extensively about Islamic reform, and Tariq Ramadan, Oxford professor and exponent of 'European' Islam, make cameos. In listing the people excluded from al-Qaradawi's *Ulama Union*, Zaman mentions 'dissident Iranian intellectual' 'Abdolkarim Soroush, exiled 'Egyptian scholar' Nasr Hamid Abu Zayd, and 'Syrian civil engineer' Muhammad Shahrur and explains why they do not belong. The exclusion of women like Siti Musdah Mulia, former head of the Indonesian Council of Ulema's research division; American theologian and gender-justice advocate Amina Wadud; or Moroccan sociologist Fatima Mernissi passes without comment, seemingly too obvious to mention. But why should this be so?

We read about Qaradawi and early-twentieth-century Egyptian scholar Muhammad Rashid Rida's discussions of marriage but what of their female interlocutors? Even if Rida did not directly engage the flourishing turn-of-the-century Egyptian women's press debate on polygamy, he was undoubtedly aware of its contours. And anyway, might it not have been instructive for Zaman to compare the register in which he defended polygamy to that in which his countrywoman Malak Hifni Nassef, writing as Bahithat al-Badiya, lambasted it? When Qaradawi gives his seal of approval to *misyar* marriages, second-class unions in which women relinquish rights to support and regular visitation, he implicitly engages with Muslim women's objections; Zaman notes his calculated rhetorical appeal to female choice. Wouldn't it be important to know what these women say, if only to better understand what is significant in the argument of the *ulama*?

It is no secret that the interpretive monopoly of the *ulama* has been broken, nor that many *ulama* still wield considerable power in interesting ways. The exclusion of women's ideas and contributions gives an impoverished picture of the intellectual and social climates in which these men work. Rather than an atavistic force mired in the past, the *ulama* have been, in Zaman's phrase, 'custodians of change'. In the process, they stake their claims to authority in ways that require accommodation to new conditions. To compete in modern discursive arenas, the world of the online fatwa and global satellite programming, they must offer an attractive product.

Women may not be full conversation partners, or even subordinate consultants, in *ulama* circles. Nevertheless they are part of the *ulama's* clientele, part of their audience, part of their flock – and, increasingly, part of their competition. Laymen and women, modernists, Islamists and traditionalists, approach issues differently today in part because of another major change in the period Zaman studies: the emergence of women scriptors since the late nineteenth century as participants in debates over religious issues, foremost, but not exclusively, those concerning women.

Interlude 1

In October 2011, I participated in a meeting of Muslim and Orthodox Jewish scholars and religious leaders in New York. I was a last-minute replacement for a male scholar who had to bow out. Everyone else on the programme was male. The Jews were rabbis; the Muslims included professors, a chaplain, and the Sudanese-born president of the Islamic Society of

North America, Mohamed Magid. The daytime sessions were by invitation only and the audience was mostly male and academic; the evening session, open to the New York community, was a better mix. That night, my rabbi counterpart and I each gave a lecture on 'Foundational Texts,' to which two people – two men – from each tradition responded, including Magid. And then, in the question-and-answer session, someone lobbed in a leading question about scripture, gender, and family authority, which I had chosen, after some internal debate, not to talk explicitly about. (I didn't want to be the woman who always talks about women.)

Magid addressed it head on. He brought up the frequently quoted verse of the Qur'an, 4:34, which is usually understood to affirm male authority over women and to direct men who fear 'women's "rebelliousness"' to 'admonish them, leave them alone in bed, and strike them'. Magid said that when community members ask him about it, and the authority it seems to grant husbands to hit their misbehaving wives, he insists that they read it in the light of the egalitarian verse with which the chapter begins.

Two things struck me at the time as vital in Magid's response. First, he understood equality in 4:1's creation narrative ('Oh people, revere your Lord who created you from a single soul and created from it its mate and from the two of them brought forth many men and women spread far and wide') not merely as a statement about men and women's equal worth as human beings but as directly relevant to questions about male authority and disciplinary power. Second, even more fundamental, he took for granted that that passage's narrative actually was egalitarian. If this seems obvious now, it was anything but three decades ago.

Magid's remarks illustrated a point I had made in my lecture about shifting norms of interpretation within Muslim communities. It is not just the key ideas that have changed but the ways in which the text is approached: often in isolation from its longstanding commentaries, directly, by people not trained as traditional scholars. As US-based Pakistani scholar Riffat Hassan had pointed out in the late 1980s, Muslim commentators had almost universally assumed the first human was male and the second, created from him, female and therefore 'ontologically secondary and derivative.' She objected; the only evidence for this came from the tradition of the Prophetic hadith; the Qur'an says no such thing. African-American scholar Wadud's groundbreaking *Qur'an and Woman*, which was first published in Malaysia in 1992, brought new considerations to bear, largely those of Arabic grammar. Its grammatical explanations mirrored classical commentary, but it bypassed other elements of that tradition, most signally, engagement with the works of other commentators. Wadud was not playing insider baseball.

Her constituencies included the Malaysian organisation Sisters in Islam, with whom she had worked, and small communities of academics, including Pakistani-born Asma Barlas, who followed up, refined, and departed from Wadud's arguments in her *Believing Women in Islam*. These and an increasing number of essays and books, written in English, engaging with theories about reading and the creation of meaning, were not aimed at the traditional *ulama*, but they did engage with male Muslim thinkers. Wadud cites Egyptian Islamist Sayyid Qutb, but is most profoundly influenced by Fazlur Rahman. Neither is a member of the traditional *ulama*.

Departing from tradition

If Zaman's story is an analysis of the *ulama* and their internal debates, and Wadud's intervention is a deliberate move away from the tradition, Sherman Jackson's *Islam and the Blackamerican*, published in 2005, is a hybrid. Jackson, a Sunni Muslim who holds the King Faisal Chair of Islamic Thought and Culture at the University of Southern California, examines Black American history and theology. He brings the classical Sunni Muslim tradition, including a few of its recent interpreters, into conversation with an African-American intellectual tradition, largely Protestant. The people whose ideas he discusses are again overwhelmingly male. The index names 187 men and eight women, just over four per cent. The fact that the cover photo is of 'Nation Sisters' might lead a reader to expect that gender issues would get a significant airing; instead, Jackson presents a paragraph of very intriguing hypotheses about hyper-masculinity and feminisation in American Christianity and Islam. He notes that the issues deserve 'serious attention,' but fall outside the scope of the work. He indicates his hope to address them in later studies. Unfortunately, gender issues recede further into the background in *Islam and the Problem of Black Suffering*, a ground-breaking work published in 2009, interweaving Sunni theological ideas and African-American religious thought to construct a viable Black-friendly Sunni theology in the face of ongoing racial harms. And individual women fade too: its

index names four women, including a fourteenth century Damascene acolyte of the theologian Ibn Taymiyyah, and 137 men; still better than Zaman
but nonetheless dismal.

An insistence that the topic of women is too important to be dealt with
briefly can serve to defer it continually. In his slim but influential book
Common Questions, Uncommon Answers, the late Algeria-born, France-based
scholar Mohammed Arkoun begs his readers' pardon 'for not having undertaken a detailed analysis of numerous verses that for centuries fixed the
status of women.' He blames limitations of space. The chapter 'Women'
stretches over four pages. The chapter 'The Person' occupies twenty. There
is no chapter on men.

Despite his postponement of any sustained discussion of gender matters,
Jackson addresses two points that bear directly on women's intellectual
contributions. The first is his argument for engagement with the classical
tradition. In *Islam and the Blackamerican*, he proposed mastery 'of the super
tradition of Islam' as essential for Black American Muslims. Such mastery
involves extensive training, linguistic skill, and possibly personal apprenticeship. By *Islam and Black Suffering*, though, he had come to believe that standard 'both unreasonable and unnecessary'. Rather, one need only 'gain
enough facility in Tradition to display the requisite degree of 'rhetorical
etiquette' to be recognised as playing by the rules of Islamic 'public reason'
when vindicating, crafting, or critiquing doctrinal and practical positions' .

In theory, the lowered bar for participation in Islam's tradition is good
news for women, who confront significant obstacles in obtaining traditional
education. As Zaman discusses at length in *Modern Islamic Thought*, the
dichotomy between madrasa and secular education no longer holds and
university education at least supplements when it does not replace traditional textual learning. And, in any case, women are seeking out various
forms of hybrid religious education, including in the West.

No, the problem here is the passive 'to be recognised'. Recognised by
whom? This assumes that someone in power is willing to recognise someone
outside his (ethnic, scholarly, class, or gender) circle as an acceptable participant. Jackson recounts an incident where Egypt's Grand Mufti Ali
Gomaa bestowed the status of legitimate disputant by virtue of 'rhetorical
etiquette' on Qutb, the ideologue of the Muslim Brotherhood, by calling

him *shaykh* Sayyid Qutb. Like a nineteenth century London men's club, to enter the ranks of shaykhs, one needs to be sponsored by a member.

Interlude 2

I pointed out to my department chair that with a recent retirement and a promotion, all the full professors in my department at Boston University are male, and all the associate professors female (the assistant professors are a mix). He was puzzled: Why should that matter? I replied that since only full professors deliberate and vote on the promotion of associates, when the first of us comes up for promotion, there won't be a woman in the room. I hadn't thought about that, he said. And then, to his credit, he did.

Provincialising Men

Discounting Muslim sexism by describing non-Muslim sexism is a cheap trick. But it's fair game to describe how patriarchal traditions align to prejudice women. It is not just scholars of Islam, in any sense of that phrase, who ignore women in favour of their male counterparts; women's perspectives and contributions to thought are routinely discounted in Western contexts. Lists of major Western thinkers, key intellectuals, or important reformers display similar bias. I have an unscientific but long-standing practice of noticing this sort of list. Sometimes there are no women at all, or only one, in a list. For example, Oneworld's *Makers of Muslim History* biography series contains 28 men, 1 woman; Harper Collins' *Eminent Lives* 12 men, 0 women. Occasionally, women approach a fifth or even a quarter of a group as in *Penguin Lives*. But women usually comprise between 10 and 15% of any given list of key people. A local university's list of high-profile lectures for the upcoming year, 'Seven Thought-Provoking Evenings of Diverse Opinions and World Perspectives,' included only one woman among its luminaries. Might the selection bias in each of these instances result from choices made by high-ranking shapers of opinion at universities or publishing houses? No, it applies to crowd-sourced determinations of significance as well. Historian Claire Potter recently showed that women are dramatically underrepresented in Wikipedia contributors and articles. (Her blog is entitled 'Prikipedia.')

So, the downplaying and omission of women as significant thinkers is not exceptional to works on the Muslim tradition, but it is pervasive there. The recent list of the Institute of Ismaili Studies' Mohammed Keshavjee is typical, putting Fazlur Rahman alongside 'activist thinkers like Tariq Ramadan, Mohamed Talbi, Abdolkarim Souroush, Mohamed Shahrour, Ebrahim Moosa and Abdullahi An-Na'im'. Smaller groupings are even less likely to include women, even where they are attentive to geographic diversity. Carol Keersten's *Cosmopolitans and Heretics: New Muslim Intellectuals and the Study of Islam*, focuses on Arkoun, Indonesian Nurcholish Madjid, and Egyptian Hasan Hanafi. David L. Johnston's pamphlet essay 'Evolving Muslim Theologies of Justice' selects again 'three contemporary Muslim thinkers': Egyptian Jamal Al-Banna; Malaysia-based, Afghan-born Mohammad Hashim Kamali; and US-based Egyptian Khaled Abou El Fadl as its subjects.

Not every work excludes women completely. An edited volume on *Modern Muslim Intellectuals and the Qur'an* contains chapters on Madjid, Arkoun, Rahman, Abu Zayd, and five other men, including a Syrian, a Tunisian, a Libyan, an Iranian, and a Turk. Wadud rounds out the ten figures. In her chapter, Barlas observes that 'Wadud is the only woman in this group' which attests to both 'her own achievements in a male-dominated field and her charge that, historically, women have been excluded from Muslim interpretive communities.'. Indeed, Wadud is one of the few figures semi-regularly mentioned when Muslim thinkers are brought up (though Jackson, despite his focus on African-American Islam, does not discuss her). She is the only woman among the eleven Muslim and non-Muslim respondents to Abou El Fadl's *The Place of Tolerance in Islam*, a *Boston Review* volume from a series which packages an essay with responses by noted figures. The cover proclaims 'Khaled Abou El Fadl with Tariq Ali, Milton Viorst, John Esposito, and Others.' Wadud, appropriately enough, is an Other.

Georgetown professor Esposito's own list of Muslim reformers in his book *The Future of Islam* (2009) has a far better ratio of females to males than any of these works: three women, including Wadud, out of eleven figures. He aimed for 'a representative sample.' He explains that his 'primary criteria for selection were that each enjoys a significant following or audience and that together they provide a spectrum of religious and lay as well as traditionalist, or perhaps more accurately neo-traditionalist, and modernist voices for change in the twenty-first century.' He lists Pakistani preacher and educator Farhat Hashmi and Egyptian political scientist and internet entrepreneur (she co-founded Islam Online) Heba Raouf alongside Wadud.

Perhaps it is because his category is 'reformers' rather than intellectuals or thinkers that women comprise slightly over a quarter of his main examples, though quite a number of other male figures are mentioned in passing. Even so, the women do not get the same depth of attention as the male reformers. After noting that the three are 'are Islamically and Western-educated scholars from very diverse cultural contexts' he highlights their femaleness and their concern with gender: 'Hashmi, Wadud, and Raouf are female reformers who often have diametrically opposed positions on women in Islam.' Raouf is mentioned on only one other page; Hashmi and Wadud appear twice more. Televangelists Amr Khaled (Egypt) and Indonesian scholar Abdullah Gymnastiar merit three index citations apiece, Madjid has four and Ramadan five, as does Ali Gomaa. Mustafa Ceric, Boznia-Herzegovina's Grand Mufti, has six. The other two figures mentioned, England's Timothy Winter (aka Abdul Hakim Murad) and, again, Qaradawi, merit, respectively, eight and nine index citations, including some under the subheading 'gender issues.'

Not only do people writing about Muslim reformers generally fail to take women seriously, so do reformers themselves. Ramadan is the most egregious offender here. His *Radical Reform: Islamic Ethics and Liberation* (Oxford, 2008) makes a broad argument that one must approach current problems in new ways. Like Zaman, Jackson, and Esposito, he signals the interdependence of 'Western' and religious educational systems and quotes people – men – from various backgrounds. He argues that 'text scholars', the *ulama*, must collaborate with 'context scholars', by which he means specialists outside of the religious sciences. Instead of formalist fatwas that seek to accommodate Muslims to the modern world, there must be a broader project of transformation.

Ramadan's book, like Zaman's, contains copious references to women's issues (Marnia Lazreg, author of *Questioning the Veil*, refers to his 'tantalising yet limited ideas about women'). Unlike Zaman, Ramadan rhetorically welcomes women into the fold of scholarship, religious and especially worldly, stating over and over that 'men and women' or, twice as often, 'women and men' must contribute to the reconsideration, reformulation, and reconstruction he describes. Yet despite Ramadan's insistently inclusive language, the main text is entirely devoid of female scholars, thinkers, or reformers, present or past. It is practically void of women at all. Ramadan names only four Muslim women, all from the Prophet's time. Of these four, two are Muhammad's wives and one is his daughter. One long endnote – twice as long as any other – lists numerous works by Muslim women, including a book of mine, but marginalises female thinkers and female scholarship from the body of the work. Ramadan exhorts women to leap into the fray but pointedly ignores those who do. Relegating women's books to a note, he segregates women and fails to engage our 'interesting contributions' on their merits, postponing such critical reflections to some possible future in which 'women and men' will radically reform the world.

The late Abu Zayd does a little better: he criticises women's scholarship. In *Reformation of Islamic Thought* (2006), he offers a stark, though not entirely unfair, assessment of the accomplishments of Muslim feminist Qur'anic interpretation, claiming that it is 'unable to go beyond existing male hermeneutics,' that the approach to certain verses positing differences between men and women 'is neither new nor original,' and will flounder 'as long as the Qur'an is dealt with only as a text – implying a concept of author.' Abu Zayd, who was also deeply critical of the approaches to the Qur'an taken by male reformists, saw a major shift in the understanding of scripture and its relationship to community practice (and law) as necessary for social transformation. Female exegetes' accomplishments in shifting the debate so that even conservatives must offer at least lip service to principles of justice and perhaps equality meant nothing in the face of their failure to offer something substantively new and theoretically cogent. The broader victory Wadud and others have won, changing what is taken for granted about women in the Qur'an and Islam, is insufficient. Abu Zayd takes women as intellectuals seriously enough to condemn their scholarship on the same grounds that he condemns most men's, but his failure to recognise the real-world objectives female scholars have attempted to meet means that he has failed to appreciate significant elements of women's interpretations. American scholar Aysha Hidayatullah's forthcoming *Feminist Edges of the Qur'an* provides an equally critical but also sympathetic, contextualised, and ultimately constructive account of women's encounters with scripture.

If Wadud's writing gets perhaps less attention than it should, the same cannot be said of her occasional public acts. Magid's predecessor Ingrid·

Mattson, the first female, first convert, and first North-American born president of ISNA, headed that organisation during the controversy that followed Wadud's leading of a public mixed-gender Friday prayer in New York in 2005. Mattson struck a presumably sincere and also carefully calibrated balance, weighing in against women's imamate for male worshippers, but in favour of significantly greater attention to women's perspectives in all matters of leadership and authority. As she has since pointed out, 'It is my observation that when this religious leadership does not include women, their experiences, concerns and priorities will not be well represented. I am aware that there are those who would argue that this is not inevitable. There are those who are convinced that men are capable of guiding and leading the Muslim community in a just manner without female peers. I would argue that common sense tells us that even the most compassionate and insightful group of men will overlook some of the needs and concerns of the women of their community. More compellingly, experience teaches us that when women are not in leadership positions in their communities ... they have few means to access the rights they possess in theory.'

One need not impute dastardly motives to male authorities to observe that they often fail to observe things women notice (like my department chair), and that their perspectives are not somehow universal and impartial while women's are limited and particular. Women's exclusion from the ranks of the religiously authoritative has profound consequences, including, the reinforcement of the notion, as Wadud puts it, that 'the normative Muslim is male.'

Interlude 3

I was in a meeting where the antics of a few senior male faculty members at another university were being discussed. One person used the term diva. Another said prima donna. I pointed out the irony in using feminine terms to discuss oversized male egos. All the women and most of the men around the table laughed. The ranking male at our host institution chided me, though, for analysing things 'too deeply.'

The Right Question

Some years ago, in a characteristically brief and incisive essay, Jewish feminist scholar Judith Plaskow argued that in addressing her tradition's marginalisation of women, 'the right question is theological.' It is not merely a matter, she stated, of patriarchal or misogynist men's textual interventions or social restrictions. Rather, it is a fundamental question about the nature of God, and God's relationship to humanity. Legal and liturgical tweaking can go only so far. As the problem is deeply rooted so must be the solutions.

In the case of Islam, I think the right question is epistemological. Yes, theological questions have got short shift in Muslim feminist thinking, which has mostly been concerned with scriptural interpretation and, to a lesser extent, law. Recent provocative and rich meditations on the nature of revelation, justice, and human personhood by Laury Silvers, Islamic studies scholar at University of Toronto, and Sa'diyya Shaikh, the feminist thinker at University of Cape Town, among others, promise interesting conversations to come. I would contend, though, that underpinning these theological issues and the more mundane ones about legal and practical aspects of Muslim life, there are questions of epistemology. How do we determine what constitutes valid knowledge? As Wadud asks in *Inside the Gender Jihad*: what ways of knowing are possible? Are there gendered dimensions to epistemology? Does women's personal experience play a role, and if so, what sort of role? How can experience be communicated and verified? How and when can one generalise from one's own experience to say something broader about Islam, about humanity, about the world we inhabit?

Of course, diverse experiences of the world do not arise only through gender difference. Geographic diversity, race, and economic conditions can also lead to divergent perspectives. As Barlas notes in her essay on Wadud, she was also the only convert among the ten 'modern Muslim intellectuals' profiled in the book, which 'leads her to raise questions about Islam that people who are born Muslim often do not consider asking.' The same is obviously true for African Americans, as Jackson argues, and women. Therefore, excluding women from positions of religious leadership, Mattson notes, will curtail ordinary female community members' access to religious education, prayer spaces, and support of various kinds.

I have moved from women's absence from scholarly books to women's absence from mosques. There is not a unilinear, causal relationship in either direction. But the two absences reverberate. When women, women's ideas, and Muslim women's ideas in particular, are dismissed by 'religious scholars,' by academics, and by ordinary Muslims, not only are Muslim communities negatively affected but scholarship about Muslims is impoverished. I have lumped together Zaman's analytical study of the Muslim tradition with works of committed, confessional scholarship by Jackson and Ramadan. Zaman aims to elucidate an aspect of the tradition; Jackson and Ramadan aim to shape it. Zaman focuses on the Arab Middle East and the Indian subcontinent, Jackson on Black America, Ramadan on Europe. And yet they are united by their pervasive, consistent, insistent failure to take women's ideas seriously. In Ramadan's case, his rhetorical gestures towards the inclusion of women only highlight his failure to practise what he preaches.

Excluding women from studies of the Muslim 'tradition' isn't just about the fact that women are not present, though. With no women around, and their absence unremarked, men are taken to represent 'human beings.' With no women's books discussed, men's books are assumed to tell the whole story. Even without putting women in the narrative, simply registering women's absence as noteworthy would mean that maleness would cease to be an unmarked category.

In *Radical Reform*, Ramadan argues that Muslims must respond to the challenges of today's world not merely by adapting to it but by transforming it. Feminist historians have long made a similar argument for history. Instead of attempting to repair the deficiencies of the dominant male-centered narrative by adding women and stirring, they have argued that taking women's experiences as foundational both requires and makes possible historical scholarship that better reflects many facets of human experience.

If feminism, as the saying goes, is the radical notion that women are people, then perhaps Muslim feminism is the radical notion that Muslims are, at least sometimes, women. If so, then it makes sense for scholars of Islam to pay attention.

OTHER THAN MEN

Asma Afsaruddin

Official pre-modern histories of Islam typically tell the stories of prominent men and their lives. Unofficial chronicles and literary sources, however, muddy this picture for us – occasionally, they preserve for us accounts of prominent and not-so-prominent women who made a difference in the life of their communities and without whose contributions the Islamic tradition would not recognisably be the same.

One of these women is Umm 'Umara. You are in good company if you ask: 'who was she?' There might even be an obvious reason why her name has receded to the sidelines of history, even though early biographers paid quite a bit of attention to the details of this early Muslim woman's life. Umm 'Umara, after all, was the kind of woman who makes many men (and some women) feel uncomfortable. She asked questions, she sometimes loudly protested the lack of fairness she saw around her, particularly in regard to women, and she was active in various public events. The truth of the matter is that she was typical of the early Muslim women from the generation of the Prophet Muhammad in the first century of Islam and through most of the early medieval period. Umm 'Umara was one of the well-known women Companions of the seventh century and is particularly valorised in the early literature for her courage on the battlefield. According to the ninth-century biographer, Ibn Sa'd (d. 845), she fought fearlessly in a number of the early battles in Islamic history. During the battle of Uhud, she defended the Prophet himself against a particularly ruthless enemy and as a consequence was fulsomely praised by him for her matchless bravery.

Another very important reason to remember her name is that she is cited as the reason for the revelation of a significant verse in the Qur'an. Most verses in the Qur'an have what is known as an occasion of revelation behind them; in other words, commentaries that recorded the specific historical event in the Prophet Muhammad's life which prompted the revelation of a particular verse. It is reported that Umm 'Umara remarked to the Prophet, regarding the Qur'anic revelations up to that point: 'I see that everything pertains to men; I do not see the mention of women'. As a result, this particular verse was revealed:

Those who have surrendered to God among males and females; those who believe among males and females; those who are sincere among males and females; those who are truthful among males and females; those who are patient among males and females; those who fear God among males and females; those who give in charity among males and females; those who fast among males and females; those who remember God often among males and females – God has prepared for them forgiveness and great reward (33:35).

In Islam, and I would assume in most faith traditions, God clearly listens to women and is responsive to their needs. Women who can read and understand the Qur'an for themselves draw their power and strength from the Qur'an itself. The Qur'an, as we see in this passage for example, specifically addresses women and uses language deliberately inclusive of them. This verse, above all, maintains the absolute religious and spiritual equality of women and men – no ifs or buts.

The Qur'an also confers specific legal rights on women, some of which had not previously been granted to women and were quite revolutionary in their consequences. Thus the Qur'an gives women the right to contract their own marriages, to hold property in their own names even after marriage, to seek divorce under specific conditions, although this is a practice not encouraged either for men or women, and to expect fair and equal treatment from their husbands and fathers in particular. Islam also recognises the special gifts that women are endowed with as compassionate caregivers and nurturers within the family. A famous saying of the Prophet places the position of the mother far higher than the father in terms of the respect and love she is entitled to from her family. Another saying of the Prophet glowingly asserts that Paradise lies beneath the feet of mothers.

The early Islamic community was also inclusive of women regarding political rights and citizenship. Political rights for women are usually assumed to have been born in the modern period and as a consequence of the rise of the modern nation-state. Prominent among such rights is the right to vote, the most graphic indicator of modern participatory citizenship. Early historical and biographical sources contain valuable information that allows us to state that there was a recognised public, political space for women from the very inception of Islam in the seventh century. When the Muslim community was established in Medina by the Prophet Muhammad in 622, the early converts to Islam personally had to make a pledge of allegiance to the Prophet, which signalled their formal entry into the Muslim polity. This pledge, known as *bay'a*, was required equally of men and women. The terms of the oath were similar for both, except that the women were not obliged to militarily defend the community. Early biographers like Ibn Sa'd (784-845) provide us with extensive details about some of these remarkable women who made the arduous trip between Mecca and Medina often under very dangerous conditions and sometimes with irate male relatives in pursuit. A number of these women came on their own, leaving behind families and oppressive social circumstances to seek spiritual fulfillment in the new Muslim community. They found the Qur'anic message of the complete equality of men and women before God and the recognition of their independent moral and social status highly empowering. Modernist Muslims today see in the *bay'a* as an early precursor of the electoral vote, by means of which their predecessors had registered their approval of the leader of their community. The fact that the Prophet took the *bay'a* from all the faithful, regardless of gender, as a prelude to membership in the Islamic polity is pregnant with all kinds of ramifications for the contemporary period. It particularly allows us to draw the conclusion that women were equal participants in the early Muslim polity during the time of the Prophet and that the *bay'a* was a concrete affirmation of the political enfranchisement of Muslim women from the very beginning of Islamic history. All of this stands as a stark contrast to the late 'Abbasid period when women's public roles were considerably circumscribed.

Women's presence in the public sphere in the first century of Islam is rather dramatically underscored by the fact that A'isha, the Prophet's widow, assumed a prominent political role after her husband's death. She is notably remembered for having led a revolt against the fourth caliph 'Ali ibn Abi Talib in 656 for not having brought the assassins of his predecessor 'Uthman b. 'Affan to justice. She made a public speech in the mosque at Medina, rousing supporters to her side, and went off to the battlefield with her army, mounted on her camel, thereby conferring the name 'Battle of the Camel' on the battle itself.

A'isha was clearly exercising her right to 'command good and forbid wrong,' a moral imperative that is equally binding on men and women, according to verse 9:71, which states: '(Male) believers and (female) believers are the natural partners of one another; they command the good and forbid wrong and they perform prayer, give the obligatory alms, and obey God and His messenger. They are those upon whom God has mercy; indeed God is Almighty, Wise'. Read from a contemporary Islamic feminist perspective, this verse is understood to be very empowering of women within a religious and moral context. Women and men are described as enjoying an unqualified equal partnership with one another – because of what they do and the qualities they share in common. The criteria of faith and righteousness are invoked equally for men and women and are not gender-specific. However, male commentators in the classical, medieval, and modern did not stress the equality of this partnership (*al-wilaya*) in their interpretations of this verse but went on instead to construct hierarchical gendered identities consonant with their own milieu. Muslim feminists are interpreting this verse in a manner that they believe unlocks the full potential of gender egalitarianism in the Qur'an. They are revisiting the highly-gendered social roles crafted by pre-modern male Muslim scholars and have cogently argued that their perspectives subverted the original intent of this and a number of other verses in the Qur'an which mandate the full social and ethical partnership of faithful men and women.

Ibn Sa'd, once again, can be invoked as an authoritative source for documenting the numerous instances of women's public activities of a religious, intellectual and humanitarian nature during and after the time of the Prophet. These activities included transmission of Qur'anic verses and the sayings of the Prophet, the two basic sources of Islamic law. A'isha and Umm Salama, widows of Muhammad, transmitted many prophetic traditions which were recorded in the most reliable collections of these reports. The *Sahabiyyat*, or women companions, ran makeshift hospitals in the mosque at Medina, tended to the wounded on the battlefield, and led — usually other women — in prayer, among other activities. There is also one recorded instance in which Umm Waraqa was appointed the prayer leader over her entire, mixed household by the Prophet because she was the most learned in her family.

History also informs us that the second caliph, 'Umar b. al-Khattab (d. 644) appointed a woman, Shifa binti Abd Allah, as the public inspector of Medina, a position roughly equivalent to that of a city mayor today. It is also worth noting that Umar entrusted his daughter Hafsa with the safekeeping of the original manuscript of the Qur'an, which became the basis of the final codex of the Qur'an in less than ten years after Umar's death. Of course, Umar could have given it to one of his sons, but he preferred his daughter over them for this enormously important task. The reasons were quite clear: Hafsa was better known for her intelligence, piety and charity than his sons, and gender was irrelevant in 'Umar's selection.

Umar also provides an example that illuminates for us the status and role of women in the public sphere during the first century of Islam. Umar once publicly announced in the mosque at Medina that he wanted to cap the amount that women can claim as their *mahr*, or bride-gift. As part of the Muslim wedding contract, the groom agrees to pay this monetary gift which is contingent on his financial circumstances and the consent of the other party. This gift is the bride's alone; and no one else can lay claim to it. During the Prophet's time, no cap was placed on the amount but Umar wished to impose a ceiling. Upon hearing this, an older woman present in the audience cried out to Umar that he was overstepping his bounds and unjustly imposing a restriction on women's rights where none existed. At that 'Umar is said to have felt ashamed and retracted his decision. Moreover, he acknowledged the woman's courage and correctness of opinion by publicly declaring, 'Umar is wrong and a woman is right'. This anecdote is remarkable because of a number of inferences we can draw from it: it informs us that women freely attended the mosque in Medina; that they publicly took part in legal interpretation along with the caliph; and that their views were accepted when deemed correct and appropriate. This is all the more remarkable when we observe today that ultra-conservative countries like Saudi Arabia and a number of the Gulf states, which claim to adhere strictly to Islamic principles, prohibit women from going to mosques.

And yet the fact that Muslim women were highly visible and active in the early period should not come as a surprise to us. Religious communities which emphasise the value of faith and piety over wealth, lineage, descent and kinship, like the early Muslim and Christian communities, have in fact little regard for gender. However, regretfully, the memory of women's robust roles in the early Muslim community has all but evaporated.

But recent scholarship reveals the productive educational, social and economic roles that women continued to perform throughout the medieval period. During this time, that is before the rise of modernity, wealthy Muslim women who had exclusive control of their property continued to endow charitable foundations and establish institutions of higher learning that sometimes bore their name. In religious scholarship in particular, women played outstanding roles as teachers and scholars. The Qur'an insists on the obligation to acquire knowledge for the believer, whether male or female, as does the *sunnah*, or example, of the Prophet Muhammad. Therefore, the right to study the Qur'an and learn about the religious law remained a fundamental right for women, even as some of their social and economic rights became restricted during the Middle Ages. Our historical records show that girls and women, especially from the upper classes, studied alongside males in private homes as well as in more institutionalised settings and became conscientious and beloved teachers. We know this important fact because male scholars gratefully included the names of their female teachers in their lists of prominent scholars and testified to their extensive learning.

There is nothing therefore in Islamic injunctions themselves that disallows women's participation in the public sphere, including the political realm. If anything, the early record shows that Islamic principles of egalitarianism and high regard for learning empowered women in both the private and public spheres. The later gradual diminution in the public rights of women is a consequence of culturally conditioned, masculinist interpretations of the religious law, whose effects are still with us today.

An example of some of these drastic changes is provided by the twelfth-century conservative legal scholar Ibn al-Jawzi (d. 1201), who remarked, in a manual he wrote for the edification of men, that they should not consult with women in any matter: compare this statement with the reports we find in early biographies of the Companions of the Prophet that the male Companions eagerly sought the advice of A'isha and other knowledgeable women after his death. The memory of the first generation of Muslim women must have grown so dim for Ibn al-Jawzi that he, unintentionally one is inclined to think, insulted the widow of the Prophet as not worthy of being heard and consulted by the male Companions of the Prophet. Such transformations remind us that attitudes can change drastically when one loses touch with the foundational history of one's faith and community.

These historical facts concerning early Muslim women seem strikingly incongruous with the situation of many women today in Muslim-majority societies. Women in Afghanistan continue to be harrassed by the Taliban for example, for seeking education and employment outside the home. Highly educated women in Saudi Arabia are restricted in their movements by male guardians, are not allowed to drive, and find their job opportunities severely limited. Granted these are extreme examples that have been severely criti- cised by other Muslims and there are many Muslim countries, such as Malaysia and Turkey, where women obtain advanced degrees, hold jobs, and definitely drive, even if some are veiled. However, the majority of women in Muslim countries lag behind men in education and earning potential and cannot aspire to the topmost managerial or leadership positions. True, the Muslim world has produced many female presidents and prime ministers but in terms of widespread, concrete economic and civic rights, women fall behind men, if we compare them within the same educational, social and economic categories. One may then logically ask the following question: when the foundational texts of Islam, the Qur'an and the examples and sayings of the Prophet Muhammad, uphold a woman's inalienable right aspire to full equality with men, why has that not produced societies where gender equality is the norm? Why is there such a disjunction between nor- mative prescriptions and the reality on the ground?

The answer is complex. First, we have to consider the historical reasons for these transformations that happened progressively. Our sources indicate that starting sometime after the ninth century, the position of women slowly began to change. The religious, social, and legal rights that have been given to women by the Qur'an began to be slowly whittled away as the nature of Islamic society itself began to change. Outside cultural influences from the Hellenist and Persian worlds began to impact upon Islamic socie- ties. Both the Hellenist and Persian societies were very hierarchical in nature and enforced social divisions among people on the basis of lineage and occupation. This led to rigid and authoritarian societies in which every- one was assigned a specific social status based on these critieria. Since women typically did not have professional occupations, they were usually placed at the bottom of the socio-economic pecking order. Hierarchical systems therefore encourage patriarchy, a social system based literally on the 'rule of the father.' Under patriarchy women are subordinated simply on the basis of their gender, masculine values are considered intrinsically superior, and social structures are designed to maintain male privilege. These positions are or should be problematic for Muslims because they undermine basic, core principles in the Qur'an. These four verses from the Qur'an clearly challenge these patriarchal notions:

1. 'O humankind, verily We have created you from a single (pair) of a male and a female, and have made you into nations and tribes, that you may know each other. Indeed the most honored of you in the sight of God is the most righteous' (49:13).

2. 'O humankind! Be careful of your duty to your Lord Who created you from a single soul and from it created its mate and from them the two has spread abroad a multitude of men and women'. (4:1)

3. 'The believers, men and women, are protectors of one another…' (9:71)

4. '[Wives] are your garments and you [husbands] are their garments. (2:187); here 'garments' is a metaphor for mutual comfort and joy and the equal rights shared by wives and husbands vis-à-vis one another in the marital relationship).

With the rise of patriarchal societies, many of the progressive and liberating teachings of early Islam, particularly concerning women, began to be compromised – never completely eradicated, but definitely compromised.

Second, we need to consider how the sacred texts are interpreted and by whom. Typically, almost without exception, sacred texts like the Qur'an, the Bible, the Bhagavad Gita, have primarily been interpreted by men throughout centuries. It is their interpretation that has become authoritative. In the early period of Islam, there were women interpreters, the foremost being A'isha. She had disciples of her own and her interpretation as transmitted by her disciples has been preserved for us in various commentaries. If there were other female commentators from the early period, their names have not become part of the official record. As a result, masculine perspectives became privileged in Qur'anic hermeneutics since only their commentaries survive. Viewing the Qur'an through a masculine lens meant that the well-being of society was understood to be equivalent primarily to the well-being of men. Although the text of any scripture is stable and the words themselves do not change, any text, particularly, a religious text, can be read and understood by different people in different ways in different times. Androcentric interpretations leave their imprint on a number of Qur'anic verses that have been used to assert the husband's special prerogatives within marriage. For example, polygamous union with up to four women is said to be permitted in the Qur'an for men on the basis of a particular verse which states:

If you fear that you cannot act equitably towards orphans, then marry such women as are seemly to you, two and three and four; but if you fear that you will not do justice, then only one or what your right hands possess; this is proper, so that you may not stray from the right path (4:3).

Those who look favourably upon polygamy read this verse as a general permission provided that a man can treat all his wives absolutely equally on all fronts — economically, socially, and emotionally. Those who are not inclined to accept polygamy read this verse as allowing polygamy only as a concession during special circumstances, such as war, when the death of a large number of men can leave many women and children in dire circumstances. The verse does specifically refer to women with children with no male provider – and it is helpful to remember that we are talking about a time when a woman, if not independently wealthy, was inevitably financially dependent on a man. Muslim modernists arguing against polygamy as a regular, rather than a highly exceptional practice, point to another verse which states, 'you are never able to deal fairly among women, even if it is your ardent desire' (4:129). Reading these two verses together, these interpreters insist that the Qur'an actually states very clearly that no man is humanly capable of treating more than one woman justly, and thus effectively considers polygamous unions, under normal circumstances, beyond the realm of possibility.

Scholars – women scholars in particular – have now started to reclaim women's voices throughout history in an attempt to separate what is genuinely Islamic from culturally conditioned interpretations of Islamic principles. Muslim feminists tend to argue that the main tools for countering social injustice towards women lie in the Qur'an and authentic examples of the Prophet Muhammad and that being a feminist within these parameters means being true to the highest religious and social ideals of Islam – ideals which lead to the promotion of the human rights of women. Religious feminists of other faiths make similar statements based on their own faith traditions. Questions have been raised, however, about the credibility of such claims, particularly by those who believe that human rights derive from secular notions of the dignity of human beings and that religious claims often undermine them.

Such questions are influenced by the fact that human rights in the European context sometimes had to be developed in opposition to the clergy and organised religion. To ensure certain basic rights, the state had to step in and create new laws. Thus it was not until the nineteenth century that the Married Women's Property Act was passed in Britain finally giving the married woman the right to own property in her own name rather than having the husband automatically gain control over her assets, as was the case until then. In Muslim societies, women have always had the right to own property in their names. In the pre-modern period, Muslim jurists also developed a human rights scheme according to which every individual (male and female) had the right to protect their own life, property, religion, progeny and intellect. This is why most Muslims continue to argue for human rights based on Islamic values that are understood to be consistent with the universal notions of human rights. However, it is important to realise that there remain certain issues and limitations that have not been adequately addressed in the modern period. Thus, according to pre-modern interpretations of the religious law, a woman's legal and social status was inferior to that of a man's and remains so, at least on the books, in a number of Muslim societies today.

Muslim reformists have therefore been calling for a reinterpretation of the Shari'a since the nineteenth century. But the Shari'a is not law as we understand it in the modern period. It is a broad set of moral and ethical guidelines, some of which, but not all, have legal implications. Through their ability to reason, what in Islamic terminology is called *ijtihad*, human beings study the Shari'a to derive specific legal rulings from it. Through *ijtihad* Muslims have the ability to interpret and reinterpret the religious law in order to make it consistent with certain basic moral principles and objectives that are regarded as unchanging. Thus Muslim reformers argue that if the objective of the law is to promote equality, justice, and tolerance, and these basic moral principles cannot be compromised, then the understanding of the Shari'a and the specific rules that are developed from it must always be consistent with these objectives. This means that over time, as our conceptions of what constitutes justice, equality, and tolerance change, our application of the law has to change accordingly. With regard to gender justice, our notions have changed quite drastically in the last few decades. Now we take it for granted that women have equal rights to education, employment and compensation; anything less would be considered unjust. Such arguments are beginning to be increasingly heard in Muslim societies; in Egypt, for example, the Egyptian Supreme Court recently allowed women the right to initiate divorce, that is to petition for divorce on their own in cases of abuse or desertion by the husband. Although it sounds revolutionary, this is a right that has always existed for women under Islamic law, although not extensively practised or even well-known among Muslims.

Women's rights advocates in the Muslim world base their arguments on specific interpretations of the religious law that promote gender equality and are woman-friendly. They also draw upon the early history of Islam to establish that gender-egalitarianism is a strong and integral component of Islamic belief and tenets. The recuperation of scripturally mandated rights and concepts is the driving force behind the scholarship and activism of a considerable number of Muslim women and men. This is a courageous enterprise that often faces strenuous opposition from ultra-conservative religious ideologues.

But the effort continues.

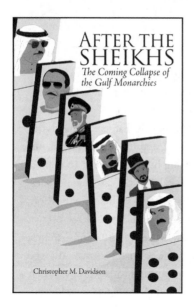

Christopher M. Davidson

ISBN: 9781849041898
£29.99 / Hardback / 224pp

After the Sheikhs

The Coming Collapse of the Gulf Monarchies

CHRISTOPHER M. DAVIDSON

The Gulf monarchies have long been governed by highly autocratic and seemingly anachronistic regimes. Yet despite bloody conflicts on their doorsteps, fast-growing populations, and powerful modernising and globalising forces impacting on their largely conservative societies, they have demonstrated remarkable resilience. Obituaries for these traditional monarchies have frequently been penned, but even now these absolutist, almost medieval, entities still appear to pose the same conundrum as before: in the wake of the 2011 'Arab Spring' and the fall of incumbent presidents in Egypt, Tunisia, and Libya, the apparently steadfast Gulf monarchies have, at first glance, reaffirmed their status as the Middle East's only real bastions of stability. In this book, however, noted Gulf expert Christopher Davidson contends that the collapse of these kings, emirs, and sultans is going to happen, and was always going to. While the revolutionary movements in North Africa, Syria, and Yemen will undeniably serve as important, if indirect, catalysts for the coming upheaval, many of the same socio-economic pressures that were building up in the Arab republics are now also very much present in the Gulf monarchies. It is now no longer a matter of if but when the West's steadfast allies fall. This is a bold claim to make but Davidson, who accurately forecast the economic turmoil that afflicted Dubai in 2009, has an enviable record in diagnosing social and political changes afoot in the region.

'What is the secret of the Gulf monarchies' survival? There are numerous reasons. The support of Western powers, oil wealth and an effective secret police are among them. But in this exceptionally argued book, Christopher Davidson concentrates on the prime reason: the Gulf monarchies enjoy considerable legitimacy from their populations.' — Ziauddin Sardar, *The Independent*

WWW.HURSTPUBLISHERS.COM/BOOK/AFTER-THE-SHEIKHS

41 GREAT RUSSELL ST, LONDON WC1B 3P
WWW.HURSTPUBLISHERS.COM
WWW.FBOOK.COM/HURSTPUBLISHERS
020 7255 2201

BEYOND THE CROOKED RIB

Saleck Mohamed Val

As a teenager I used to squabble with my sister over things we both wanted to possess. Sometimes, it would be as trivial as a small basket made up of palm tree leaves to keep dates, at others, it would be as loveable as a small plastic 'camera' through which you could see pictures of the Ka'aba, the black stone, the green dome and the mosque of the Prophet. Our self-indulgent quarrels always ended up with the intervention of my grandmother who would tell me: 'leave it to her my beloved son! You are a man dear! She is woman! She is a crooked rib and deficient in mind and in religion!' These words, though powerful enough to let me give up my case for the camera, the basket or any other worth or worthless object, recurrently struck at the core of my limited vision of womanhood.

The notion that women emerged from Adam's rib is deeply rooted in a traditional society like Mauritania where I grew up. It is iconised in the title of the novel *From A Crooked Rib* by the celebrated Somali writer Nuruddin Farah. It tells the story of a nomad girl who manages to escape an arranged marriage to a much older man. The view is justified on the basis of numerous alleged sayings of the Prophet Muhammad, hadith, and stories that originate from the Jewish and Christian traditions known as *Israiliyyat*. Both these hadith and *Israiliyyat* are heavily quoted in the classical Muslim commentaries on the Qur'an that my grandmother read judiciously. Not surprisingly, she had internalised that misogynistic representation herself.

The classical commentators, such as Ibn Jarir al-Tabari (d. 923), whose *Jami' al-Bayan* is regarded as a foundational interpretation, and Ibn Kathir (1301–73), generously used Biblical creation narratives in their works. For example, commenting on the Qur'anic verse 7: 19-24, where the Qur'an details the creation account, Tabari states: 'when Adam ate from the forbidden tree, God asked him, "why you have disobeyed me"? Adam said, "it was Eve who told me to eat from it". Then God said: "As a punishment for your act, you, Eve, shall always suffer the hardship of labour and menstruation"'. Tabari goes on to justify this with a string of hadith, most, as Barbara Stowasser notes, 'blame the woman, as it was the majority opinion of theological experts by Tabari's time that it was only through the woman's weakness and guile that Satan could bring about Adam's downfall'. Ibn Kathir offers a similar explanation in the famous *Tafsir al-Qur'an al-Azim*, while commenting on 4:1:

God ordered his servants to worship Him alone and not to have associates with Him. He points out to them his power and supremacy through creating them from a single soul that of Adam. He 'created, of like nature, his mate'; that is Eve who was created from his left rib while he was asleep…It is narrated by ibn Abbas that 'the woman was created from man, so that her desire would always be to him, while man was created from earth so that his desire would always be to it, you have then to incarcerate your women.' The Hadith also says: 'Treat women nicely, for a woman is created from a rib and the most curved portion of the rib is its upper portion, so, if you should try to straighten it, it will break, but if you leave it as it is, it will remain crooked. So treat women nicely.'

The commentaries of Ibn Kathir and al-Tabari are the basis of Muslim traditions and have established the inferior and secondary nature of women in traditional societies. Modern commentators of the Qur'an have accepted these views uncritically and slavishly. The prominent Mauritanian-Saudi scholar Mohamed El-Amine al-Shinqiti (1905–74), for example, states in his influential commentary, entitled *Adwa' al-Bayan*, that 'women, unlike men, suffer from a natural deficiency. They are physically and mentally weaker than men. Their deficiency appears in their persistent need for ornaments and jewellery while men are not in need of that because they are naturally perfect and superior to women'.

This 'textulisation of misogyny', to use the words of the American Pakistani scholar Asma Barlas, has been criticised and totally taken apart by feminist scholars such as Aziza al-Hibri, Amna Nosseir, Nimat Hafez Barazangi, Amina Wadud and Barlas herself. But my grandmother does not read feminist works, particularly in English. So to debunk her position and change her mind we need to look elsewhere – to the work of traditional Muslim female scholars.

Fortunately, there is no lack of traditional female scholars attempting to overturn the misogynist interpretations of traditional, conservative scholarship. While it is true that traditional commentaries were always written by men, and incorporated the experiences of only men, or presented women's position through the male gaze, this is increasingly not the complete story. In Mauritania, for example, traditional women scholars have played a very important part in shaping religious knowledge. Women such as Khadija Mint al-Aqil, Mariam Mint Hin, and Fatimetou Mint Abd al-Fattah had an extremely important influence on the Mauritanian traditional Islamic teaching. One would expect conservative male scholars to ignore or downgrade the contribution of these women. Thus, these distinguished intellectuals are omitted from the *Biographies of Eminent Scholars from Mauritania and the Western Sahara* by Muhammad al-Buruti, published in 1981. As the Moroccan scholar and anthropologist Chouki El Hamel points out:

Some women even became *shaykhs* of *mahdara*, poets, writers, etc. The example most repeated in Moorish writings is Khadija Bint al-Aqil. She lived at the very beginning of the nineteenth century, and was a teacher and writer. She is best known for a commentary on *as-Sullam al-Murawnaq* (a book on logic) of al-Akhdari. It is curious to note that al-Burtuli did not say anything about this woman even though she lived in his time and he knew her family because he wrote a biography about her brother Ahmed b. al-Aqil. His silence could be explained by the fact that he maintained a very conservative attitude towards women, believing that their place was in the harem and that they did not represent serious scholars.

Perhaps a more important question is: why have feminist scholars neglected these women? Indeed, it seems that the debate of feminist scholars is largely conducted between themselves; they tend to look down on the work of traditional female scholars, or dismiss it as a product of a patriarchal tradition.

During my visits to Morocco's famous religious educational institutions, such as Al-Qaraouiyine in Fez and Dar al-Hadith al-Hasaniyah and al-Rabita al-Muhammadiyya in Rabat, I discovered a significant heritage of commentaries and exegetical works by women scholars. Conversations with female scholars of the Qur'an such as Farida Zumrrud of Dar al-Hadith, and Nusayba al-Ghalabzori and Rashida Nasser from al-Qaraouiyine, further established that traditional women scholars have been and are very active in developing women's perspectives on the Qur'an.

It was at Dar al-Hadith and al-Qaraouiyine that I first came across the work of the Egyptian female scholar Aicha Abd al-Rahman (1913–98), who wrote under the name Bint al-Shati (Daughter of the River Bank). Bint al-Shati was not only the mentor of some of the men and women I met in these Moroccan religious educational institutions, but was also the first Muslim woman in the twentieth century to undertake the arduous task of interpreting the Qur'an. Her commentary, *The Rhetorical Exegesis of the Qur'an (al-Tafsir al-Bayani li-al-Qur'an al-Karim)* was published in 1967. Though *Rhetorical Exegesis* is an incomplete literary interpretation of the Qur'an, the exegetical methodology adopted by Bint al-Shati reveals a subtle discourse. She insists on a topical reading of the Qur'an, arguing that it is the best way to get near the original egalitarian meaning of the Sacred Text. In the introduction to *Rhetorical Exegesis*, she states:

This method of Qur'anic exegesis...is concerned with the topical or thematic reading of the Qur'an. Deploying this method, the scholar will study one particular Qur'anic theme and collect as much information about it as to come to an accurate and valid understanding.... It is actually a method that differs from the common traditional approach that often looked at Qur'anic verses atomistically; detaching them from their overall Qur'anic context, a fact which often led to misinterpretation and diversion from the original meaning of the sacred text.

Thus, Bint al-Shati's method involves collecting verses on one topic from different parts of the Qur'an and interrogating them collectively to discover the overall intent of the text. She emphasises the historical context of the verses, avoids reading any extraneous elements into the Qur'an, and looks at classical and modern commentaries to systematically critique them for robbing the text of original meaning. But what is really intriguing about *Rhetorical Exegesis* is Bint al-Shati's subtle evasion of gender-related verses of the Qur'an. Undoubtedly, a thematic reading of the verses on the creation account, for example, would have been a tremendous contribution to the clarification of the Qur'anic positioning on women, particularly as a response to the traditional misogynistic commentaries. The chapters she chooses to write about were revealed in Mecca, before the Prophet migrated to Medina, and do not have any legal content. So, one could argue, that there seems to be a deliberate attempt to avoid discussion of verses relating to women. But I would suggest that there are other concerns at play here. *Rhetorical Exegesis* is focused on developing a methodology, which in the 1960s was quite original. And, initially at least, she was more concerned with the spiritual aspects of the Qur'an.

However, any suggestion that Bint al-Shati, being a traditional scholar, wanted to shy away from challenging traditional male perspective on women in the Qur'an simply evaporates with her next work, published two years later in 1969, with the explicit title: *A Treatise on Men: Quranic Discourse (Maqal fi al-Insan: Dirasa Qur'aniyah)*. Bint al-Shati tackles the creation story head on. Not only does she refer back to the Qur'anic notion of *khilafah* (trusteeship), that is both men and women are equal trustees of God on earth, but also vehemently critiques the hadith which states that women were created from a crooked rib. After a long analysis, she concludes: 'There is no evidence whatsoever in the Qur'an that Hawwa (Eve) was created from Adam's rib. Rather, what the Qur'an has often emphasised is that they were both created from a single self. Those who put forward this notion,' she writes:

often rely on the hadith where the Prophet compares women to a rib....If this hadith is valid, one should not take it as indicating women's origin, rather, it stands as a metaphor for the careful treatment of women. The Prophet, for example says "be careful with the clay-pots", are women then created from clay-pots?

Both the arguments and views of Bint al-Shati are not far removed from those of modern feminists like Amina Wadud and Asma Barlas. Wadud's book, *Qur'an and Women*, was first published in Kuala Lumpur in 1992 – almost a quarter of a century after Bint al-Shati's seminal *A Treatise on Men*. But while Wadud is lionised, Bint al-Shati remains invisible. Is this because one is a modern feminist, while the other is a traditional scholar? Why have those feminists who have produced a volume honouring Wadud, whose oeuvre is limited to two books, not produced a *festschrift* in honour of Bint al-Shati who has left a considerable body of work, not just on the Qur'an but also fiction, poetry, Arabic literature and what today would be called 'subaltern studies' (one of her books is entitled *The Problem of the Peasant*, published in 1938). Is this a case of the pot calling the kettle black?

But Bint al-Shati is not the only traditional scholar to challenge patriarchy from within the tradition. During the last few decades, a number of female scholars have emerged from Al-Azhar University in Egypt, an institution most feminists and quite a few modernists consider as a bastion of traditionalism. Consider, for example, Zainab al-Ghazali's *Views on the Book of God (Nadharat fi Kitabillah)*, Fawkiyah Sherbini's *The Simplification of Exegesis (Taysir al-Tafsir)* and Kariman Hamzah's *Pearl and Diamonds of Qur'anic Exegesis (Allu'luwa al-*

Marjan fi Tafsir al-Qur'an). I would argue that the exegetical contribution of these scholars is just as important as that of their feminist counterparts, even though it differs from the interpretations offered by feminist scholars. Moreover, my grandmother, and other traditional women, will have no problem in embracing their insights.

In her interpretation of 2: 34-36, Zainab al-Ghazali removes all Biblical references from the story of Adam and Eve's fall from paradise, and shows that according to the Qur'an it was Adam and not Eve who disobeyed God:

Allah called upon Adam and his wife to dwell into the Garden and warned them not to eat from a particular tree. Apart from that, they could eat from whatever bounties there and whenever they wanted. But *Iblis* (Satan) maliciously kept pushing them towards eating from the forbidden tree telling them that it was the tree of eternity and ever-lasting sovereignty. Adam finally succumbed to Satan's whisperings and ate from the tree so his *awrah* (parts of the body that must be concealed) was revealed to him and he started covering it with leaves from the trees in the Garden… He looked at his wife, but she was also like him. Eventually, they were both expelled from the bounties of the Garden due to their transgression.

Here Zainab al-Ghazali explicitly goes against the interpretations of classical authorities such as al-Tabari and Ibn Kathir. There is not even a trace of the classical exegeses which attribute humanity's sin and misery to the foolishness, mental deficiency and seduction of Eve whose moral and intellectual inaptitude has made her an easy prey to the guile and deviousness of Satan. But traditional scholars, like most scholars — including the feminists — have limitations. Despite reframing the entire creation story, Zainab al-Ghazali shies away from tackling the controversial issues of male-guardianship and women's political leadership.

Fawkiyah Sherbini's views are not too far from those of Zainab al-Ghazali. We ought to remember that these women were working in a pretty constrained and oppressive environment. Sherbini was a student of Sheikh Mohamed Mitwalli al-Sharaawi (1911–98), a conservative but popular preacher who also served as Egypt's Minister of Endowments, and who was adored by the Saudis. Not surprisingly, Sherbini is very subtle and cautious in her endeavour to challenge the classical perceptions of women in the Islamic scholarly corpus. Indeed, it can even be argued that she is an orthodox scholar. Despite that, *The Simplification of Exegesis* caused quite a few problems for Al-Azhar; when it was eventually published in 2008, it had gone through over five years of careful scrutiny and inspection from the Islamic Research Academy of the University. *Simplification* adopts some subtle methodological mechanisms that shows her awareness of the misogyny of classical commentaries and reveals the difficult conditions under which she is working. As she boldly states:

I did not have recourse to the *Israiliyyat* traditions, though I found them heavily quoted by al-Tabari and Ibn Kathir. The *Israiliyyat* had caused a lot of damage and scepticism amongst Muslims, so I chose to avoid using them... We do not also have to rely on the prophetic traditions that contradict reason especially when interpreting the Qur'an. An interpreter should make sure to avoid the Biblical and extra-Biblical lore that led to a lot of confusion in the past.

Indeed, when Sherbini comes across a misogynist hadith, she demolishes it pretty quickly with a sharp rebuke. For example, when the she comes to 4:1 ('People, be mindful of your Lord, who created you from a single soul, and from it created its mate, and from the pair of them spread countless men and women far and wide; be mindful of God, in whose name you make request of one another'), she finds that classical scholars quote a hadith, narrated by Abu Hurairah, which states 'treat women well, the woman was created from a rib', to justify their position. Sherbini asks that when the Qur'an says 'we have sent you a messenger from amongst yourselves', does that mean that God took Muhammad from our souls and created him? No, it means that the Prophet was from our human species. It is therefore reasonable to assume that Adam and Eve were created in a similar way. The rib just does not enter the equation!

Sherbini's reading of the creation verses shows the extent to which she was able not only to discard the *Israiliyyat* traditions but also to elucidate the story in a manner that emphasised its divergence from the Judeo-Christian account. In clarifying the meanings of 4:9-23, she shows that Eve was not responsible for the act of disobedience. 'Satan's whispering and seduction', she writes, 'was directed at both Adam and Eve. Eve was not the one who initiated the act of disobedience but rather it was Satan who seduced both into sin'. She emphasises the mutuality of the transgression and repentance of both Adam and Eve in the Qur'anic narrative when commenting on 2:35-38. Moreover, Sherbini illustrates how 'Adam' is a generic term for humanity, and includes both Adam and Eve. For example, in 2:37, which states 'then Adam learnt from his Lord words of inspiration, and his Lord, turned towards him, for he is oft-returning, Most Merciful', the term 'Adam', Sherbini argues, is generic. Adam stands for the couple who are created from a single self, and refers to humanity as a whole. It is humankind that 'received words of repentance from the Lord who accepted it grieve and regret'.

True, Sherbini strategically avoids directly challenging the traditionalist corpus and her Azhari mentors for that would be simple and inevitably lead to the exclusion of her views from the mainstream traditional scholarly domain. No doubt, this position would be seen by the feminist scholars as a clear betrayal of their cause. But this, I would argue, patronising view assumes that a women working in a traditional environment is unable to articulate her voice; in fact, Sherbini's voice is loud and clear in *Simplification*. Indeed, she has a very sophisticated and subtle position that is far more efficient in claiming the egalitarian spirit of the Qur'an. A thorough reading of her work and the social, political, cultural and even academic circumstances in which it was written and came to light, reveals its true revolutionary nature. Both Sherbini's audacious articulations of her position and her daring involvement in a male-dominated arena where interpretation is the exclusive right of male scholars is worthy of praise.

Kariman Hamzah's *Pearls and Diamonds of Qur'anic Exegesis*, published in 2010, also had to undergo microscopic scrutiny and consequent revision, by the Islamic Research Academy of Al-Azhar. It is difficult to say which sections of her commentary she had to revise and which parts were suppressed. But the Islamic Research Academy itself was quite enthusiastic about her exegesis and declared it to be 'the first interpretation of the Qur'an by a woman' (clearly, the luminaries at Al-Azhar have difficulty in counting). Sheikh Abdul Zaher Abu Ghazala, Director of the Research, Translation and Publication Department at the Academy and member of the committee who subjected Hamzah's commentary to a 'careful review' told *al-Sharq al-Awsat* newspaper:

Kariman Hamzah's interpretation of the Qur'an is fully consistent with previous Qur'anic interpretations, and that it contained no inconsistencies or contradictions with Islamic Sharia Law. He denied that this is a new Qur'anic interpretation providing a female point of view, emphasising that this interpretation addresses men, women, the youth, and children, just as the Qur'an itself speaks to all. Therefore there is no such thing as a "male interpretation" or a "female interpretation" of the Qur'an; he said that "what is important for us is that the interpretation is consistent with the Qur'an itself, and does not contradict Islamic Law".

There are a couple of interesting points worth noting about Hamzah. She is widely known as a television presenter of Islamic programmes in Egypt; and, unlike Fawkiyah Sherbini and Zainab al-Ghazali, she is not a graduate of Al-Azhar, nor of any religious institution. And her interpretation, written in a clear and precise style, is aimed at young people.

Hamzah uses modern Biblical scholarship. She starts her commentary on 7: 19-25 by describing the creation story as it appears in the Bible and then deliberately emphasises the differences in narration and perception in the Qur'anic account. One of main differences, she notes:

Between the creation story in the Qur'an and the Bible is that in the latter one finds that all the blame is laid on Eve who was thought to be behind the act of eating from the forbidden tree: "she gave to her husband and he ate too". Because of this fact, Eve stood as a symbol of sin, seduction and disobedience in the Judeo-Christian traditions. In the Islamic traditions, on the other side, Adam and Eve were created to be Allah's vice-regents (*khalifah*) on earth. The Qur'an does not speak about the notion of original sin, rather it says: "no bearer of burden can bear the burden of another."

But Hamzah glosses over the important distinction between the important implications of the story of creation in the Qur'an and the Bible. In her reading of 4:1, which states, 'People, be mindful of your Lord, who create you from a single soul…', she does not recognise that the Biblical story with its account of Eve creation of Adam's rib contradicts the text of the Qur'an, which makes no mention of the rib. Instead, Hamzah opens her commentary by asserting that 'most commentators state that the "the single soul" is Adam, and that Eve was created from it; a meaning that could be literally found in the Bible; Genesis.' Unlike Bint Shati, who was fully conscious of the danger of the *Israiliyyat* traditions to the extent that she totally ignored them in her commentary, Hamzah finds herself immersed in a deeply misogynistic discourse, from which she struggles to get out. Part of the problem is that Hamzah seems to rely too heavily on conservative commentators such as Sheik Muhammad al-Ghazali, Sayyid Qutb, and a string of Al-Azhar scholars. Perhaps she was forced to do so by the Islamic Research Academy of Al-Azhar. Nevertheless, one can detect a questioning attitude in her work as well as an attempt to develop a new understanding of the Qur'an. Her primary concern seems to shape a Qur'an-centred project of women's liberation.

Although I have only dealt with the creation story, issues of authority, method and legitimacy are also central to the work of these traditional women scholars. The work of Bint al-Shati, Al-Ghazali, Sherbini and Hamzah, while totally neglected in modernist and feminist circles, demonstrates that traditional women are able to stand up against oppressive tradition, even within its bastion. One could argue that the restraining conditions of Al-Azhar prevent the emergence of a genuine female perspective on the Qur'an. However, this does not diminish their courage, nor does it undermine their attempts to subvert male authority and break free from the deep-seated misogyny of traditionalist thought. It only underlines the acute problems of working within the tradition, orthodoxy and canonical mainstream.

Traditional women scholars have frequently been accused, in feminist quarters, of flirting with patriarchy, and labelled as 'conspirators to their own subjugation'. But it would be much better for feminist scholars to stop beating their chests and talking amongst themselves and instead to start embracing their more traditional sisters. They have far greater appeal for women like my grandmother, and millions like her, who need to be persuaded about change. And they want to move forward with their tradition and sanity intact.

THE GROOMERS

Shamim Miah

One of my daily rituals is to go for a short walk to the local park, adjacent to my house. The Werneth Park is part of Oldham's historical legacy; it used to be the property and residence of Dame Sarah Lees, one of Oldham's celebrated philanthropist and industrialist politicians. In 1920, Dame Sarah Lees became the first female mayor of Oldham, only the second woman in England to hold such a position. An inscription on one of the memorial fountains situated in the centre of the park aptly summarises her life and work: 'Dame Sarah Lees – trusted God and served its people'. The Park now attracts a wide range of people, from elderly Muslim women doing light exercises, dog-walkers, to children playing on the swings. The neighbourhood has also, over more recent years, become home to affluent Muslim communities.

On a summer's day last year, I entered the park and saw a group of young Muslim men, in their early to late twenties. One of them was listening to hip hop music on loud-speaker, while his friends were pre-occupied, watching something on a phone. What they were watching clearly excited them. As I walked closer to the group, their 'enjoyment' grew increasinly loud and rowdy. The sociologist in me was intrigued to find out what they were watching. Judging by their verbal exchange and the references they made to the female anatomy, it became apparent that they were viewing pornography. As I walked past the group, one of the lads made eye contact yet continued in the banter concerning the nature and content of the mobile footage. He was unperturbed by the fact that I realised they were watching pornography.

This random encounter highlights a crucial aspect of behaviour of certain types of Muslim men in Britain. It shows that consuming pornography is now regarded as natural by certain gangs. Indeed, pornography has become, for many, a part of everyday life; it is not confined to the most intimate,

private space. Rather, it now ruptures the barrier which hitherto had separated the public and the private. Consuming pornography is no longer
merely a private act; and neither is the location from which pornography is
consumed. The now ubiquitous nature of 'porn' means that people can have
access to it instantly, unlike in the past when it was something which had to
be searched for in restricted places. It can be casually watched in the most
idyllic of places and in a most bizarre and contradictory manner. Second,
pornography plays an important role in how the female body is viewed and
sex-role stereotypes are developed. This is crucial because pornography,
consumed in this way, is then used to inform present and future relationships with the opposite sex. The consumers expect women to behave as
they behave in pornographic films and videos, giving rise to certain expectations of sexual relationships.

The recent disturbing cases of 'sexual grooming' in a number of cities in
Britain should be seen through this prism. The sheer scale of the incidents,
the calculated and orchestrated approach used against victims, and the way
young, underage girls were viewed by perpetrators is truly shocking.
Between June 2009 and May 2013, eight different groups of Muslim Pakistani men were convicted of sexual grooming in Oldham, Rotherham,
Derby, Nelson, Telford, Rochdale and Oxford. One can almost describe it
as an epidemic of Muslim male perversion. Many of the perpetrators are
brothers: for example, two of the seven, Ahdel Ali (25) and Mubarek Ali
(29) in Telford are brothers; in the Oxford case of May 2013, there are two
sets of brothers: Mohammad Karrar (38) and Bassam Karrar (33), and
Akhtar Dogar (32) and Anjum Dogar (31). Most of the men involved are
married with children. Some are regular mosque goers; one was even a
religious teacher in his local mosque. Almost all are semi-literate.

The first case of sexual grooming to gain national notoriety involved the
murder of Laura Wilson in October 2009 in Rotherham, South Yorkshire.
She was groomed by a group of Pakistani men from the age of 12, degraded
and passed from man to man. When she had a child with one of them, she
was murdered, aged 17, for – get this – bringing shame to the family! In a
text message, Ashitaq Asghar, who confessed to her murder, wrote: 'I am
gonna send that kaffir bitch straight to hell'. In the January 2011 Derby
case, twenty-seven young girls were involved, the youngest was twelve
while the oldest was eighteen. The pattern is always the same: gangs win

the trust of young white girls, shower them with gifts and displays of affection, ply them with alcohol and drugs, then pass them around to be brutally raped. If the girls try to run away, they are threatened with beheading or their homes are firebombed. In the May 2013 Oxford case, the gang risked the life of a twelve-year old girl by performing a crude, unsafe abortion on her themselves before branding her with a scalding hairpin so she would know that she was their property.

Long before the groomers appeared on the British landscape, a similar case created headlines in Australia. It involved the gang rape of Australian teenage girls, some as young as fourteen, in Sydney in 2000. The gang leader was a man called Bilal Skaf, and all his gang, aged between sixteen and twenty-two, were of Lebanese Muslim heritage. The notion of the 'Muslim sexual predator', creating a new folk-devil and generating heightened moral panic, first emerged after the Skaf case. The British grooming cases further entrenched this image, establishing within the public imagination a link between sexual grooming and the image of the menacing Muslim male. The national debate was given particular impetus following the sentencing of the Derby ringleaders Mohammed Liaqat, 28, and Abid Saddique, 27, and six of their accomplices in January 2011. Three of the accomplices were convicted of making child pornography with their victims. The subsequent intervention of the former Home Secretary, Jack Straw MP, strengthened the link between culture and crime. He argued that the best way to make sense of these cases was not through an individual criminal model, but rather through the cultural fabric of Muslim societies. Part of the 'cultural reading' involved an explanation of sexual grooming based upon Pakistani culture, seen to be responsible for perceiving young white girls as 'easy meat'. Straw clearly articulated this in a Radio 4 interview in January 2011:

There is a specific problem which involves Pakistani heritage men... who target vulnerable young white girls. We need to get the Pakistani community to think much more clearly about why this is going on and to be more open about the problems that are leading to a number of Pakistani heritage men thinking it is OK to target white girls in this way. These young men are in a western society, in any event, they act like any other young men, they're fizzing and popping with testosterone, they want some outlet for that, but Pakistani heritage girls are off-limits and they are expected to marry a Pakistani girl from Pakistan.

The link between ethnicity, religion and sexual grooming was etched further in the public consciousness after the Rochdale sexual grooming cases in the north west of England in May 2012. A total of forty girls, a number of them from care homes, were identified as victims. Nine men were convicted. One of the men was a father of five and a religious studies teacher at a local mosque. The ring leader of the gang was fifty-nine-year-old, Shabir Ahmed (also known as the 'daddy'), from Oldham. He was convicted of thirty charges of child-rape and jailed for nineteen years. Compared to the Derby and the Rotherham cases, the Rochdale cases were even more grotesque. Victims were forced to have sex with several men, several times a day. One of the victims recalled how she was raped by twenty men, one after the other. In the Oxford case, the perpetrators were selling their victims for £600 at a time.

The grooming cases have raised a number of challenges. First: if both the local and national media are to be believed then the problem is essentially cultural, it emerges from the deeply engraved DNA of Muslim youths which allows them to behave in such a manner. There is an assumption that Muslim masculinity is fixed by social structures prior to social interaction. If this were the case, then all Muslim men of a particular age would have a propensity for acts of sexual deviance. This type of logic can generate widespread hysteria if left unchallenged. For example, there was a case of a young Muslim man from the south who happened to be in Heywood, Rochdale, during the media sensation around the Rochdale case. He had been looking for a particular address and was obviously lost. He stopped to ask some young white girls if they knew the address. The young girls, frightened at the prospect of a Muslim man in an expensive car asking for directions, walked away before taking an image of the driver, the registration number and the make and model of the car. Before long the information and the photograph of the individual went viral through Facebook. The police investigating the matter had to reassure the community that the man that they thought was a potential 'groomer' was in fact an innocent locum pharmacist.

Second: it reinforces a general perception of Muslim masculinity as violently patriarchal, rooted in crimes which display a desire to control vulnerable white girls through force, sexual violence and exploitation. In other words, it paints all Muslim men with the same brush; the deviancy and criminal behaviour of a score of individuals is projected on the whole

Muslim community. All Muslim men become potential perpetrators and sexual menaces, patrolling the streets and closely keeping a watchful eye for the next target. Contrast this with the Jimmy Savile affair, the case of the BBC presenter and celebrity who abused young girls on an industrial scale from 1958 to 2008. Over 600 victims have come forward. A joint report by the Metropolitan Police Service and the National Society for the Prevention of Cruelty to Children (NSPCC) concluded that 'Jimmy Savile was one of the UK's most prolific known sexual predators. Indeed the formal recording of allegations of crime on this scale is, to the best of our knowledge, unprecedented in the UK'. Several other presenters, producers and artists have been implicated; and the BBC itself has been shown to have turned a blind eye. Yet no one is accusing the BBC of being a den of paedophiles; or even an establishment that provides favourable accommodation to sexual predators. Or the case of sexual abuse in North Wales where systematic abuse and rape of children went on in eighteen child care homes over three decades. Again, no one is accusing the Welsh of harbouring a child abuse gene nor indeed is anyone describing the people of Europe as being innately prone to child abuse despite the mushrooming of paedophile networks throughout the region. Can we not attribute all this to cultural influences, accepted gender roles, and notions of masculinity that see women as 'easy meat'?

Patterns of racialising minority groups have a long history within the study of race in Britain. For example, the academic Stuart Hall, in his landmark study, *Policing the Crisis*, studied the emergence of a new and frightening form of crime and social threat, namely, muggings carried out by some black young men in the 1970s. Similar to the 'grooming' offences, Hall noted how in the 1970s muggings were objectified and transformed to cause moral panic despite the absence of a legal definition of mugging as a distinct crime. Hall's collaborative study further demonstrated how certain racialised minority groups were singled out and located at the centre of the causes of moral panics. The state then, all too quickly, uses the strong-arm of the legal system to maintain law and order in reaction to this perception.

But we are still left with the basic question: where do these violent thugs come from? What has shaped their notions of violent and perverted masculinity? I think some of the answers lie in pornography and hip hop.

Inner city Muslim youth are deeply influenced by hip hop; and urban Muslim youth culture derives some of its notions of masculinity from this genre of music. But it has to be noted that hip hop culture is not a mono-lithic entity. While some critics have dismissed it as 'dead letter of brazen stereotype-mongering among the severely undereducated' or that the 'defi-cits of hip hop are amplified because they blare beyond the borders of ugly art to inspire youth to even uglier behaviour', others have praised it as a deep and noble tradition of speaking 'truth to power'. Tony Mitchell's 2001 book *Global Noise* demonstrates the global reach of hip hop with Italian artists promoting Marxist politics through music, Basque rappers using punk-rock hip hop syncretism to espouse their nationalist cause and French artists of Moroccan and Algerian heritage challenging social issues in France and questioning France's role in the Algerian civil war. Mitchell attempts to question the monopoly over hip hop of African-American culture, by dem-onstrating how 'rap music and hip hop culture has in many cases become a vehicle of various forms of youth culture'. The links between Islamicate culture and hip hop can be traced back to the early pioneers of rap music and Black separatist groups, such as the *Nation of Islam* or the splinter group *Five Percenters*. In fact, the success of these groups led some commentators to declare: 'Islam is hip hop's official religion'.

There is, however, a much cruder and misogynistic aspect to hip hop that has its origins in America, as illustrated by a song like *Me so Horny* by the Miami-based group The 2 Live Crew, which came to prominence during the 1980s. The song and accompanying video caused immense controversy with its sexually explicit content and deeply misogynistic lyrics. Following the public backlash, The 2 Live Crew responded with an angry and explicit album, entitled 'Banned in the USA'. Despite the controversy it caused, the album went on to sell over 2 million records. In fact, Luke Records went on to release a number of other albums during the 1990s including *Back at Your Ass for the Nine-4*.

The 2 Live Crew is not an anomaly in the hip hop scene nor in youth culture. In fact, they represent the growing trend in the 'Dirty Rap' genre, with a number of prominent rappers including 50 Cent, with his song, *Magic Stick,* and Akinyele, with his EP release *Put it in Your Mouth*. While these artists focused on using the lyrics to conjure up images of women's bodies, drawing upon crude misogynistic and highly sexualised stereotypes, it was left to hip hop's legendary rap artist, Snoop Dogg, to push the hip hop music scene into the porn industry by releasing his mixed hardcore porn and hip hop music video, *Doggystyle*. Not only was this the first video listed by *Billboard*, an international music magazine, but the location of the scenes was given a personal touch; most of them were filmed at Snoop's mansion in California. It was Snoop who merged the porn industry with the hip hop youth subculture by giving it a touch of 'class', 'respectability' and a degree of 'coolness'. This resulted in the synthesising also of 'dirty words' and 'dirty thoughts' within urban sub-culture. Given the close proximity between much of Muslim youth culture and urban, hip hop 'coolness', it is not surprising to see a slippery slope of acceptability and respectability, with hip hop and pornography shaping constructs of masculinity.

However, we cannot ignore the cultural and religious dimension altogether. The fact that all the grooming cases involve Pakistani Muslims cannot be brushed aside. Some of the answers lie in how women are perceived in certain Muslim circles. A good example is provided by Sheikh Taj Din Al-Hilali, the Egyptian Imam of the Lakemba Mosque, Sydney, in response to the 2000 Skaf gang rape case. The good Sheikh declared:

If you take out uncovered meat and place it outside... and the cats come and eat it... whose fault is it, the cats' or the uncovered meat?...The uncovered meat is the problem...If she was in her room, in her home, in her hijab, no problem would have occurred.

This is not an uncommon reaction amongst Imams, Mullahs and religious scholars – to blame the victim for luring men by dressing in a particular way. She was asking for it. And what is a Muslim man whose lust has been aroused to do, 'except' as another great religious luminary explains on the web, 'to marry or possess a female slave?' This particular line of thinking is based upon the notion that women, in most of the cases, are responsible for unlawful sexual intercourse because they have the power of enticement. The web, from where many urban Muslim youth get their religious ideas, is full of declarations by religious scholars describing women in a most atrocious manner, declaring them to be property of men, and giving more than a hint that *kuffar* (non-Muslim) women are fair game. Many Muslim men think that there is some kind of religious sanction for their behaviour.

Shiekh al-Hilali, the self-appointed Grand Mufti of Australia, isn't the only prominent religious leader to articulate this view point, but he was the first Muslim to reverse the 'cultural' argument by claiming that there is something inherent in 'white' non-Muslim culture that makes white women legitimate targets of rape.

I have conducted extensive interviews with youth workers, community activists and young people in Oldham, Rochdale and Rotherham regarding the 'sexual grooming' cases and I have detected a distinct shift in attitudes. Back in 2006, when Oldham Council's 'Operation Messenger' was established following the child-sex exploitation in Oldham, the dominant reaction of most of my interviewees was 'disgust' and outright contempt for the perpetrators. In fact, I found it difficult to find anyone who even attempted to justify the actions of these perpetrators. But by the time the Rotherham and the Derby cases were reported in 2009, the mood had changed. Now, a clear cultural argument, similar to that of Shiekh Taj Din Al-Hilali, became the dominant reaction, often with religious overtones. 'Com'on bro!', I was told, 'these white gals were asking for it, dressed up like that and flirting with the bro's with the bling…'; 'you won't get good gals hanging around on the street at night. You know they are after one thing…'; and 'the reason why the victims are all white is because there is something in white culture which glorifies sex and promiscuity'.

But the 'uncovered meat' metaphor is not something which is confined within Muslim discourse; it seems also to have influenced professional attitudes toward some of the young girls who have been sexually groomed and assaulted. The Rochdale Borough's Safeguarding Children's Board Review of Child Exploitation, the work of a multi-partnership structure between the police and the various care professionals, documented systematic, institutional failures in protecting vulnerable white, working class girls in care. The report also documented how, despite repeated complaints to the police and social workers, young girls were not protected by the professionals who were paid to protect them. The framing of young working class girls through cultural lenses was seen to be partly responsible for the exploitation. In fact the Interim Report by the Office of the Children's Commissioner (OCS), an organisation that was established in the UK and is underpinned by the United Nations Convention of the Rights of the Child, clearly highlights how young people were often described by professionals in many local authorities as engaging in 'risky behaviour'. Some of the frequent phrases used by professionals echo Sheikh Taj Din Al-Hilali's observations; for example, young people were often described as 'sexually available', 'asking for it' or 'prostituting themselves'.

In the light of this institutional misogyny it is not surprising that the total scale of sexual exploitation of young people is unknown. The statistics that are usually cited by agencies refer only to the tip of the iceberg and fail to reflect the true nature of the problem. As we have seen in both the Rochdale and the Oxford cases, many victims and their parents routinely reported the crimes to a range of professionals who failed sometimes to take any notice, or did not record the crimes, or take the victims' testimonies seriously. Finally, a combination of under-recording, under-reporting and under-detection of crimes of sexual exploitation makes it exceptionally difficult for us to paint a picture of the perpetrators.

For example, out of the 115 submissions received to the OCS report on the victims, only thirty agencies submitted data on the perpetrators. Information on them was provided in full in only 3% of the call for evidence, with a staggering 68% of the submissions having no perpetrator data. This suggests that some agencies are only keen to record the ethnicities of some perpetrators while ignoring others.

While we cannot ignore the cultural component of the grooming cases, it is only a part of the story. The bigger story, involving perpetrators from a range of cultural backgrounds has yet to be told. What we can say with some certainty is that hip hop and pornography have played an important part in these cases. One of the key, yet silent, aspects of these cases is that the men were acting out particular fantasies of hip hop songs and pornographic films – in, for example, sharing the girls amongst friends and wider networks, performing certain acts of sexual violence (described by one victim as 'sexual torture'), and using certain terminology to describe their victims.

The sexual objectification of women is not an essential characteristic of hip hop, neither is it an essence of Black or Muslim youth culture, nor is it a problem confined to inner city ghettos. Rather, it is a complex mechanism through which young men internalise negative stereotypes which are prevalent within society. The role of pornography in shaping young men's perception of women is the 'elephant in the room' and is rarely investigated in academia or reflected in public debate. Yet, for most youth workers the casual and routine encounters with pornography by some men, and boys as young as twelve or thirteen, is a particular problem. During my research, I have met young Muslim men who have clear memories of the date of their first encounter. In fact, for some, viewing pornography is seen as one of the rites of passage. There are those for whom pornography blurs the boundaries between expected, required and acceptable forms of sexual conduct. That pornography is now associated with what is 'cool' in Asian youth subculture, through the medium of hip hop, is a serious and present danger.

QUTB: POET AND ISLAMIST

Tanjil Rashid

A crystal is not made of ice, but is a more complex composite of atoms or ions. A leopard is not a cross between a lion and a panther, but a creature more untameable than either. And a pontiff is no builder of bridges. The Argentine short story writer, Jorge Luis Borges, observed these ironies of etymology in his 1940 essay on the description of a fascist. Today, the Muslim man everyone is trying to describe is 'the Islamist'. An Islamist is not made of Islam, Borges might have noted. He is a more complex composite of ideas and influences.

An Islamist is not a cross between Islam and some 'ism or ocracy' but a creature that escapes taming by either. Increasingly, the Islamist is called a 'salafist', an acolyte of the *salaf*, Islam's first generation. In truth, the salafist is the most novel of Muslims, his infamous aversion to *bid'a*, 'innovation', in fact precipitating the most extraordinary intellectual innovation. He is less a spiritual fundamentalist – like the muftis of the famous seminary of Deoband, India, or the Ayatollahs of Qom, Iran, self-effacing in ethereal expectation of the afterlife – than a materialist, motivated by that worldly amour-propre behoving only an inhabitant of the present day. The Islamist stands not in the tradition of Islam's flat-earth cosmologists, Islam's iconoclastic photography-forbidders, who know only the Qur'an; he stands instead in the cosmopolitan tradition of the first to call themselves 'Salafists'. These were the nineteenth-century reformers like the itinerant, whisky-swilling, polyglot Jamal al-Din al-Afghani (1839–97) or the respectful correspondent of Tolstoy, the Mufti of Egypt, Muhammad Abduh (1849–1905), both canonical figures in the Islamist tradition, yet whose examined lives barely correspond to the vision both Westerners and Muslims now have of fanatics and philistines.

Note the Borgesian ironies in the case of the very first Islamist. Commemorated on stamps in the notoriously censorious Islamic Republic of Iran; intellectual godfather to the Egyptian Islamists who stabbed the novelist Naguib

Mahfouz (1911-2006) to near-death; and widely-read among the book-burn-
ing, Buddha-blasting Taliban: the Islamist ideologue and one of the founders
of the Muslim Brotherhood, Sayyid Qutb (1906-1966) is not a man whose
followers are known for admiring the arts.

Yet the man was an artist himself, a poet of some repute, as the landmark
publication in Egypt of the *Complete Poetical Works of Sayyid Qutb* established last
year. It took seventeen years to edit, includes some thirty-five unpublished
poems, and illuminates overlooked chapters in the life of Islamism's seminal
thinker. According to the leader of Al-Qaeda Ayman al-Zawahiri, Qutb is 'the
nucleus of the modern Islamic jihad movement.' A reputation holding equal
sway over his detractors: Martin Amis, British turned American novelist,
describes him as 'the first framer of Islamism' while neoconservative cabinet
minister Michael Gove proclaims him 'Islamism's most influential thinker'.
They count among the millions who have read *Milestones*, a screed every bit as
influential as Marx's *Manifesto*, decreeing that 'attacking the non-believers in
their territories is a collective and individual duty'. That's the Qutb seized on
in the age of Islamist terror. As American journalist Andrew Sullivan sarcasti-
cally asks: 'Is there anybody in America after 9/11 who isn't an expert on
Sayyid Qutb?'

Such 'experts' would be very surprised to see in the *Complete Poetical Works*
that Qutb proved more prolific as a progressive poet than a religious rabble-
rouser. But should an Islamist ideologue's sensitive scribbling be so startling?
Consider this:

I am a supplicant for a goblet of wine
From the hand of a sweetheart.
In whom can I confide this secret of mine,
Where can I take this sorrow?

These lines were written by none other than the Qutb-admiring Ayatollah
Khomeini (less noted for his poetry than his infamous literary criticism, writing a nearly literal hatchet-job on Salman Rushdie), while the recent,
acclaimed publication of *Poetry of the Taliban* similarly jogs our perceptions of
Islamists by anthologising the inner lives of Taliban fighters.

It happens that the man the arch-American atheist Sam Harris calls 'Osama
bin Laden's favourite philosopher' had a similarly sorrowful side, penning

poems like this *cri de coeur* from 1929, where he sounds less like an Islamist ideologue than an adorable adolescent seduced by the *Sturm und Drang*:

Is this life or is it an inferno,
with its agitated furnace aflame?
My soul's sorrow in life
is greater than in death.
To whom shall I complain?
Who can clarify my feeling?

Despite initial opposition from Egypt's religious establishment when the book's editor, Aly Abdel-Rahman, first proposed the tome, the clerics of Al-Azhar are now behind its publication. So is the movement Qutb inspired. The Muslim Brotherhood's supreme guide Mohammed Badie believes the world must see Qutb's creative side, 'for it is creativity that led him to Islamist thought.'

But in a sign of the ideological battle over Qutb's legacy, his brother Muhammad, formerly schoolmaster to Osama bin Laden himself, suppressed the inclusion of Qutb's romantic novel, *Ashwak* (*Thorns*). We are familiar with Western novels about doomed love affairs, from Theodor Fontane's (1819–98) *Effi Briest* to Ian McEwan's *On Chesil Beach*, but little acknowledged is Sayyid Qutb's own Arabic contribution to this genre; with relationships impeded by antiquated honour codes and a consequent inability to communicate, *Ashwak* is reminiscent of both. In his other novel *Saturday*, McEwan posits a psychological gulf between Western rationalism and violent terrorism – might the bizarre parallels in the literary output of representatives of both worlds suggest otherwise?

These flippant questions are posed to expose our hidebound conceptions, to shake our inadequate vision of Islamism out of the inertia that grips it. An equivalence between Qutbism and Western liberalism is not at issue, already disproved by the Islamists' embarrassed disavowal of Qutb's harmless novel for its apparent autobiographical roots in the young Qutb's romantic failure. But *Ashwak* is in fact a crucial clue in tracing Islamism's overlooked intellectual contexts.

On publication in 1947, the novel boosted Qutb's reputation, garnering a generous review from Naguib Mahfouz. Indeed, this rising star of Egyptian letters owed his own reputation to Qutb, by then a leading critic. Far from a mad mullah, Qutb's career rather resembles somebody like Matthew Arnold (1822–88), holding a day job as a school inspector while pursuing his calling as a poet, and like Arnold it was as a cutting-edge culture critic that he achieved the greater fame. The first literary critic to discover Mahfouz's nascent genius, relations between the Islamist ideologue Qutb and the liberal scion Mahfouz were warmer than people realise.

In reviews that would bewilder the Qutbists who knifed the novelist in 1994, Qutb acclaimed Mahfouz's *Khan Al-Khalili* 'an Egyptian dish on the dining table of world literature' and recommended *The Struggles of Thebes* 'be distributed in every house for free'. Qutb did more than anyone to lend literary legitimacy to Mahfouz, but also did more than anyone to legitimise the insurgence that so menaced Mahfouz. 'Qutb was a superb poet, story-teller and writer,' mused Mahfouz, 'but he inspired the Islamic groups from whose ranks emerged the person who attempted to kill me. It's a paradox.'

Indeed, Qutb's career is stamped not by the cast-iron conformities his admirers and revilers propound, but by paradoxes. *The Enchanted City*, Qutb's novel about a Prince and a rustic damsel, is sodden in imagery of caves and wildernesses that bespeaks his mysticism, more Paulo Coelho than Ian McEwan – yet its author developed the infamous, influential *takfiri* ideology that declares more mystical-minded Muslims *kuffar* (non-believers). The shrine-smashing Shabab today terrorising Somalia claim to honour Qutb's ideas.

If contemporary Qutbists were to have come across Qutb in the 1930s, they would likely have targeted their intellectual progenitor using the very *takfiri* framework he himself would come to theorise. The reformist Canadian Muslim thinker Ibrahim Abu-Rabi describes how Qutb 'opted for a modernist approach in language, mental outlook, and cultural orientation', moving in the worshipful orbit of progressive poet Abbas al-Aqqad (1889-1964) and the 'dean of Arabic literature', Taha Hussein (1889-1973). As a measure of their orientation, note they were proposing Egypt's curriculum be overhauled to introduce compulsory Ancient Greek, just as the West began phasing it out of its own. That current beleaguered the religious reactionaries of the 1930s who, as Qutb's biographer John Calvert writes, 'believed they were under siege by the secular, iconoclastic agenda of the literary modernists'. That agenda's staunchest defender was Sayyid Qutb, disparaging 'religion, religion… the battle-cry of the feeble-minded.'

He was religious, only his variety of piety was unconventional. Some of his poems are spiritual verging on blasphemy. The opening salvo of a poem entitled *Ibadah Jadidah* ('A New Deification') rings of Rumi: 'To beauty alone I owe my worship!', his verse thus tainted by the sin of *shirk*, idolatry, for which Qutb's followers have mercilessly murdered. Such a Sufi-suffused sentiment contradicted his later religious stand during the 1950s and 1960s.

While Qutb's Islamist hagiographers and Western critics fail to realise the extent of his non-Islamist inclinations (it muddles the simplistic narratives they peddle), academic aficionados explain the discord between Qutb's two (seemingly) distinct faces as two distinct phases. In 1949, the Ministry of Education fobbed him off on a fact-finding fellowship to America; to this secular stateside sojourn is imputed the metamorphosis from progressive poet to fundamentalist philosopher, even the very genesis of Islamism. 9/11, Martin Amis explained, 'all goes back to Greeley, Colorado.' A novelist can't resist such a dramatic story arc, but even the respected American journalist Lawrence Wright, contends: 'al-Qaida had really begun in America, not so long ago.'

Certainly, in his political writings, as much memoir as manifesto, Qutb vindicates his ideology with recollections of the New World, rather like Alexis de Tocqueville (1805–59), but concluding the opposite about democracy in America. Other Egyptian intellectuals betray a similar trajectory, like Columbia-educated literary critic Abdel-Wahhab el-Messeiry (1938-2008) who became an Islamic political theorist, and Egyptian author and literary critic Safinaz Kazim, a student of the avant-garde New York theatre scene, who veiled herself in 1972. America was supposedly a turning point for Qutb. Either that, or the torture his CIA-schooled jailers meted on him in the 1960s, or the rejection of the lover he fictionalised in *Ashwak*, and so on.

For the terrorism-pundits and scholars, interpretations of Qutb hinge on turning points. Unable to square his paradoxes, all insist on a chronological cut-off from man-of-letters to ideologue, precluding cognitive dissonance. Scholars tend to buck the complicated truth that thinkers often think two contradictory things at the same time. Like economists, they presume rational coherence in the object of their analysis. The Qutb scholars, indeed, have taken a leaf out of the economists' book who have long grappled with the only comparable case of a patently paradoxical intellectual legacy of such political significance: 'Das Adam Smith Problem', the contradiction between

Smith's *Wealth of Nations* and his *Theory of Moral Sentiments*, between the capitalist economist and the moralist philosopher. Just as Smith's moralist philosophy has been notoriously written out for political convenience, so has Qutb's literary career.

Aly Abdel-Rahman, the editor of the collected poems, has a novel solution to Das Sayyid Qutb Problem: to judge Qutb's work as a whole. Abdel-Rahman notes that Qutb never renounced his earlier writings, even as he cultivated his radical reputation. It cannot be argued there was no contradiction – he went from being an employee of the liberal state to the most articulate advocate of its overthrow. But there is some curious continuity between the two phases.

Writing of Qutb, Martin Amis asks 'whether love can be said to exist…in the ferocious patriarchy of Islamism'. An odd question when set against *Ashwak*. Or the love poems he now and then composed, like *The Dream of Life*:

O! dream that portrayed her
Every day with another exquisite picture,
All of them look – and how many they are! –
Sweet, attractive glimpses, and transparent.

More scandalously, he advocated public nudity (for salutary reasons). But his political writings do not evade his erotic obsessions. On the transatlantic liner, a temptress in a cocktail dress bursts into his cabin to seduce him. In a D.C. hospital, a nurse's 'thirsty lips… smooth legs… provocative laugh' impress him. Intrigued by sexual freedom, he cites the newly-published Kinsey Report and Britain's Profumo Affair (given *Milestones'* circulation, the names John Profumo and Christine Keeler must be better known in the Muslim world than in the English-speaking one). In an episode evoked in Adam Curtis's 2004 BBC documentary, *The Power of Nightmares*, he attends a parish ball where, in Michael Gove's words, 'The strains of "Baby It's Cold Outside" inspired him to a furious philippic against the bestial carnality of yankee youth.' Qutb conjures the scene with almost Joycean lyricism in the original unpunctuated Arabic: 'the hall swarmed with legs arms circled arms lips met lips chests met chests the air was full of love.'

The poet and the ideologue are clearly closer than has been let on. As a poet, Qutb was a Romantic, palpable in his imagery of poisoned chalices, wilted roses, his novel's eponymous thorns. As a critic, he admired English writers Samuel Coleridge (1772-1834) and William Hazlitt (1778-1830). As an ideologue, too, he drew on Romantic themes. His political concept, *jahili-yyah* (ignorance), was an ancient appellation for the annals of pagan pre-Islam, its barbarism redux in the modern West. Against this, Abu-Rabi notes that Qutb romantically envisioned 'the present and the future... pregnant with possibilities outside the pale of the past.' That desire to escape history is a classic characteristic of Romantic utopian thinking, particularly popular in America – think of Ralph Waldo Emerson (1803–82), the leader of the Transcendentalist movement, when he asks, 'Why should we grope among the dry bones of the past?'

Qutb's poetry can stir more intriguing comparisons. 'O weariness of men who turn from God!' opens one verse. Not Qutb's, though: that's from TS Eliot's *Choruses from 'The Rock'*, but an almost identical sentence crops up in Qutb. There are passages from Eliot's *Idea of a Christian Society*, too, that could be seamlessly transplanted into *Milestones*, even Eliot's critique of the West refers to 'Modern Paganism', paralleling *jahiliyyah*. In Qutb's talk of 'the rubbish heap of the West', novelist Jonathan Raban fancifully detects an allusion to Eliot's *Wasteland*, noting how both share 'a pessimistic and apocalyptic vision of the West's decline'. Embracing literary modernism and anti-liberal politics, Qutb's career has shades of his Bloomsbury contemporary's. Obviously, Eliot never called to arms a violent, global movement, though, in another illustrative parallel, Ezra Pound (1885–1972), American poet and critic of early modernist movement, did. Like Qutb, he was a modernist poet seduced by violent politics.

Sometimes influences lean far-left. Qutb appropriates Marxist-Leninist concepts like the 'vanguard'. The opening of *Milestones* recalls *The Communist Manifesto's* first lines: 'Mankind today is on the brink of a precipice... The turn of Islam has arrived.' It becomes less astounding that a revolutionary anti-clerical ideology should percolate Islamist ideology when viewed against Qutb's belletrist clues. His novella, *A Child From The Village*, mocks 'the cleric who rarely takes a shower', and anti-clerical contempt equally informs Islamism. Counter-intuitively, the great anti-clerical threat to world religion today is radical Islamism, rivalling even Bolshevism's annual mosque-destruction count.

Even as an ideologue, he retained a poet's sensibility. In prison he authored *In The Shade of the Qur'an*, a 'commentary that consistently pays attention to the way the Qur'an achieves literary and psychological effects,' writes Robert

Irwin: 'he did not favour an unduly literalist reading of the text.' Although Qutb himself selectively quotes the Qur'an in *Milestones*, he's far from the fundamentalist brand of philistine, literalist Qur'anic interpretations.

Martin Amis considers Qutb 'marked by intellectual vacuity'. On the contrary, Qutb is a veritable plenum chamber dense with the flotsam of Western intellectual influences (no small number of which influence Amis too). For example, Jonathan Meades, the British writer on architecture and culture, talks of Qutb's origins in 'the late nineteenth-century European tradition of anti-urbanism that calumnises cities as licentious and decadent and calls for moral renewal.' The soundbite about 'mediaeval' fundamentalists and the fundamentalists' own rhetoric of a return to Islam's early-mediaeval, salaf origins is ironic, for Islamism is a modern mutation from the lineage of the European post-Enlightenment, which liberals and Islamists both define in contradistinction to Islamism. The Romantic, modernist and Marxist imprimaturs in Qutb's literary writings testify to this relationship. But Qutb's admirers and revilers are none the wiser. Amis condemns Islamism as 'a massive agglutination of stock response, of clichés, of inherited and unexamined formulations.' That's as true of the Islamist as it is of Amis's (and others') responses to Islamists like Qutb. Both sides ignore Qutb's poetry and fiction to keep their simplistic narratives simplistic.

Such blinkers do our understanding of the makings of an Islamist no favours. Remember, the 9/11 bomber Muhammad Atta was an architect. His dissertation considered the erosion of historic Aleppo's venerable Arab cityscape amid modern development. It would be misleading to attribute aesthetic motives alone to the Islamist insurgence. But it is no less a mistake to ignore Islamism's complex aesthetic dimension. Popular perception denies the Islamist's inner life. In fact, what goes in those recesses may well be the most revealing, even if it unveils a complicated co-existence of contradictions that pedagogues, pundits and propagandists alike are unable to square. Qutb's most famous work may well be called *Milestones*, but his life entailed less of a milestone in America than everyone simplistically imagines, and his poetry shows the enduring dissonance of his thoughts. However, if there was one thing he did learn anew in that country, it was perhaps gleaned from the wisdom of the novelist Scott Fitzgerald (1896–1940), doubtless then doing the rounds, that 'the test of a first-rate intelligence is the ability to hold two contradictory ideas at the same time.'

HARUN YAHYA'S FAST FOOD

Stefano Bigliardi

There exists a substantial group among Muslim men who hunger for simple answers. These men suffer from an acute inferiority complex regarding their religion and are perpetually engaged in proving the superiority of Islam over all other religions, ideologies and worldviews. They are devoted to a special type of popular literature known as *ijaz*, or 'scientific miracles of the Qur'an'.

The tendency to read science in the Qur'an has a long history, dating back to the beginning of the twentieth century. However, it received a boost with Maurice Bucaille's *The Bible, the Qur'an and Science*, which was published in 1970, translated into numerous languages, and exists in several editions. Many simple-minded readers see Bucaille's assertion that the Qur'an is full of scientific facts as a positive proof of its Divine origin. The *ijaz* movement was institutionalised when the Saudis established the well-funded *Commission on Scientific Signs of the Qur'an and Sunnah*, which went on to hold numerous international conferences. Despite the fact that 'considerable mental gymnastics and distortion is required to read scientific facts or theories in these verses', as Ziauddin Sardar notes, 'this height of folly has become a global craze in Muslim societies'.

The new and undisputed champion of *ijaz* literature is Harun Yahya, the Turkish author and religious leader. Yahya serves a lavish meal for those who hunger for 'scientific miracles' in the Qur'an and have a thirst for a Muslim religious identity. His works, as well as Yahya's self-representation, aim to demonstrate that Muslim faith is in harmony with science and compatible with a hyper-technological lifestyle. Indeed, there are plenty of them: almost 300 books in Turkish have been published under the name 'Harun Yahya' and more than 200 translated into English. Yahya's official website lists over 2000 articles in Turkish, and approximately 1300 in English. Translations are available in another sixty languages, all widely advertised through more than 150 constantly updated websites. These figures are constantly increasing. If reading is food for thought, Harun Yahya clearly offers a wide range menu through a very large chain of outlets.

The actual individual associated with the name Yahya is Adnan Oktar (b. 1956, Ankara). Oktar came to the fore in Istanbul in his late twenties while studying philosophy and interior design. In 1986, following the publication of a book dedicated to conspiracy theories, Oktar was charged with promoting a theocratic revolution and served nineteen months in jail, the first of a long series of legal troubles. He eventually dropped his studies and managed to gather around himself a group of students from well-off families that gradually took on the form of a sect, whose activities and internal dynamics repeatedly raised the attention of Turkish authorities. To date, Oktar's biography includes episodes of hospitalisation in a psychiatric institution, several imprisonments, legal troubles for possession of cocaine, sexual harassment, and blackmailing of collaborators. All these troubles and legal indictments, some still pending, have been widely reported in Turkish media; Oktar himself makes no mystery about them, narrating the vicissitudes of his life in interviews and other texts published on the web. The man is presented as extraordinary and outstandingly devout, and his troubles are described either as the result of the occult agencies he boldly fights against, or as God's tests which he patiently endures. Oktar demonstrates a charismatic and self-assured attitude and is constantly portrayed in very elegant, fashionable clothes; similarly dressed collaborators often accompany him and address him as *hodja* (preacher) and *agabey* (big brother).

Despite a maimed reputation in his home country and his outrageous TV appearances, some of which have become viral YouTube clips (especially those where he flirts with heavily made-up young women), Oktar/Yahya still enjoys worldwide respect by readers, who are either unaware of his most whimsical traits, or do not attach any importance to them. In 2010, Yahya was selected among the top fifty most influential Muslims by the Royal Islamic Strategic Studies Center in Jordan. A request for his books is likely to raise some eyebrows in Istanbul bookshops, yet they can be easily found in mosque bookshops in Cairo as well as in Toronto.

The real dimensions, sources, the reach of Oktar's activities, as well as the networking of people and institutions, are hard to see behind the flood of multi-coloured books, websites, TV programmes and the inexhaustible self-promoted information on, and praise of, Oktar's life. Oktar founded the

Scientific Research Foundation (SRF: in Turkish, *Bilim Arastırma Vakfı*, BAV) in 1990, followed by the Foundation for Protection of National Values (*Millî Degerleri Koruma Vakfı*, or MDK) in 1995. The goal of the SRF, which boasts on its website an organisation of over 2600 scientific events in Turkey and abroad, is the 'establishment of a worldwide living environment that is dominated by peace, tranquillity and love,' and it seems principally devoted to the defence of creationism, while MDK seems more focused on Turkish issues. However, their real extent and their connections, besides official statements, can only be estimated. Clearly, his immense output, global marketing, and massive free distribution suggest huge financial backing. Furthermore, the pressure that he was able to exert on the Turkish government on several occasions to block certain websites perceived as hostile, most notably that of the militant atheist British biologist Richard Dawkins, indicates that he is a powerful person.

Yahya has apparently discovered not only the recipe for uninterrupted productivity, but also a source of fabulous wealth. All books under his name, besides being available in glossy, fully-illustrated editions, can be downloaded for free in different formats. This extraordinary diffusion means that, sooner or later, a bookshop customer or Internet user bumps into one of the texts associated with his name. In addition, in 2007 Yahya prompted the curiosity of potential readers by sending his gigantic and luxurious tome *Atlas of Creation* (768 glossy pages, 5.4 kg, 275 x 375 mm, images in motion on the hard cover), unsolicited and free of charge to science teachers, research institutions and libraries throughout Europe and North America.

His books are written in plain if stilted language; they are highly repetitive, and seem to be mainly composed with a bold copy-paste technique, with a system of quotations far below acceptable standards of academic and popular communication alike. The books are sprinkled with de-contextualised quotations from major scientists along with more controversial and questionable figures, with no distinction between them. However, they have the advantage of a clear communication and they are efficaciously eye-catching.

So what's on the menu? According to Yahya, Darwinian evolutionist doctrines are the source of all the violent and repressive phenomena of the last centuries such as terrorism, totalitarianism, communism, fascism and racism as well as romanticism, capitalism, Buddhism, and Zionism (which at present he explicitly distinguishes from Judaism, after a flirt with Holocaust denial in the 1990s). Yahya considers them all interconnected because, in his view, they all stem from and foster materialism, atheism, and pessimism. He claims that they were propagated throughout the millennia by freemasons, who he argues are the principal occult actor of history in all its anti-religious manifestations. Darwinism is rejected by Yahya for its supposed moral consequences, but also as a pseudo-scientific doctrine that lacks concrete proof, as a theory that excludes divine agency and that has been exaggerated and idolised.

Yahya sees Darwin as the major advocate of evolution. Moreover, he also claims that evolutionist doctrines date back to the ancient Greeks and Egyptians. To fight more efficaciously against materialism, Yahya endorses a philosophical theory of the inexistence of matter: matter does not exist and its illusion is constantly re-created by God. Despite the fact that his work seems mainly modelled on Christian creationism, Yahya refuses to be compared to the advocates of 'intelligent design' who hold that the complexity of the biological world can only be explained by the intervention of a divine designer. Yahya points out that Christian creationists do not make explicit reference to Allah and that the very reference to a 'design' limits the concept of divinity. He subscribes to the idea, rejected by a considerable host of Christian creationists, that the Earth is a million years old.

Against the evils that affect contemporary society, Yahya endorses an ecumenical and messianic form of Islam, based on a return to religious values, which has its symbols and examples in the Prophets. According to Yahya, the arrival of the Mahdi, the 'Guided One' of Islamic eschatology who will rid the world of evil, is imminent. He will appear and begin his activity in Turkey, the country that Yahya considers endowed with moral superiority and therefore apt to take up the leading role in an Islamic union. Despite refusing to explicitly identify with the Mahdi, Yahya constantly describes him in a way that, curiously, fits his own profile.

While subscribing to the known doctrine according to which the miracle of the Qur'an is its beauty and inimitability, what Yahya emphasises are its 'scientific miracles'. In his *Allah's Miracles in the Qur'an*, Yahya propagates the idea that the Qur'an mentions natural phenomena that were not known in detail (or wrongly known) at the time of the revelation, as well as later technological inventions. He mentions eighty-seven cases that include the Big Bang; amongst the historical events and technological developments that, according to Yahya, the Qur'an predicts are: the preservation of the mummified body of the Pharaoh who pursued Moses, the Moon landing, coronary bypass surgery, and atomic technology. Furthermore, according to Yahya, the Qur'an displays patterns of word repetition which, associated to numerical values, have a correspondence with reality or special symbolic values. For example, the word 'day' occurs 365 times; and Sura 54, 'The Moon', with a numerological interpretation, gives 1969 – the year of the successful Apollo 11 mission.

Yahya constantly celebrates nature, which is lavishly illustrated in his books, and describes natural phenomena as miracles. In this sense, the whole universe is, as the title of another of his books suggests, *A Chain of Miracles*. All the features of the universe are regarded by Yahya as signs of divine artistry, and therefore as clear proofs of the existence of God. According to Yahya, everything in the universe is necessary, necessarily made for life, and undoubtedly points at the existence of God. Yahya usually describes a natural phenomenon in plain language, enriching the description with some schemes full of numerical data, and generously sprinkled with quotations from the Qur'an, together with passages from prominent scientists. He insists on the necessary character of the phenomenon with a sort of 'counterfactual reasoning': if the phenomenon in question did not exist, life would not exist either – therefore God exists and/or is good. This scheme has been applied by Yahya to numerous single phenomena as 'miracles': animal migration, ants, atoms, the blood, the heart, cells, cell membranes, DNA, electricity in the body, enzymes, eyes, honeybees, hormones, human creation, the immune system, molecules, mosquitos, photosynthesis, plants, protein, seeds, spiders, talking birds, termites, smell and taste.

The ideas that Yahya relentlessly propagates under the label of 'creationism' are his most resilient and visible ones – and the ones that have ensured him a worldwide readership amongst Muslims in need of simple answers. The term 'creationism' comes with a positive connotation for anybody who is religiously inclined, and particularly from a Christian background. If 'creationism' indeed means that the universe should be seen as coming into existence through, and dependent on, God's creative action, the term sounds like a platitude for any believer and a trait to be necessarily included in any religious worldview. This is analogous to advertising fast food as 'natural' and 'tasty': who would want to consume food that is not genuine and palatable? Yet to demonstrate that the specific food you are selling is healthy and naturally nutritious, simply printing its trademark in green on the background of a rural landscape is insufficient. What matters are the actual ingredients. 'Creationism' has to be examined for its ingredients, the specific collection of ideas on nature and science distributed by Yahya.

Yahya's reading of the Qur'an is not limited to highlighting references to natural phenomena and invitations to observe them but, following the principles of *ijaz* literature, he emphasises 'scientific facts' purportedly contained in the Qur'an. The Qur'an is thus a repository of detailed scientific descriptions of natural phenomena whose presence in the revelation a long time ahead of their observation by the scientific community proves its divine origin. This kind of analysis does violence to both science and the Qur'an. It sees science simply as a collection of facts rather than an enterprise based on paradigms, theories, mathematical models, empirical work, experiments and refutation. Moreover, it renders the demonstration of the Qur'an's divinity dependent on some specific formulations of 'scientific facts' that might be revised by the scientific community — think, for instance, how Pluto was reclassified in 2006 as a dwarf-planet — or a theory that may be falsified and replaced by a new theory.

One could engage in a piece-meal refutation of the supposed objections to biological evolution put forth by Yahya, as several authors, Muslim and non-Muslim alike, have done. However, the real intellectual risk inherent to Yahya's production, that cannot be completely identified with any of the specific and unsound ideas that he popularises, has rather to do with the general conceptual structure that his works represent and encourage. Returning to the fast food analogy, one can of course debunk commercial slogans, and engage in a systematic nutritional analysis of the ingredients, but what is really detrimental to the consumer's health is not a single element, nor the single, occasional consumption of a meal. It is the general habit of consuming fast food, camouflaged by slogans evoking genuineness and tastiness. Yahya can be more substantially criticised for the internal logic that his works encourage and on which they rely, rather than the specific ideas he advocates from time to time.

The landscape of daily life is interspersed with sophisticated devices. Technology constantly invades our sensorial field and is insistently equated with contemporary natural science and modernity, even if human beings have been successfully trying from time immemorial to extend the capacities offered by their own bodies through devices that are not to be directly found in nature. Laypeople tend to overlook the conceptual and mathematical structure of scientific enterprise; physics is instead conceived as the collection of 'facts' regarding the natural world, while technology evokes such 'facts', which are constantly represented in documentary films and advertisements through pictures of spectacular celestial bodies and collisions of subatomic particles.

The internal logic to Yahya's works is twofold. On the one hand, Yahya encourages the hasty and superficially equates technology, natural science, and 'facts' that are visually accentuated in his books. Such reduction ignores such defining traits of science as knowledge, technology as practice, and physics as the understanding of the natural world through experiments and mathematical models. Then Yahya tries to bestow on his religious discourse the prestige and respectability commonly attached to science itself; that is, he presents his discourse as reputable knowledge. His style mimics that of scientific popularisation, and his discussion attempts to present itself as 'more scientific than science' by targeting as its antagonist a famous name connected to science, Darwin; he apparently discusses evolution as an expert in the field, on an equal footing with established biologists and evolutionary scientists of the world, criticising it, offering 'proofs,' asking for counterproofs and so on. The result is a maimed, caricaturised understanding both of science and Qur'anic exegesis.

Paradoxically, despite the fact that he is commonly perceived as the most vocal advocate of Islamic creationism, Yahya's discussion of 'Darwinism' is extrinsic to his work; it is just a consequence of the deep internal logic of a 'scientified' religious discourse. Darwinism is attacked in order to appear 'scientific,' while discussing some theory that is famously associated with science. As a result of such a strategy, Yahya might well have decided, or may decide one day, to offer criticism of the physics of the black holes or attack the speed of light; for instance, he might claim that they are an insult to God's power, argue that they are not observable, or vocally challenge Stephen Hawking.

Now it may well be that the person behind the name 'Harun Yahya' has good intentions. It may well be that his own faith is strengthened by such a twisted logic. After all, anybody can arrive at faith, or strengthen it, in her or his own way and, conversely, no one is entitled to stand in judgement over someone else's faith. What one can seriously object to is this: projecting a confused, oversimplified and extremely flawed version of science on the Qur'an, and indissolubly blending the two seriously damages the credibility of Islam. It belittles Islam and its Sacred Text. In the final analysis, it is extremely dangerous to the mental health of Muslim individuals and society.

For those who are interested in adopting a more balanced approach towards Islam and science, there are plenty of alternative diets. The Qur'anic verses referring to the natural world can be seen as a sign of God's creative power and an invitation to take science seriously. One can say that contemporary Muslim societies lag behind in terms of scientific education and that the believers have a religious duty to work actively to reduce this deficit. One can also engage with the verses of the Qur'an from the perspective of science; there are authors who actually do this in the light of a sound appreciation of science. By 'sound' I mean an appreciation of science that accepts and incorporates biological evolution and presents science as a dynamic enterprise that involves the collection of empirical data and their interpretation through mathematical models. Indeed, there is a group of Muslims with a background in natural sciences that is trying to develop a more meaningful discourse about Islam and science. One can mention Ziauddin Sardar's *Explorations in Islamic Science*, published in 1989, as a serious attempt to develop a new discourse on Islam and science grounded in a sound view of science; incidentally, he also vigorously attacks what he calls 'Bucaillism', which is nowadays described as *ijaz* literature. More recently, the Algerian astrophysicist Nidhal Guessoum has explored the relationship between Islam and science on the basis of knowledge and thoughtful reflections, while debunking the *ijaz* literature, in his *Islam's Quantum Question*. Furthermore, the Jordanian molecular biologist Rana Dajani, while discussing Guessoum's ideas, has aired 'a new Einsteinian theory of evolution which involves the dimension of time and human cognition.'

One might perhaps say that such attempts are currently far from being complete and articulate: they display all the fascination and promises of an enterprise that has just begun. On a pessimistic note it can also be pointed out that the production and distribution of good products will always have to compete, in terms of velocity, quantity and mass, with low-quality ones. Nonetheless, experiments aimed at finding a synthesis that solves the hunger for thinking soundly, both religiously and scientifically, are in progress. The outcome is uncertain, the task thrilling. Meanwhile, we need to avoid fatty comfort food widely served by the likes of Harun Yahya and the purveyors of *ijaz* literature.

THE FORGOTTEN GENDER

Leyla Jagiella

My life has largely been defined by talking about 'not being a man'. I am a transwoman. That means I was born with what society normatively calls a 'male body'. But I define myself as a woman; and am usually seen and treated as such by people around me. Some people do sometimes ask me, in what I perceive as quite an insensitive way, if I 'had once been a man'. I confidently answer: 'no'. I have never been a 'man' in the precise meaning of the word. I have been a boy – at least in the eyes of society - but have been living as a woman since late adolescence and have been feeling very comfortable in my feminine gender ever since. I relate to men in exactly the same way many heterosexual women relate to men: they are a part of my life that I do not want to miss but too often I perceive them as 'the other' and frequently doubt that I will ever truly understand what's going on in their lives, hearts and minds.

Genders are culturally constructed narratives. Not all men – not even all heterosexual men – are alike and neither are all women. Almost no human being will perfectly fit into a culturally defined 'gender box'. We know that not all men make great warriors and not all women are good at doing the household chores. There are men who fail in natural sciences but excel in learning languages. And some of us may even have heard of women who loathe shopping for shoes. Even though our culture tries to neatly classify all human beings into two gendered categories, a more careful analysis will tell us that individual human beings actually fall into a continuum of numerous gendered behaviours and identities; and even quite a number of biological sexes (if we talk about the numerous variants of chromosome combinations with which babies are born every single hour). One could almost say that in some way or other all human beings are transwomen or transmen. All of us struggle with fulfilling the expectations that society has imposed on our masculinity and femininity and try to live up to some of these expectations while failing with regards to others.

My sense of myself as a woman has often clashed with cultural and social expectations of 'being a man'. Even though I never ever saw myself as someone who was destined to become a man, I lived my childhood and my youth in 'a man's world' – and an important part of that in a 'Muslim man's world'. For most people being born with a male anatomy automatically means privilege and entitlement. But not for me; for me it has meant a great deal of pain and suffering.

I was born in 1980 in a small town in a rural part of Germany. The birth was not easy. Apparently I did not really have an interest in being born and felt much more comfortable with the oceanic semi-consciousness that preceded birth. The labour had to be induced; and I had to be pulled out into this cold world. When I was born I was assigned the male gender. I was my parents' first child, my younger brother would be born about four years later.

A few days after my birth, I was baptised into the Protestant Church. My maternal grandfather was a Lutheran and sprinkled the sacramental water on my head. My parents see themselves as secular German Protestants. But they both have peculiar cosmopolitan and multi-religious family histories that have influenced me from my childhood. My father's family is originally of Polish and Lithuanian origin, which gave me my melodious non-Teutonic surname. My mother's family has ties to Russia and the Netherlands. Both family histories had been shaped by what one could call a good portion of 'colonial hybridity', with several connections to the Muslim world, notably Turkey, India, Pakistan and Indonesia. In my childhood home there was a peculiar black-and-white photograph of my paternal great-grandfather in Istanbul, dressed in 'Muslim regalia' and smoking a hookah; and my grandmother kept several old lithographs once belonging to my maternal great-grandfather, depicting Muharram processions in Southern India. Tales about ancestors in and from other countries and the presence of some visual traces of Islamic culture in my childhood environment may have ignited my love for Islam and the Muslim World. But what really fed this fire in my heart was my parents' adventurous love of travelling which introduced me to several countries and different cultures even before the start of my school education.

One might say that I was aware of Islam and of human cultural diversity long before I was truly aware of the painful reality of gender. I am not totally sure when I first realised that I had a male body. I do however know that from my earliest days on I was always interested in what others usually called 'girls' stuff'. I liked to play with dolls and watched with fascination when my mum put on her make-up. The only typical boys' game that I liked to play sometimes was 'Cowboys and Indians' because that had something to do with 'different cultures' (I always wanted to be the 'Indian', and 'my Indian' was always some kind of shaman). However, the social expectations regarding my body were in conflict with how I felt about myself. My parents and grandparents worried about my preferences but they loved me, they wanted me to be happy, and they tried not to be too perturbed with my choice of games and toys. In any case, they knew that they had done nothing wrong. My younger brother, brought up with exactly the same principles and in exactly the same environment as me, grew up as a normative male boy with many stereotypically masculine interests.

Nevertheless, conflicts surrounding my gender variant behaviour were ever present. Neighbours, the kindergarten staff, and later primary school teachers, commented on my ways. Other boys treated me badly at times, and other girls did not want to play with me because I was a boy. I cried a lot as a child; and felt horribly lonely.

My childhood taught me that I was a 'strange child', 'not normal', who had to change to conform to society. At times my parents tried to change my behaviour by suggesting other interests and hobbies to me. They also tried different educational methods. But I was who I was and wanted, just like everyone else, to do what I felt comfortable with and what didn't hurt others at all. I did not understand why my interests were seen as a problem. When I realised for the first time that this whole drama had something to do with my physical existence as a biological male I started to express my regret over having been born as a boy. I began to dream of a morning on which I would suddenly wake up as a girl. Indeed, I even created a fantasy alter-ego for myself: I pretended that I was actually some kind of alien princess from another world who only had to spend a few years in a strange body in this strange world to fulfil some mission necessary for the survival of my race but would very soon return to her true home and her true self. I hung on to this fantasy all through my primary school days, I think.

There were advantages to growing up in this way. The struggle made me question the things that I was told and taught at a very early age. While people were constantly telling me that something was 'wrong', deep down in my heart I simply knew that nothing was wrong. This apparent discrepancy made me think about the nature of human life and I learned never to take anything for granted. I started to wonder about the meaning of our existence and developed a strong interest in philosophical and religious questions. My grandfather, the Lutheran, could answer some of my questions. But he was not able to answer all of them. My interest in the diversity of human cultures and our family's frequent travels to several countries in Asia and the Near East had already introduced me to people with different religious backgrounds. So I started to study Buddhism, Hinduism and Islam as well as other spiritual traditions.

Even though I grew up in a secular Protestant Christian household, I had known about Islam from my childhood. For example, I was familiar with the basic movements and words of Muslim prayer even before I could read or write properly. I felt a deep inner relationship with Islam, a relation that was based as much on Islam as an aesthetical culture as on Islam as a system of theology and religious practice. I was twelve years old, I distinctly remember, when I decided to leave Germany's Protestant Church to embrace Islam by taking *shahadah*, the Islamic affirmation of faith. Two years later, at the age of fourteen, I started to visit a local mosque and began to seriously observe Muslim religious practices.

It was a time when my body was changing rapidly. Puberty had arrived; the age when hormones flood your body and change its appearance for ever. The time when you become aware of your own sexuality. Until that age my gender variant behaviour had been of an innocent nature. But puberty suddenly changed everything. Nothing was innocent anymore. I discovered that in addition to my existing interest in supposedly feminine things, I was also developing a romantic interest in boys. This new interest felt as natural to me as my childhood interests, there was nothing strange about it. Society, I discovered again, saw things differently. I watched jealously when some of my female friends started to flirt with boys who certainly appreciated their attention. However, boys categorically did not appreciate my attention. For some time I saw myself as gay and I wondered if I could find love and fulfilment in the gay community. But it became quickly clear to me that it was not what I wanted. I did not want to be attractive to a man 'as a man'. I experienced myself as a young woman, with the feelings and desires of a young woman, albeit with a body that increasingly felt at odds with my inner feelings and self-perception. I felt as if in a prison. A prison whose walls were getting narrower and narrower every day, threatening to crush me.

The situation became even more complicated because of my involvement in the local mosque. There I entered a world that was strictly defined by gender segregation. I was perceived as a boy and had to conform to the standards created for boys. I was not allowed to pray with women and girls to whom I felt much closer emotionally and in whose company I felt much more secure. Eventually I created a double life. At school I was with my female friends, talking about make-up and the latest boy bands, while at the mosque I tried to be a 'good Muslim boy'. Both were part of my life and both were important to me but I couldn't see any way of reconciling these two parts of my life. In numerous Friday sermons, I learned that homosexual and cross-gendered feelings were supposedly sinful. From time to time I tried to 'repent', to 'pray the gay away', as they say. I threw away all the make-up that I had started to use at school and when I was spending time with non-Muslim friends, and devoted myself to strenuous religious exercises that were supposed to make me 'normal'. Alas, they never made me 'normal'. What they did, however, was suppress my vital character traits and feelings, which returned after a short while in a self-destructive and devastating backlash of uncontrollable negative emotions and desires that left me sexually and spiritually unbalanced.

My parents also became concerned about me and my 'eccentric behaviour'. There was a moment when I confessed to my parents that I 'might be gay or something similar'; their reply was that they would always love me but would nevertheless prefer me to keep my 'sexual orientation' to myself. They became increasingly unhappy with me when I declared my conversion to Islam. Not because they had any private reservations about Islam as a religion but because my new religion contributed to whispers and rumours about me in our small German town. At one point my parents accused me of being egocentric and declared that my gender issues were all about attracting attention. This was, I thought, their way of coping with the challenges that my strange behaviour caused them.

Thus my teenage years were spent fighting simultaneously on different fronts. There was the discovery of my own identity and sexuality in the midst of a cruel environment of hormone-intoxicated teenagers. There was my constant struggle at the mosque and with my Muslim friends to present myself as a 'normal boy' devoted to Muslim orthodoxy. And then there were regular skirmishes with my family. Sometimes I could hardly bear the pressure. Dealing with constant criticism from several sections of the outside world was one thing. Even worse was the fact that I internalised what others told me. Even though I knew with all my heart that I was doing nothing wrong, and felt and acted the way that was most natural for me, I developed feelings of guilt and self-loathing. When insults such as 'fag' or 'sissy' were thrown at me, I put all the blame on myself. I became depressed and suicidal. I probably would not have survived without my strong faith in God and the support of some very good friends.

When I was nineteen and about to finish my school education, I realised that I had to change my life if I were to survive. If I would not make a clear decision to stand up for who I was and how I wanted to live I would have no future whatsoever. This became evident when insistent demands for gender conformity turned into a flood from my Muslim sides; Imams and friends constantly advised me to get married (to a girl!) as soon as possible. I also realised that I would leave my parents and my hometown very soon to start my university education. After yet another dramatic attempt to change myself and to become 'normal', which ended in suicidal thoughts, I decided to start life as a woman. That was the only way for me to feel natural and socially adjusted. As soon as I made that decision, I remember, I felt happy and relieved. There was nothing about that decision that felt 'strange' or 'queer'. It was just what I had been waiting for since I was born. All I had to do now was to transform this decision into my everyday reality. I needed to find a way forward.

The way forward came shortly after my twenty-first birthday. I found myself in India. More precisely at the shrine of the twelfth-century Sufi saint Moinuddin Chishti, known popularly as Khwaja Gharib Nawaz ('Benefactor of the Poor'). It is located in the city of Ajmer in Rajasthan. I spent the first day of my life as a woman at the *urs*, the annual festival that commemorates the death anniversary of Khwaja Gharib Nawaz. After the six-day *urs*, I joined the *hijras*, the traditional transgender community of India and Paki-

stan, in Delhi, diving deeper and deeper into the ocean of an Islam that was
so radically different from the Islam that I knew from my German small-
town mosque. I considered India to be my second 'country of birth'.

Since that felicitous day in Ajmer I have been living my life as a Muslim
transwoman. While I do not regret having chosen this particular path I must
admit it is not the easiest path that a human being can walk. The Muslim
community is not the most welcoming place for lesbian, gay, bi-sexual and
transgender (LGBT) people, or even for other people who do not live up
to gender expectations, such as those who refuse to marry or who are
unable to give birth. Large parts of the current Muslim community are
strongly influenced by very rigid attitudes regarding gender and sexuality
and these can make life difficult if not impossible not only for transwomen
but also for many 'normal' heterosexual Muslim men and women.

I have heard many heart-breaking stories from LGBT Muslims. The level
of pain and suffering that some Muslim brothers and sisters have to experience just because their romantic desires or their gender representation
digress from the norm created by a non-understanding majority is deeply
worrying. For many Muslim transwomen and transmen, especially in the
Western diaspora, it is quite difficult to hold on to their faith. In theory one
might be able to separate an idealised 'Islam as a religion' from 'Muslims as
a cultural group with certain cultural norms' but in practice this is often
quite difficult since community is essential for spirituality and the lack of a
supportive community quite often leads to the loss of faith. I know several
cases of transwomen with a Muslim background (born Muslims as much as
converts) who left Islam for other religious communities where they found
more tolerance and acceptance. I have also wondered whether I would have
been better off had I converted to Buddhism. But the idea of *tawheed*, unity
of God, appeals to me as a theology, and my heart opens up whenever I
read a single *surah* of the Qur'an.

Muslim societies are deeply ignorant of LGBT issues. Mullahs, Imams,
and religious scholars who ask us to suppress our atypical gender characteristics, give up our romantic feelings and become 'good Muslims' simply
do not know what they are talking about. There are countless men in our
communities who insist on lecturing on subjects about which they have no
knowledge and on commenting on the lives of people they do not know or
understand and from whose life experiences they are as far removed as

possible. The more sophisticated try to back up their position with pseudo-science such as reparative therapy for homosexuality. They ought to read well-established scientific studies about sexual orientation and gender identity first. These deeply ignorant people, who insist they know what it is to be a man or a woman, risk hurting and even killing members of LGBT communities simply because they are unwilling to open up a putrid and petrified traditional discourse.

The refusal of traditional scholars to deal with the needs of LGBT Muslims feeds into an all too common hypocrisy amongst Muslims. In many modern Muslim cultures, a transwoman is seen as promiscuous simply by virtue of her transgender. The idea that all transwomen are prostitutes is as prevalent in Istanbul as it is in Lahore or Jakarta. This is the basic premise of men I have encountered in Muslim countries as much as within the Muslim diaspora in the West, things that happened to me as much as to other transwomen. Many Muslim men are quite willing to condemn transwomen as 'sick perverts' when it comes to defining the official social and religious discourse, while at the same time happy to seek them out when it comes to relieving sexual pressure. Some Muslim men tell me that this only happens in some parts of the Islamic World but that it does not happen with 'real Muslim men', those who are truly devoted to the 'Islamic cause'. But I know too well from personal experience that this is not the case.

But intolerance and hypocrisy are not specific to Muslims. Whenever I am asked about the insults, prejudices and discrimination I have suffered, there is always a supplement question: 'do you experience these kinds of things more often in Muslim than in non-Muslim circles?' No I do not. In recent years, I have had far more painful homophobic and transphobic encounters with non-Muslim White Europeans, mostly men, in the West than with Muslims in the Islamic World or the Muslim diaspora. But when it comes to the younger generations I do sense a trend that gives me hope. Young Muslims, especially in the Western diaspora but also in certain parts of the Muslim world, are increasingly becoming more accepting and tolerant of LGBT people; and more and more are interested in developing a new, open Islamic discourse that is supportive of progressive and feminist projects and questions old assumptions. In contrast, being a young gay or gender variant person has become even tougher in recent years in many Western societies than it was in my times.

The huge diversity of Muslim cultures also gives me some confidence. Historically, the Muslim world often offered an accepted social space for transgender people. The strict and almost 'Victorian' attitude to sexuality and gender that we find amongst many Muslims today is certainly not the historic norm; it is more a product of colonial encounters than of an essentialised Islam. Some traditional Muslim cultures acknowledged that not all human beings fit neatly into binary gender divisions, and in these societies we find far more dynamic ideas on gender and sexuality than we might expect. The culturally embedded status of the *hijra* community of the Indian Subcontinent is a good example. Similar examples can be found amongst Muslim cultures in Africa, Asia and even early Islamic Arabia. Even some traditional scholars, especially amongst Shi'a Muslims, have issued official fatwas on the acceptability of transsexuality as a natural condition that is part of God's creation. And more progressive scholars have now started to develop new and inclusive discourses that create open spaces for everyone in the *ummah*, regardless of race, gender or sexual orientation. What I see and experience every day as a Muslim transwoman is that there is not simply one single Islam that discriminates against 'people like me'. Rather, there are 'several Islams', both modern and traditional, some of which are more open towards gender variant people and some of which are less so. Living in today's global world we are in the fortunate position to draw water from several of these cultural springs.

When I feel sad, desperate or hopeless, I turn for comfort to the principal source of Islam: the Qur'an. There are people who have used the words of this revelation to hurt other human beings, human beings like me. But I came to Islam as a teenager by questioning what others presented to me as obvious and self-evident. Now I question the interpretational sovereignty of those who think they have the right to interpret for me, who use the Sacred Text to preach hatred and ostracism of people who are different from them. And I put my questions directly to the Qur'an.

For me, one of the most significant teachings of the Qur'an is that the diversity that we find in this universe is a direct expression of God's will; and that love of God must manifest itself through love of diversity. In 30:21, the Qur'an tells us that 'amongst His signs is the creation of the heavens and the earth, and the variations in your languages and colours. Verily, in that are signs for those who know'. And to those who think that these verses do not apply to gender and sexuality, it says: 'He it is who shapes you in the wombs as He wills' (in 3:6); and 'He creates what He wills. He bestows male and female according to His will or He combines male and female and creates whom He wills without offspring' (in 42:49-50). Even in historical times, these verses were sometimes used by Muslim scholars to explain phenomena such as intersexuality and gender variance as part of God's plan. Personally, I understand the existence of transpeople in this world as a sign of God, just as all of creation needs to be understood as a sign of God. That every single thing and every single life speaks about God is a teaching repeated over and over in numerous verses of the Qur'an. We are required to listen to this message, to open not only our ears but also our hearts. And that pertains as much to that part of the speech that we deem 'normal' as to the part that we deem 'unusual'.

I cannot tell you how many times these words of the Qur'an have inspired me to go on, to never give up, when I have felt hopeless. I have found special solace in the story of Jesus' mother Maryam, as told in 3:19. Something in me stirs up whenever I read the words of Maryam's mother: 'My Lord! I have delivered a female', and the subsequent words, 'But God knew best what she delivered; for the male is not like the female' (3:36). Maryam's mother had certainly expected something else when she had dedicated the child in her womb to the service of God. But God was not concerned about the social expectations that Maryam's mother had attached to her child's biological sex. He had a plan for Maryam. And that plan was important, even though it clashed with the gender norms of her society. Her people told the young single mother: 'Oh Maryam, you have indeed done an amazing thing! O sister of Aaron, your father was not a wicked man, nor was your mother a loose woman'. Tears roll down my eyes every time I read Maryam's words in 19: 23: 'Would that I had died before this and been long forgotten'. Words that mirror what countless transwomen have repeated so often in their lives, but which in the Qur'an only foreshadow a promise of hope that God grants to the hopeless.

What do Muslim transwomen want? To be accepted, respected and loved. Like everyone else. Just like you.

ARTS AND LETTERS

THE AESTHETIC OF PROMISE

Marjorie Allthorpe-Guyton

The Venice Biennale is regarded as one of the most prestigious cultural events in the international calendar. Its history dates back to 1895; since 1998, it has sought to place new work in a relationship with the past and promote a stronger dialogue with the viewer. The Biennale has expanded exponentially to eighty-eight national pavilions, shifting its historic North American and Eurocentric axis to embrace an infinitely wider cultural and political agenda. It is no surprise that the Holy See participates for the first time in the 55th International Art Exhibition (1 June – 24 November 2013) with a pavilion of works inspired by the first eleven chapters of Genesis. There are ten new countries this year, each paying a fee of 20,000 euros plus tax for the privilege: Angola, the Bahamas, the Kingdom of Bahrain, the Ivory Coast, Kosovo, Kuwait, the Maldives, Paraguay and the remote Poly-nesian island nation of Tuvalu with a population of 9,847. Like Venice, Tuvalu faces the threat of rising sea levels. It is banking on art to get some action on climate change after science and politics have failed. The Venice Biennale has become a fast moving turntable, a carousel of conflicting geo-political agen-das which only the strongest artist and curator can ride with impunity. Sift-ing out the art from state propaganda and the dead hand of the largely US-driven art market is the litmus test of disinterested critical judgement. It is a challenge few critics meet.

It is even more difficult to review the Pavilions of newer entrants to the Biennale who need to make their mark in Venice and satisfy expectations at home. The historical and cultural context for the Middle East, Asia and Africa are daunting – certainly for the woefully uninformed western art critic. But when addressing artists working in the glare of extreme political and social events, the art itself can be so shadowed or compromised by its context that the notion of 'relational aesthetics' is tested to its limits. Critical judgements may have to be tempered by consideration of cultural difference, conditions of production, availability of resources, and the degree of the artist's exposure to an international art world. But ultimately the art speaks or it does not. When the work triumphs it can cross conceptual and cultural borders and achieve iconic status. A good example is *The Throne of Weapons*, a chair made of cannibalised AK47s from arms dealers the world over by the Mozambique artist Cristovao Estevo Canhavato, known as Kester. It has not only been signed by the artist but also by termites, who regularly damage African wooden sculptures. Bought by the British Museum in 2005–06, it has accumulated meaning and veneration throughout the UK and Ireland. It is regarded as one of the most 'eloquent objects' in the British Museum; and was featured in 'A History of the World in 100 Objects', the ground-breaking British Museum/BBC radio programme broadcast in 2010. Few works translate so readily. The means of presentation, site and positioning are crucial and for both artist and curator Venice is a cruel mistress.

In the congested and overwhelming main Biennale exhibition, *The Encyclopaedic Palace*, it is possible to entirely miss the series of exquisite miniature paintings by Pakistan artist Imran Qureshi, Deutsche Bank's Artist of the Year 2013. *Moderate Enlightenment* 2006–09, harnesses the style of Mughal courtly painting to present the paradoxes of traditional Islamic life and the daily pursuits of contemporary Pakistani men and women, a subtle challenge to western perceptions. The Pavilions of Kuwait and Iraq both aim to puncture preconceptions and to engage the viewer in a dialogue on nationhood and values, but their sites and their curatorial approaches make for very different experiences

Kuwait has waited thirty years to participate in the Biennale. It has a Pavilion north of the Rialto Bridge, a fair walk. *National Works* presents the national sculptor Sami Mohammad and the internationally exhibited photographer Tarek Al-Ghoussein, son of a former Kuwaiti Ambassador to the UN, who lives and works in Abu Dhabi. The curator is Ala Younis, an artist based in Amman. The Pavilion is an unfurnished marble palazzo, the installation spare and minimal. The exhibition guide claims that *National Works* 'disassembles symbols of past glorious times in an attempt to re-interpret Kuwait's modernisation project'. The curator's essay reverentially and diligently explains the conditions of production, of commission from ruler to subject, 'of national works by the state for the people and the people for the state'. Artists, especially sculptors, were harnessed to the wheel of urban

Imran Qureshi, *Moderate Enlightenment,* series 2006-2009

reconstruction. Sami Mohammad's gigantic honorary statues of the 11th and 12th Emirs of Kuwait are exceptions; they were commissioned by a private newspaper, *Al-Rai Al-Aam*, and are not typical of his work. They are apparently not well known in Kuwait and could not be shown in a public space because of 'the general public's dissatisfaction with figurative art and their association of them with idolatry'. The statues were cast in London. Their story is told in the Pavilion by a bronze bust presented on a plinth and photographs. The statues' hieratic woodenness is a telling contrast to the artist's signature impassioned and bound screaming figures of struggle and suffering, which are not shown. Sami Mohammad tells the story of how during the Iraq invasion he escaped the fate of a celebrated sculptor forced to make a statue of Saddam: 'If I were caught I'd refuse to make the sculpture and the soldiers would execute me and if I'd agreed to do it, the Kuwaitis would'. What is most interesting about the Kuwait pavilion is not so much the work, but the back story of Kuwait's independence, oil, war, and of the Free Atelier founded in 1959 to train artists for change. The school hosted Andy Warhol in 1977. In the Palazzo's chilly spaces even Tarek Al-Ghoussein's fine photographs of bleak urban landscapes look dull and generic.

In contrast, the Iraqi Pavilion takes us to a different space. I had a compelling reason to see it. In 1981, the Iraqi Cultural Centre, then in Tottenham Court Road, London, held an exhibition of drawings, prints and photography: *Iraq: The Human Story* which I was asked to review. I declined: the exhibition was nationalist propaganda, a justification for the invasion of Iran and a glorification of Saddam Hussein whose achievements and life story were published in a pamphlet to accompany the exhibition. Military images and drawings also illustrated the catalogue text by the centre's director who described Saddam as 'the symbol of bravery and prudence, standing for the eternal Mesopotamian, one hand holding the sword, the other, the pen'. Thirty years on, the centre hosted a lecture by Sir Terence Clark, British Ambassador to Iraq from 1985 to 1989, during the run up to the Gulf Wars. Clark was one of the signatories to the letter from fifty-two former senior British diplomats to *The Guardian* (27 April 2004) condemning the US/British conduct in the war in Iraq. He charmed the audience with his fluency in Iraqi dialect, his archaeological knowledge, illustrated with photographs of Iraqi heritage sites by Gertrude Bell, or Miss Bell as she was fondly known in Iraq. He spoke of a religiously tolerant society where even ancient sects, neither Christian nor Muslim, lived undisturbed.

A vision of a revived, healed and an eternal Iraq, a country with nine thousand years of cultural history and accomplishment, is at the heart of Iraq's National Pavilion. Against all odds, the Iraqi project *Welcome to Iraq* succeeds where others fail. The Pavilion is supported by the Kurdistan Regional Government of Iraq and the Minister of Culture, Baghdad, corporate and private sponsors, and is commissioned by the Ruya Foundation for Contemporary Culture in Iraq, which aims 'to build a platform that will enable Iraqis in the arts, the young in particular, to benefit from, and participate in international events'. The Foundation was set up by Reem Shather-Kubba and Tamara Chalabi, daughter of Ahmed Chalabi, historian and author of *The Shi'is of Jabal 'Amil and the New Lebanon*. They admit the project was 'a logistical nightmare'. It made good press, *The Sunday Times* magazine covered the curator Jonathan Watkins, Director of the Ikon Gallery, Birmingham, as he toured Iraq from Basra to Kurdistan under armed guard to meet and select artists, returning at night to the fortified Chalabi family compound in Baghdad. The choice of a curator from a former occupying country is unsurprising; British curators and artists have a long intellectual engagement with the Middle East as 'official war artists'. Artist and celebrated filmmaker Steve McQueen worked in Iraq and artist David Cotterrell made solo journeys to Afghanistan in 2007. Both are represented in the Imperial War Museum, London. Jonathan Watkins also had form as a broad based international curator with strong interests and experience in the Middle East, and has curated Biennials worldwide, including in Palestine and Sharjah.

Watkins' decision to move away from art of the diaspora to try to work with artists living in Iraq was a departure from the Middle East presence at the 54th Venice Biennale when the main focus was on established international artists. The inaugural Iraqi Pavilion had six émigré Iraqi artists and the major pan-Arab exhibition, *The Future of a Promise*, showed works by twenty-two artists including the two well-travelled and exhibited Iraqi artists, Janane-Al-Ani and Ahmed Alsoudani. As Hassan Janabi, Iraq Ambassador to UN agencies in Rome, noted: 'getting Iraqi artists who live in Iraq is not an easy job....it could be tedious and possibly create tension... Instead, they sought out artists living in the outside who could truly reflect what constitutes an Iraqi artist'.

Iraq Pavilion, Ca' Dandalo, Venice

In challenging that view, Watkins took the risk that in a war-depleted country he would not find work which could hold its own on an international stage. His mission would have failed had he sought to make a conventional exhibition. Some of the work is undeniably weak and would pass unnoticed in an art school degree show. But by conceiving the Pavilion as an act of hospitality he brings about a powerful connection between the artist and the viewer, the host and the guest, which is rare. Watkin's curatorial strategy is not new. It takes its premise from the 2012 Liverpool Biennial and the accompanying book *The Unexpected Guest* which is an anthology of texts addressing hospitality from perspectives of colonial history, spatial politics, citizenship and the exercise of power. The question is: does the overall work stand up to that of the nomadic internationalist artists of the Venice Biennale whose art is hawked around the world, has high 'production values' and speaks the language of resources and money? How does it fare alongside the craftily polished sculpture and paintings of the British celebrity artist Mark Quinn? Quinn's inflatable replica of his nude marble sculpture of Alison Lapper, an English artist who was born without arms, which once sat defiant on the plinth in Trafalgar Square, now queens it over Venice, like one of the gross cruise liners that dwarf the Venetian skyline. Watkins answers this by declaring that 'we are not so hung up on art and similarly value found objects and artefacts. The Iraq Pavilion itself is an extraordinary found object'. Moreover, 'the exhibited work is inextricably bound up with this context'.

He shows works by eleven artists of two generations: cartoons, paintings, sculpture and installation in lofty first floor rooms, with light flooding from the tall windows of Ca'Dandolo, a Venetian *palazzetto* overlooking the Grand Canal and conveniently facing the San Toma vaporetto stop. Such an accessible and prominent site attracts locals, tourists as well as professional Biennale visitors. They are enveloped by the gentle ambience of the Iraq Pavilion where they can sit in comfort among fine Kurdistan carpets and rugs, watch laptop short films, listen to the haunting music of the Oud, drink tea in the customary delicate glass and eat sweet *kleytcha* biscuits warm from the kitchen. Everywhere there are neat piles of well chosen books on Iraq from the Iraq National Library and Archive, enough for weeks of browsing. Works of history, literature and politics sit alongside children's books: *Babylon's Ark: the Incredible Wartime Rescue of the Baghdad Zoo*, *The Iraqi Cookbook* and *Shoot an Iraqi: Art, Life and Resistance Under the Gun*. The latter could be the by-line for

Welcome to Iraq. It is a place of respite from the circus of the Giardini, the main Biennale site where queues blocked the entrances of the habitually self-important US, German and French Pavilions which have swopped sites in a trite gesture of inverted nationhood.

At the Iraq Pavilion the guest enters another world. I was hosted by two of the artists who work together in Basra as WAMI, Yareen Wami and Hashim Taeeh. They talked about the conditions of the Iraqis and of their own artistic isolation, the lack of resources, galleries or any art infrastructure: 'nothing has changed for us'. Over 5,000 works of art, looted in 2003 from the National Museum of Modern Art in Baghdad, are missing or destroyed. WAMI make finely crafted sculpture and furniture from cardboard. Every ridge and corrugated furrow counts. The faux minimalist aesthetic of Muji, the Japanese retail store, is used to coruscating effect in an eerily monastic bedroom installation that speaks volumes about confinement and making do and getting by, on nothing. Cardboard, as cheap ubiquitous material, is common currency in the British art room, but it is rarely recycled with the simplicity, subtlety and wit of WAMI's figure and portrait reliefs which quote their Sumerian heritage and nod to Western modernist influences from Klee to Braque.

The work of Bassim Al-Shaker, a painter living in Baghdad, evokes an earlier landscape art, the naturalistic realism of the nineteenth century French artist Jean-Francois Millet. Al-Shaker fluently paints the vast water lands of the southern Marsh Arabs who were displaced when the marshes were drained and degraded by Saddam Hussain and are now being slowly restored. Paintings of date sellers, reed harvesting, herding and milking hang in place of the marine paintings which usually grace the walls of the Ca'Dandolo.

Shaker's works may look romantic, bucolic and are hardly contemporary, but like Millet's great *Angelus* of 1857, these are paintings of both mourning and celebration, full of meaning for contemporary Iraqis. The more overtly political works of conflict by Jamal Penjweny, who was trained at the London Institute of Photography, are known and have been published internationally. He now lives in his birthplace in Kurdistan, Sulamaniya, where he runs an art café. His photographic series *Saddam is Here* of ordinary Iraqis holding an image of Saddam in front of their faces are both memorial and curse. As the artist says: 'they cheered for him, they beautified his cruelty… Saddam is here'. This is the closest any of the works come to commentary

Ca'Dandalo installation, WAMI (Yaseen Wami, Hashim Taeeh)
Untitled 2013

Ca'Dandalo bedroom installation, WAMI (Yaseen Wami, Hashim Taeeh)
Untitled 2013

on sectarian divisions.   Penjweny's film Another Life made a powerful impression on everyone I spoke with. It is a roughly edited day-in-the-life narrative of the fate of mostly young Muslim men forced through poverty to smuggle crates of alcohol from Iraq into Iran. One holds up bottles of Scottish liquor, another shot has the label 'Danzil Vodka Made to Chill'. The boys are angry, some laugh, desperate in the knowledge that on every mule run they face murder by the customs officers they have not paid off. They die. We are left feeling anger with their paymasters, with the hypocrisy and the venality of those in power.

Abdul Raheen Yassir, Miscellaneous cartoons 2003-2013

The Iraq pavilion shows the plight and the resilience of artists living now in Iraq where roiling bloodshed has killed hundreds of thousands. It is of course incongruous that their works furnish the theatre of a Venetian palazzo on the Grand Canal, but they represent actors in a much larger drama: where the sweep of history is before us and Baghdad, Arab City of Culture 2013, becomes again Dar-es-Salaam – City of Peace. The Iraq Pavilion stands for the promise of a civil society where artists and art have a place and value.

The catalogue is written simply, no theorising or art speak, for a general public. There is a question and answer interview with a soldier in the Iraq Special Forces:

'What is your favourite place?'
'Kurdistan'.
'Describe Iraq in one word'
'Precious'.
'What do you love most about Iraq?'
'Affinity'
'What do you hate most about Iraq?'
'Violence'
'Where is Venice?'
'Spain'.

Abdul Raheen Yassir, Miscellaneous cartoons 2003-2013

THE BEAUTY OF MEN

Alev Adil

'You have to leave now Z, before it becomes impossible.'

'How is New York?'

'Seriously Z. We're very worried, I promised Aziz I would look after you. You are no longer safe.'

'I don't need looking after Serge. I promise. I'm fine. I'm settling in. Tell me some gossip instead. How are things with you? And at the bank? With Selma's gallery?'

The distance between us, the awkwardness, is hidden in the slight time delay the ghosts of telephony bestow upon the conversation. I know he's thinking I'm heading for another breakdown. I don't tell Serge that a prophecy led me here. That would only confirm his fears.

A vision of a city that was the place I was born in, and sometimes the fugitive corners of all the other streets I'd ever wandered down, called to me insistently night after night. I walk the deserted routes of my childhood at dawn towards something unnamed. Then there is darkness and a full moon, a bright neon moon. The fist permanently clenched around my heart unfurls and an extraordinary lightness fills my chest so that a silken bolt of night-dark sky and thousands of stars emerge from within me, from this relief, this letting go, a scatter of planets and new beginnings, this release from a long exile. 'A full moon and an inheritance you thought you had lost are now returned to you.' It is a thought, rather than a voice in the dream.

Serge and his girlfriend were more than happy when I left the apartment on 79th and East River in their care. Selma can watch the sunrise and traffic

145

flow from the living room window over early morning coffee as I did. The living room is large enough for Serge to hold formal dinners. It will help his rise and rise at the bank. I told them I wanted to leave New York for a while because I wanted to renovate a traditional house, the kind I remembered from my childhood, to make a garden. I would plant jasmine and roses, mint and lemon verbena, I would grow pomegranates and figs, and there would be an orange tree. Spring would bring the scent of blossom. They were worried for me, my solicitous nephew and his fiancée, but their elation at having a four bed on the Upper East Side all to themselves meant they did not interfere or make much attempt to dissuade me as Aziz might have. Aziz's wishes still leave their traces and I feel guilty that I don't have to work harder to persuade anyone to let me disappear. I am mourning my husband. I am allowed to be nostalgic. I am a widow with dark etched shadows under my eyes and knife-sharp cheekbones. Sometimes the mirror misrecognises me for the girl I used to be, at other times for a demon, a harbinger of death.

'Give me a child until the age of seven' the Jesuit nuns at the convent used to say, 'and I will give you the man.' I wondered about the man that would

be given me. They were hoping to save my soul, my mother corrected me, laughing. There was no man. I can still hear the echo of her young laugh, something the climate retains, even if the architecture has forgotten us. I sang along with the nuns, the child at seven, but I was a pagan in my unspoken heart. I believed in the lives of trees and stones and the silent judgmental gaze of my blind dolls but had no sense of god and redemption through suffering. No, none of that.

Now I am not so much grown but multiplied, seven times seven feral children. I disguise myself as a mature woman but really I am an urchin crowd, an implacable feral orchestra of thieving, catapult-wielding orphans. The old sandstone house on Abdicavus street no longer exists. The family sold it soon after I married Aziz. Such houses were demolished decades ago and replaced by tall condos that crane their necks to gaze at the sea. The few that remain are now all boutique hotels or embassies, prettified representations of a lost world. My ghost does not ride her little red bicycle along the pavement. My neighbourhood is a shopping mall now. No trace of me endures here, nothing to grieve over. Nothing - that clenched fist around the heart.

I bought this flat on the twenty-ninth floor on the edge of the European quarter. No garden then. I did not fight for a garden. A full moon and a lost inheritance, that's what the dream has promised me. The living room window looks out over the mountains, the distinctive grey blue lights of the checkpoints twinkling in the distance, the motorway snaking into the city. I can hear the muezzin's recorded and amplified call to prayer over the traffic and the sirens. I can sense the sea, though I cannot see it from any of the apartment's windows. I am only a brisk fifteen-minute walk from the ocean, though no one walks briskly here. They drive or they dawdle.

In the mornings, before the sun has risen properly, whilst the air is still crisp, I walk the streets of the old town, the back streets tangled around the Murad Gate, up to the Castle and then down the hill, usually skirting the Kasbah and circling back to the European quartier and onto the Corniche. I rarely venture further than that. I watch the sunrise, the moon fade.

Serge's voice is distant and insubstantial, made of thin sheet metal perhaps, or seashells. 'Z, I wouldn't call you in the middle of the night like this if it wasn't serious. The city has fallen. It's really far too dangerous for you to remain. There is a UN delegation arriving tomorrow. I've arranged for

you to leave with them. You must meet them at the Swedish embassy by seven am. Bring all your papers. You remember it? Go to the garden entrance next to the Orthodox Church. You remember it auntie?'

Does Serge remember the lunch party there in Aziz's honour, over twenty years ago; he would have been at lycée then. He was such an awkward intense boy; passionate about literature although he already knew that banking was his destiny. He and I had played with the ambassador's imperious Siamese cats in the dappled shade in the garden and discussed Anna Karenina. Could it be considered a tragedy? For the ancients the tragic is that which is inevitable I told him. 'Then I don't think it's tragic at all. You choose whom you love.' I'm not sure why Serge believed so fervently in free will since he submitted with such good grace to the path mapped out for him by the family. I'm not sure what I believed then. This was before Joe.

'Yes, I remember. Yes, I'll try to make it.' I tell him, but I don't really believe I will. It's amazing how quickly you adapt to intermittent sniper fire. It feels like a bad mood, a nasty rumour, this war. There hasn't been any shelling yet but already many of the residents, all the families, have left the

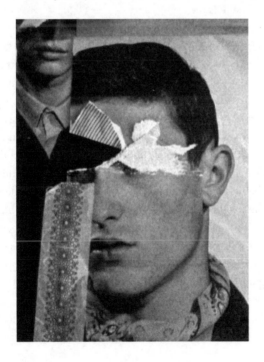

condo. The café on the ninth floor is empty. I don't have to navigate any noisy brats when I do my laps in the pool.

There is still the insistent recurrent image of a full moon and the promise of a lost inheritance that keeps me here. Such dreams have ruled my life. I only ever told one person this, Joe. I studied biological sciences at Columbia. I was a rationalist. It is not a question of faith, or an act of will. Joe understood that, his sleeping world was alive with revelation too; he saw that there are worlds far more compelling than any waking reality. The first really powerful night vision I had, I can't have been older than eleven or twelve at the time, was a hallucination that shook me with the power of a divine disclosure.

I am asleep in a tall green room, high up in the sky. The sun warms my face as a man draws the curtains. I am awakened to the beauty of a man, of the blessing of his being in the world. He is a silhouette against the window, his face obscured yet his every gesture is a gentle spell. The easy elegance in the curved line of his arm makes the light do a hazy dance along the broad slope of his shoulder.

'I can't stay,' he tells me.

I love him absolutely. He is everything to me.

'I believe we were meant to meet in New York, but I can't stay with you.'

The vision returned on three moonless nights over the next six months. I knew I had to go to New York. I worked steadily and I got into Columbia. I even won a partial scholarship. I was following a dream. Not aspirations of wealth, a good marriage, a position in society – although I was to attain all these because of my absolute fidelity to the idea of one instant in a tall pale green room, with the muffled sound of traffic far below and the magnificence of this man in the morning light, the pure all consuming physical grace of his being and the love in his eyes filling me with golden energy.

I was only in my second semester and wasn't really settling in. I'd met my parents in Paris to celebrate the New Year together and had been reluctant to be parted from them. Perhaps that's why they asked Aziz, a distant business ally of my father's, to keep an eye on me. In hindsight, from a distance it all looks quite conventional, quite arranged, a suitable match between a virginal student from an important family and one of the most powerful bankers of the Middle East. The truth was much stranger. He took me to his apartment to see the view, after a Japanese lunch and a blustery walk in the

park. We were formal with each other, until I saw the room. This was the room in that recurring time where I sleep until I am awakened by the beauty of a man. I had found the room.

He asked me if I would like some tea. He began to list the types of tea he had. I stepped out of my dress in a single efficient gesture, a dance movement. Our eyes met. The ferocity of my gaze branded him for life. We were married in the spring. Everyone came to the wedding – several retired film stars, a deposed Shah and other royal pretenders, politicians, arms dealers, politicians turned arms dealers, the heads of banks and *Vanity Fair*.

The line is dead. Serge is gone. I watch the shadows of the mountains becoming more defined as the sky lightens imperceptibly; Joe's shoulders were strong and swooping like that. The moon becomes more translucent, shimmering and almost full; Joe's gaze was as radiant. How I longed for him to be my horizon. I cover myself in a diaphanous silken fabric of dark thoughts, shadow cover, black disguise. I'll hide under it through the narrow backstreets and the round the Kasbah and then hide it in my bag when I get to the European quartier. The citizens are sleeping the last of a very uneasy

peace bequeathing the streets to us, to the sleepy soldiers, the drunks, ill-fated lovers and early morning grievers.

   The air is sharp on the Corniche, fresh with oceanic promise. A couple is sitting on some rocks, below the esplanade. She rests her head on his shoulder and leans into him, a marionette released from her strings. His back is lean and long, his arm around her, his head held high, watching for the rising sun. Fishermen are returning from night fishing, they are pulling in their boats, coiling rope and hauling crates onto the quay. Everywhere I look there are reminders of Joe. When I was younger I never really saw it. I was too aware of myself-in-the-world. The preoccupation with how I looked and seemed to others veiled my gaze. I did not look properly, I did not appreciate the divine in the beauty of men.

   I loved Aziz. I loved his hands and his stout squared-off fingers, not for themselves but because they were his. I loved his wit, his intelligence and that affection extended to his body. But it was different with Joe from the very first time I saw him, and he was only a man-boy of nineteen then. He was the first man I truly saw. He embodied all beauty. His lash-fringed green gaze, his kiss-blossom mouth were the most beautiful in the world not because they belonged to him but simply because they were perfect. To behold him was to feel connected to the possibility of an ideal world. I did not care that we had nothing in common, that he had no knowledge of Japanese cinema or Russian literature, that I knew nothing about basketball and mathematics. I only wanted to be in his presence, to watch him.

It was easy to pass off my passion as a maternal devotion to Aziz's young protégé. I lied to myself as well as to the world. Joe was an orphan, quite brilliant. Aziz was sponsoring him through Yale. They'd met through a charity circuit mentoring scheme but it went way beyond that. We'd been married ten years by then and I still hadn't produced any kind of heir for Aziz. Joe was an ideal, instant son for him. One way or another we all fell in love.

Three years passed like that, with my heart in my mouth and on my sleeve. When his fingers brushed mine a power surge charged my whole body. 'Joe, pass the salt please.' And when his gaze met mine, because his gaze did meet mine, and mine alone. 'This bread needs more salt.'

Everyone wanted more of Joe. All the girls and women watched him, cutting themselves and not the apples they were meant to be peeling with their sharp little silver knives. Joe only returned my gaze, not theirs. I watched the seasons in Central Park, the clouds against the wind, the new leaves trembling on the branch, the roses opening, waiting.

I was asleep in the tall green bedroom where I had first seduced Aziz. I opened my eyes to the sunlight streaming into the room as Joe drew back the curtains. I was filled with the extraordinary happiness of being awakened by him, the blessing of his being in the world. He was a silhouette against the window, his face obscured yet his every gesture was a gentle spell. The easy elegant line of his arm made the light do a hazy dance along the broad slope of his shoulder. The sunlight illuminated the dust so golden sparkles and diamonds seemed to float about the room. I wanted to laugh, to suggest I make pancakes for breakfast. I wasn't prepared for what he said.

'I can't stay.' His gaze was tender. Did he know he was killing me?

'I believe we were meant to meet in New York, but I can't stay with you.'

I went mad after that. Aziz tried to keep me at home, but he had to send me to the Dakota Clinic within a month. That was the only time in my life I buried myself in pure blind sleep, because of the drugs they gave me, I presume. For long dry years I subsisted on the insistent memory of that fold in time, when I felt all of love, the moment I was told it was to be only for a moment. I wanted to disappear eternally into that island of time, those seconds borne on sparkling motes of dust, before he was gone. If I was hungry, it was for him. When I looked out across the horizon, it was for him. When I was thirsty, the cool clear water that quenched me contained him. Was it love or madness? Everything was Joe and Joe was in everything, from celery seed to sandalwood. I was a holy fool trapped in that pleated repeated instant of love revealed and denied.

In contrast Aziz's love was human, constant, made of modest accretions and patience, not sudden or ever-lasting revelations. He did not mention Joe at all. Eventually he brought me back, and we achieved domestic equilibrium again. Although a baby would have been a useful distraction, my work as a research fellow at the sleep laboratory and Aziz's at the bank kept us busy. When I look back on my life I can see the years razed by madness, and yet those deserts are golden with the light of love. I can regret nothing. Joe and Aziz have taught me love, both in its splendour and in patient husbandry. I have lived for one and been saved by the other. I can deny neither.

All the shops and cafes on the sea front have their shutters drawn. It is early yet but they have a more stoutly defended, permanently abandoned air than usual. The present tense of war intrudes on my memories. Four voluptuous caryatids have gazed out to sea from the Corniche since 1893, holding up the swaggering marble edifice of the Pera Café. The large bowed windows have all been hastily boarded up. Dimitris, the headwaiter is nailing them down.

'Good morning hanoum' he greets me, 'today is not such a good day for your walk along the shore I think.'

When I hear thunder behind me I turn to see clouds but there are planes instead.

'Come inside please. The power has been cut, but luckily our stoves are gas. I will make you your coffee.'

The chandeliered main salon of the café is in darkness. The lovers from the Corniche are here. She is lying on his lap on the velvet banquet wrapped in a snowy table cloth, a red flower blossoms and grows on the fabric, I hear the gentle tap-tap drip of blood onto the parquet. He rests a gun on the table. The fishermen emerge from the shadows. They are in camouflage now. I turn to ask Dimitris where old Fuad Bey is and who these soldiers are when time is torn and the building collapses upon itself.

The purest darkness, perhaps I am dead? After a measureless interval that is the end and then the beginning there is a cold full moon. There is a fight towards the light, seven times seven feral children, an urchin crowd, an implacable feral orchestra of thieving, catapult wielding orphans and a silken bolt of night-dark sky and thousands of stars are emerging from within me in a tornado of splintered chandeliers and exploded putti. A full moon and an inheritance you thought you had lost are now returned to you.

'Commander, there's a survivor.' Their voices are frenetic but distant and indistinct. He is a silhouette against the moon, his face obscured yet his every gesture as he reaches towards me is a gentle spell. Joe. The fist per-

manently clenched around my heart unfurls and an extraordinary lightness fills my chest, relief, letting go, a scatter of planets and new beginnings, this release from a long exile. My Joe has returned for me.

'Commander, are you alright? Is it someone you know?'

If your god is a poet then it is so; but if your god is a jealous god, then your reply is 'No'.

'Powerful and important' — Noam Chomsky

REVOLT IN SYRIA

STEPHEN STARR

9781849041973
£14.99 paperback / 240pp

'This searching inquiry is painful reading, but urgent for those who hope to understand what lies behind the shocking events in Syria, what the prospects might be, and what outsiders can – and cannot – do to mitigate the immense suffering as a country so rich in history and promise careens towards disaster.' — **Noam Chomsky**

In January 2011 President Bashar al-Assad told the *Wall Street Journal* that Syria was 'stable' and immune from revolt. In the months that followed, and as regimes fell in Egypt and Tunisia, thousands of Syrians took to the streets calling for freedom, prompting ferocious repression by the authorities.

In *Revolt in Syria: Eye-Witness to the Uprising*, Stephen Starr delves deep into the lives of Syrians whose destiny has been shaped by the state for almost fifty years. In conversations with people from all strata of Syrian society, Starr draws together and makes sense of perspectives illustrating why Syria, with its numerous sects and religions, was so prone to violence and civil strife.

Through his unique access to a country largely cut off from the international media during the unrest, Starr delivers compelling first hand testimony from both those who suffered and benefited most at the hands of the regime.

www.hurstpublishers.com/book/revolt

41 GREAT RUSSELL ST, LONDON WC1B 3
WWW.HURSTPUBLISHERS.COM
WWW.FBOOK.COM/HURSTPUBLISHERS
020 7255 2201

LITTLE FLECKS OF SILVER

Tam Hussain

At dawn the view of Damascus was glorious. I loved to watch the sun rise whilst Kurdish pigeon fanciers flew their little flecks of silver over the green minarets that illuminated the city. I came to love those birds, especially the ones who never obeyed the flight course taken by the rest of the group. They seemed to have their own rhythm, their own music, and they flew in any way they pleased, slaves to no one, as if in direct communion with God. None of the clapping of the pigeon fanciers could entice them to descend unless they wished to.

I lived in Rukn ed-Deen, a Kurdish neighbourhood with winding alleyways and houses made of breeze blocks that reclined on the slopes of Mount Arba'een. I rented a flat from a chain-smoking widow whose husband was killed in the 1967 Six Day War. The widow was kind and generous and never let you eat alone during Ramadan; apart from that she left you to your own devices.

I had come to Damascus to learn the Arabic language. Initially, my reason had been to understand the Qur'an, but by my first year I had become obsessed with the language itself: the infinite meanings that triliteral roots could contain and the shades of meaning that derivative verbs could give. I was infatuated with the literature, newspapers, everything. Although I told myself repeatedly that to understand the Qur'an was still the main aim, the truth was that it had become a pious cover. The language possessed me: it was no longer a mere key to the secrets; it was the secret itself.

I picked Damascus because of its proximity to the classical language. Their dialect was clean and speaking the classical Arabic on the street might bring about peals of laughter, but the response could still be articulated in classical Arabic. You could still find a gem of a street vendor steeped in the classical verse of Abu Tammam or the bombast of Mutannabi who spoke, like the ancient Arabs, words replete with eloquence and resplendent in their subtlety, even as he offered you his shawarma.

I don't claim to have mastered Arabic literature as yet, but M'Saad was certainly one of the men who put me on that road. My meeting with M'Saad was through a mutual friend one evening in the famous Rawdah café, not too far from the somewhat diminutive parliament. I felt excited about the fact that our shaking hands and exchanging pleasantries occurred in the same spot where Adonis, the poet, had spun his verse. And I could not help but marvel at God's handiwork, because M'Saad's face was not dissimilar to a lama. His nose was unusually sharp and contrasted with the soft contours of his face and prominent forehead with hair combed to the side. On his nose perched a pair of round spectacles that were chosen not for style but for economy. I didn't think I had ever met such an unremarkable man in my life. If you threw him in the darkest dankest prison, where the sun is never seen and mildew grows on the crevices of one's body, no one would make mention of him except the one who bore him and God Himself.

In spite of his strange appearance I knew that I was sitting in the presence of a gentleman. I could tell that he disliked the scent of the shisha and the expressive profanity of moustachioed men in checked shirts playing backgammon; but since my tongue possessed the English language, he bore the situation with patience and dignity.

M'Saad had lived in Damascus for many years but had not lost the provincial look of his home, Deir ez-Zour. His shirt with its stiff collar was tucked in and possessed no trace of flamboyance or individuality. His trousers were pressed and appeared somewhat large. His shoes were the type you see grandfathers wearing, soft leather; his jacket, nondescript, serving the purpose of keeping the bitter winter winds out and body heat in. Had it not been for his straight inflexible posture he would have been inconspicuous moving quietly amongst the throng on the President's Bridge trying to catch one of the numerous white minivans that served as public transport. And if he spoke, which was a rare thing indeed, it would be the odd, 'excuse me, sir,' or, 'pardon me, friend.'

M'Saad would always be at my door at precisely seven in the evening. I would watch him through the key hole as he arrived. He always made sure he was well presented, running his hand over his pomaded hair, tucking his shirt in before knocking. Our routine consisted of me bringing in a pot of tea, setting our watch, and beginning with his hour of English first. Then the next hour I would read from Jawhar Al-Adab, an anthology of Arabic literature starting from the very beginnings of the language up to the modern period. I gained much from his expertise. After all, the young doctor was a *hafiz*, someone who had memorised the entire Qur'an and studied the other religious sciences whilst studying for his medicine degree. This was no mean feat. He was also a considerable poet, and he elucidated, with great patience, the finer points of poetry even though it was quite apparent that I had not attained that degree of competency necessary to deal with it. But because I had a hunger for it, he endeavoured to give it.

I would never say we were friends. We were too different in our temperaments and cultures. I liked to work hard and felt guilty when I was idle for too long, but I recognised that we were social animals. We needed rest, we needed coffee, tea, and even a pipe in order to socialise. Even the Arabic language has a common noun for Homo Sapiens which is '*ins*'. 'Ins' comes from the triliteral root 'A', 'N', and 'S'. Its general meaning is 'to be sociable'. The ancient Arabs understood the need for us to be in the company of others. But M'Saad did not need the company of men. When you sat with him, his rigid posture made you uncomfortable, his silence, his politeness, his unwillingness to relax, to joke, all made him bad company. He did not make any reference to the world. He did not know nonsense, women, football or anything else that one may experience in everyday life. He did not even watch TV. But the programmes he had watched in his childhood, he talked of as if they possessed a mystical significance. I was struck by his love for 'Sandokan'; he talked of this cartoon as if it held the very key to the universe.

This is not say that I didn't try to socialise with him, but our evening of coffee and a game of chess was a failure. There was only chit chat with interludes of silence, which ended with his clever deployment of Horse and Castle dominating the board, both horizontally and diagonally. Although I'm not a sore loser, the move was so calculated and so methodical that I ended up rebuking him. I said that he reminded me of Angelo from *Measure for Measure*. At first he was pleased that I had compared him to a character of such an esteemed playwright but then when he asked me why I should compare him thus, I replied that Angelo had ice running through his veins. His face became dismayed. How could he not have a sense of feeling?

'But,' he exclaimed, 'I am an Arab.'

'What does that mean? That you are warm hearted and we are cold?'

He was silent. That is what he implied; that he was a passionate Arab with more love in his heart than all of the peoples of the world combined. I said that maybe that was the case amongst other Arabs, but for me he was like a German car: '*Vorsprung durch Technik*'. His face became concentrated, as if he was focusing on the tip of his long nose. Once the information had been duly processed, he got up, gave a gentle smile and thanked me for the advice. He admitted that others, too, had called him a Terminator and that perhaps he should stop being so robotic. He shook my hands twice and looked at his watch. He was running late and asked for permission to leave. He adjusted his hair and stepped out into the jasmine-filled night. I watched him walking down Sharia Abed, his form changing from one of control and method to something more human. He became less rigid. I was even surprised to see that he kicked a can as he walked down the bustling street. I wondered if he was only a Terminator with me or if my words had taken effect.

We never played chess again. Despite our differences, there was still a bond between us, as if both of us were working for the same thing. I think he felt this more keenly than I did. After all, I was following in the footsteps of scholars who'd travelled vast distances to sit at the feet of old sages in order to absorb sacred knowledge. Few Westerners came to his country to do that. I think he admired me for speaking in the ancient language of the Quran on the streets, despite the laughter. Regardless of the fact that this young doctor earned a pittance in comparison to the money I had, he never accepted any form of payment. I was an honoured guest in his country, and the fact that I had more money than him was an irrelevance. I watched him shield me from the hawkers and taxi drivers who saw in me the wealth in my pockets. In the end this paternalism became so annoying that I rarely ventured out with him, and kept our meetings confined to my flat.

I never understood why M'Saad was so unrelenting in his desire to learn English until one cold winter's day when I met him outside the square of the Umayyad Mosque. He was kneeling throwing sunflower seeds to the doves. I watched him from afar. He was oblivious to the cries of the vendors in their tin vaulted souk with its tiny perforations that resembled little stars; only the birds seemed to matter. I did not mean to interrupt his tryst but the sound of my shoes on black stone and my tapping his shoulder startled the birds and sent them whirling up to the minaret and the clear blue sky. M'Saad jerked back, wide eyed as if a policeman had caught him unawares; he was brought back to the din of the market and laid his eyes on my khaki green army jacket that I had bought from an Armenian trader. He seemed to recoil at the very sight of it, like a Nosferatu eyeing a cross. The colour was wrong, he commented. I laughed, I was pleased with it; it fitted me well and I liked the ruggedness of the wool. I told him how cheap it was and of its utility, but I didn't convince him. So I pressed him as to why he disliked it. The jacket after all fitted in with his philosophy of life: austerity.

At first, he skirted my questions and bought me some Syrian ice cream with pistachios, hoping to keep my mouth full. As we walked down Souk Hammidiyeh I continued my questioning. His measured pace increased as we cut across the souk to Midhat Basha. His features became more animated as I pressed him. As we came out of Midhat Basha he lost his patience: and finally I beheld emotion. He said my jacket reminded him of the army.

He hadn't completed his army service and for several years he'd tried to avoid doing the compulsory two years of sitting around being impoverished, drinking maté, swearing and playing cards. He could not afford the high fees that would ensure exemption. In any case he could learn how to load a gun in six months, him and his father used to go hunting hyenas on their farm. He knew how to hunt, to kill even. Why should he spend two years under a barking officer who wouldn't allow him to pray? What they wanted was complete submission. The superiors didn't care if you whored, smoked, swore and hated your country, but they expected you to polish their boots. How could he go to one of those brothels in the outskirts of Damascus and put himself on a fleshy whore just because his superior commanded it? How was he to face his Maker? 'These are things,' he said becoming more taut and inflexible, 'I cannot do.'

He recalled how the sight of couples holding hands had been repugnant to him even as a boy. In his village on the Euphrates, if you had designs on a girl you approached the family first. Maté, cards and foul language was not the way of the honourable man. '*Ana faris* – I'm a knight!' he shouted as we strode towards Hejaz station.

'But,' I interjected, 'have you never been in love?'

He stopped in his stride. He thought for a moment, as if he were trying to reconcile the image of the Arab knight with the image of love. He flitted a glance at me; I could sense a hint of suspicion. Perhaps he was unsure of whether he should reveal such information to me, his interrogator. I was surprised: why wouldn't he reveal such a simple human emotion? Every young man had been in love, had they not? I was wounded by his distrust. I informed him that I had been in love once, hoping that he would reciprocate.

And he did: 'Yes once – during my undergraduate years.'

'What happened?'

Again he hesitated as if I might use it against him in a show trial in the near future. 'Look, M'Saad was in love once,' he said.

'Do you want to share the story?'

'I decided it wouldn't work.'

'Why not? You don't just decide on something like that.'

'She is rich and I am poor. The families would never agree.'

'Do you still love her?'

M'Saad did not answer my question but I perceived an involuntary faint nod. He looked ahead, ignoring, almost with contempt, the officer who stood outside the Hejaz railway steps smoking a cigarette and hailing a yellow taxi. M'Saad's eyes were drawn to the steam locomotive on display; the very same locomotive that once took you to the city of the Prophet.

In an attempt to reconcile him I offered my khaki jacket. He refused it as if it was an infectious piece of clothing, as if he had met righteous men whose moral fibre had been corrupted by the khaki; men who had left their prayers, men who now killed and tortured. He shuddered at the jacket that clung to me like a carcass. I laughed and quoted the lines of Al-Iyadi: 'O People Listen and take heed! Verily whoever lives will die. And whoever dies is forgotten. And all which is meant to pass will pass.'

The lines seemed to soothe him. 'You are right,' he said, resigned. 'If this is what God wills, there is nothing I can do to prevent it.'

He left me at Hejaz station; he had work to do. But a few weeks later the widow brought me a package delivered 'by that strange looking doctor.' It was the same jacket, except the colour was marl grey.

Now I understood his urgency to pass the IELTS exam. It would secure him a scholarship and an exemption from the army. The exam, however, was unforgiving. It consisted of an oral, written and a listening component, and was similar in some ways to the British driving test: three minor mistakes equalled a major mistake and failure. However, some mistakes were so grave that it meant automatic failure no matter how well you did throughout the rest of the exam. One such error was the substitution of the consonant 'P' with a 'B'. In other words, pronouncing such an innocuous word as Pepsi 'Bebsi', or passport as 'bassbort', meant no scholarship. For those of us who can pronounce our Ps and Bs it seems like a relatively small obstacle. But the Arabic alphabet does not possess the consonant P and the mispronunciation of the P has lead to the downfall of many a bright Arab student.

The error had a special significance for M'Saad because he had already failed the test as a result. To watch him pronounce a word beginning with 'P' was cruelly hilarious. He would struggle, both lips stretching back in antici-pation, and then there would be a pause during which his whole head would go backward and he would say the word as if he were sneezing it out: 'P... P...Pandemic!' If he got it right he would be triumphant, sometimes punch-ing the air. If he got it wrong he would be so harsh with himself that the rest of the words beginning with P would come out as Bs. It was a comic and tragic sight to watch a man who spoke like Stephen Hawking wage war with such a miniscule consonant. But he persevered. Sometimes a whole twenty minutes would be spent on pronunciation: Pace, Pacemaker, Pachyderm, Pacific, Pacifism, Pacify, Pack, Package and so on. On bad days he would confuse all the Bs with the Ps. Those days put him in the blackest of moods. It was during those moments that he would let himself go. His face that was usually bereft of emotion would lose its impassive stillness. Anger made his facial muscles uncontrollable as he berated the powers that be. He would throw the rules of grammar and pronunciation out of the window; he would lose his Hawkingesque way and gain his own voice.

He spoke with great fluency, even with a hint of eloquence, about his disappointment in his country. His government had failed the people, they had not educated its citizens. 'Modernise!' he would say, 'not just in our technology but also our minds! We must think! We need to be rid of super-stition, abandon this folkloric Islam. All this grave worship. *Takhalluff*! Backwardness!'

Contempt had turned his posture from one that resembled a surgical apparatus in its precision, rigidity, and cleanliness into one that moved generously, often slamming its fists down on the table. It was clear that this young doctor would make a fine officer; one not afraid of responsibility. Not afraid to die for his country. 'Not taking responsibility', he would bark, 'means destruction.'

As the day of the exam neared, his increasingly frequent outbursts became full of slogans, mottoes and revolutionary zeal. He was an ideologue's ideologue. 'They don't care about us!' he exclaimed, clenching his fist. 'Soon, my friend, soon you will see!'

'See what?'

'The end…'

'End? M'Saad, you are not making sense.'

'The end of these P.. P.. Pastards!'

Usually the 'P' would make him realise that he had spoken too much. He had exhausted the fervour of his harangue and lost his composure and so the process of contraction would begin. He would force himself into the control centre of his mind to cover up any trace of passion and fury that beat in his heart. The rigid posture of the automaton would return, his tone once again regular and robotic, his hands reaching for his mobile, his fingers removing its lithium battery. Only his eyes betrayed a sense of having committed a grave impropriety.

And for good measure, without my permission, he would remove the battery from my mobile too. I always found that habit disconcerting and strange. And one day I asked him about it, when he had gone off on one of his rants about how the Syrian government had allowed Syrians to go and fight in Iraq but now they were not allowed to return in case they caused trouble at home. I asked quite innocently whether it was still possible to cross the Iraqi border. 'Of course,' he nodded. 'Come to Deir ez-Zour!'

'And Palestine?' I asked.

'Balestine?' His eyes widened. He reached into his shirt pocket to check that his mobile was indeed incapacitated. Then he looked for my phone on the coffee table, and was reassured. He straightened himself, ran his hand over his shiny pomaded hair. He looked towards the door. He took a sip from his glass of water. I waited intently for his answer. But all he said was that everyone knew someone who could take you into Palestine. I asked him why he always removed the lithium battery from the cell phone.

'Beoble… I mean, people could be listening to our conversations through the mobile.'

I laughed; this wasn't *The Matrix* or *The Bourne Ultimatum*. How absurd. I kept on laughing and telling him jokes about the incompetence of the Syrian intelligence services whilst he stared through the window in deadly seriousness. He left very shortly after that, taking note of the exact time to be repaid to me at our next meeting. Apparently he had an appointment.

As he was about to scuttle off I apologised for my insensitivity. I tried to reassure him. 'Don't worry,' I said. 'They can't do anything to me. I'm British.'

'British or not,' he said dismissively, 'you are still my brother.'

M'Saad was true to his word. He repaid the twenty-seven minutes that was owed. But from that day on our conversations were confined to a list of subjects written down in his notebook. As his exam drew nearer M'Saad appeared increasingly tense and animated. I thought it was because of the examination. He became more and more forceful in asking for additional lessons, even if only for half an hour. But the more lessons we had, the more he muddled up his Ps and Bs. Sometimes he was extremely hard on himself even slapping himself in the face when he made those fatal mistakes. I suggested that he should take some time off to allow the information to settle. 'Everything's fine, don't worry,' he said. 'Let us go on.'

One day I awoke with a fright. I was not used to waking up so early on a Saturday; it was the day when I could sleep for as long as I wanted. But the sound of a wheezy cough and the fact that there was a woman in my room with a prematurely wrinkled face made me sit up in bed. It was the widow; she had used the spare key to let herself in. She stood there in front of my bed, her mascara eyes impatiently waiting, and coughing to wake me up. I stretched, trying to shake myself out of my slumber. I said:

'Khalti, is everything okay? You look flustered.'

'No, no, it's just my blood pressure – happens sometimes.'

I asked her what had brought her into my private space. She replied that we had to make our tenancy contract official. Why? Because a man was asking about me.

'What kind of man?'

'Mukhabarat,' she replied.

I conjugated it in my mind; *akhbara*; to inform on someone; *yukhbiru*, the present tense; *ikhbaran*, infinitive; *mukhbir*, active participle; *mukhbar*, passive participle.

I didn't say much. I didn't really have much choice. I had to go and see the local mukhtar, the local overseer. The widow waited for me outside, dressed in a black velvet shawl, a tight jacket and a curious French bag which read, 'Lou Vitton'. I got dressed and found that she had already prepared a breakfast for me: bread, za'tar, olive oil, a boiled egg and some mutabbal, with tea.

What started as a visit to the overseer ended up as a paper chase that Kafka couldn't have conjured up. We spent several days chasing after stamps and pieces of paper in the grey soulless buildings adorned with pictures of the president. We slipped a note to a moustache here and did the 'Allah tawwil 'amrak – May God extend your life' there. I even had to endure a fat walrus with blue ink-stained fingers who decided on an ad-hoc test to see whether I really was an Arabic student. He gave me a badly scrawled Arabic sentence and asked me to identify where subject, verb and object were. I was incensed. I wanted to ask the official whether he understood his own grammatical riddle or whether this was a story reserved for his friends at the café, where the cunning Arab gets one over the stupid Westerner. But I said nothing. I had seen others travelling in from the provinces, and Iraqi refugees begging for precious stamps. So I attempted and passed the test, and the ink-stained fingers made my tenancy contract official. I was so grateful that the ordeal had finally ended that I entertained the imbecile's lecture on the grammatical construction of his filthy jokes, whilst the respectful widow affected laughter and prayed again to God to extend his life. We left him basking in his own goodness, proud of the great service he had rendered.

Once outside, having checked that the contract was finally official, the widow cursed him: 'Destroy him, O Lord. Destroy him.'

M'Saad didn't visit during the days of the paper chase. In fact, for two weeks there was no sign of him. I didn't understand why. Was I an untouchable because I didn't have an official contract? Or was it because I had a khaki shirt? Why didn't he come? Why didn't he pick up his phone?

After the third week I realised that something must have happened. When I called M'Saad's mobile I was told by a stranger that I had the wrong number. Apparently that phone number had belonged to the stranger since time immemorial.

'Who are you?' the voice asked.

'I'm Ab…I'm just a brother,' I replied.

I tried to immerse myself in dictionaries and words. I told myself that everything was alright, that he was just sick. He had probably returned to Deir ez-Zour to recuperate. After all, the exam can be gruelling. But something, I don't know what, forced me to go round to the hospital where he worked. I asked the nurses in their spotless white uniforms and white head-scarves if they had seen him. They said they hadn't seen him for weeks. I asked his colleagues for his whereabouts. They all repeated the same mantra: that his letter of resignation had only arrived two days ago. Others, perhaps his friends, nervously suggested that maybe I should visit his home in Jeremana. But when I asked for the address they were reluctant to give it. 'You see,' they said politely, 'it would break employee and employer confidentiality.'

'What?' I said, frustrated, 'since when did this country care about employee confidentiality?'

Only the pretty receptionist seemed responsive. She must have been new because she happily disclosed his address. I scrawled my phone number down on a piece of paper and handed it to her in case our provincial friend turned up. As I explained his strange disappearance the happy picture of the president watched us talk. She kept on smiling and leaning forward as if she was interested in what I had to say, but the piece of paper remained on the desk. I suspect that it stayed there until the caretakers threw it away.

I found the courage a few days later to grab a taxi to Jeremana. This was a suburb of Damascus which had become part of Baghdad. The arrival of Iraqi refugees had not only put property prices up and changed the demography of the entire neighbourhood, it had also changed the Syrian street names to Iraqi equivalents. And so we drove around for a long time trying to find the address amongst the Iraqi hawkers hustling, the prostitutes punting in garish clothes, the merchants trading, delicious kebabs cooking and the sound of tinny Iraqi music reverberating through the dusty streets.

Eventually I did find M'Saad's place, crammed in an alleyway. It was a traditional Arab house that was so tired it leaned on the neighbour's mud brick home. When I knocked, no one opened. I tried this several times, as quietly as I could. Eventually I turned to leave when an unseen, muffled voice, presumably a neighbour's, said: 'He's not here.' I was startled. How long had this man been watching me?

'Where is he?' I asked. 'I haven't seen him for weeks.'

'Not sure, didn't pay his rent.'

I explained, surprised, that M'Saad was a doctor, poorly paid, yes, but he could easily afford to rent a room.

'Believe me, his flatmate ran off too. I think the landlord sent some strong men over to collect the rent.'

'Do you have his number?'

'No, M'Saad didn't have a phone.'

'Are you sure? I called him all the time.'

'I see,' said the voice, pausing. 'Who are you?'

'A brother...'

After Jeremana, I stopped searching. I just prayed for him. I feared he was deep beneath the Syrian Desert where mildew grew on one's skin. For the next six months I focused all my attention to becoming unremarkable. I kept my head down. I tucked my shirt in. I said my hellos and goodbyes and excuse mes quietly. I busied myself with studies and taught lessons to ignoble bastards who aspired to American girls and money. I made sure the conversation was confined to the list on my notepad. However, what I didn't realise then was that here one couldn't just disappear, dream or no dream.

One day as the call to prayer rang out and I was sitting on the balcony watching the birds in communion with their Maker, I spotted the brown silhouette of a bird. It flew at a terrifying speed, cutting through the air like a knife and catching in its talons that lone speck of silver that had dared to take its own course. I had previously only read about the hunting prowess of the peregrine falcon in poetry; and as I watched the falcon carry away its prey the phone call came.

'Hello?'

'*Ahlan*. My name is Mr. Haddad. I'm from *amn*. Can you come in to see us please.'

'What's this about?'

'Your brother, M'Saad.'

AS WITH MOST MEN

Mark Gonzales

As with most men, it is easier for me to give hugs than to accept them.
Lest the truth be known, men
are nothing more than emotional skyscrapers
built with glass infrastructures
spray painted the colour of steel
and nicknamed strength.
Strange isn't it
what walking contradictions are we called men?
At the age of five
men are taught to colonise one another
through games like cops and robbers
cowboys and Indians.
At the age of eight
we're given helmets
then told to hit each other in the head with it.
Bleed but do not blink
cut but do not cry.
Be a man, join the military
die for your country
and if death comes for you
look it in the eye, say
'bring it on motherfucker, I fear nothing but
intimacy.'
When it comes to intimacy
men quiver like fault
lines, crumble like cities
walking contradictions

are we called

men
sign peace accords while abusing their wives
accept the Nobel peace price while reducing health care
pledge to rid the world of terrorism
while simultaneously denying government aid
to any country that defends a woman's right to choose.
During the 1970s the United States government forcibly sterilised
an estimated fifty percent of the indigenous population of America's
Mid-West
telling them the process was reversible.
Can one say biological terrorism?
Bio meaning life body
and in a global war against terror
maybe testosterone is the real terrorist.
If so, how many of these star spangled singing
flag waving citizens would continue do so if we made
terror not racialised but gendered.
Would the US military turn its guns on itself for
sex crimes throughout South East Asia
Africa
and the Americas?
Would MTV be firebombed for its objectification
hyper-sexualisation of women of colour bodies?
Would we stop looking towards the Muslim world for misogyny
turn our sights to Madrid?
Montreal?
New York?
Los Angeles?
Now I understand my sisters when they say
every woman has a story that's been told to a maximum of one soul, maybe
less.

This is why you will never hear me call a woman
slut — cunt

bitch — dyke
no matter what she does for I do not blame her.
I blame the men who have emotionally
physically raped her
corporations who through images
tell her they hate her
then put arms on shoulders
tell her how grateful I am to god
that She created her.

Men take note:
this is how you give love
this is how you receive hugs
pressed breast to breast
till egos deflate like oxygen
till flesh crumples
like emotional origami.

TWO POEMS

Mohja Kahf

From a Former Grad Student of Imam Ibn al-Qayyim

I've kicked aside my prayer rug
and decided to pray on the rushing river
I've smashed those pinchy little spectacles
I used to need to read exegesis,
and decided to read the lightning
crackling in the horizon and the psyche
I've kissed the red lipstick of poetry
and lit the menthol lights of my soul
I've traded in my zikr beads
for the strappy high heels of ecstasy
Baby, I'm going out to get high on Love
and drunk at the Bar of Crazy Beauty,
so if any of those bearded qazi friends of yours
come around with their law books, tell them
I'll be dancing till white threads the black dawn

Prayers from the Cellar of Soft Fascism

This soft fascism
is gathering its forces
like a hurricane
Lord, why did I never hoard
batteries before,
and where
is my mental masking tape?
This soft fascism

that is rolling toward us
covering the horizon,
dark as shame,
contains many lessons
for the brave
Lord, make me one of them
This soft fascism
is hurtling toward us
like a tornado
I've always avoided Kansas,
so I thought I was safe
This soft fascism
slashes our ship in the night
Where did it come from so suddenly?
—jutting like an iceberg
before our titanic pride
I shrink before the big darkness
of this soft fascism
and the terror padding, panting just outside my door
I only want a battened cellar hatch
and beneath it, corner enough to fit a fetal curl
Somewhere far away from all the shrieking,
where schoolchildren's fingers are not being severed,
prisoners are not being raped on dog leashes,
and no one is vowing revenge
Where young mothers are not bombing themselves
in markets crowded with innocents mixed among the guilty,
armed settlers do not cheer the raze of local people's homes,
marathon runners do not think of bombs at finish lines,
weddings dancers strut safe from missile drones,

and where those who live the most cushioned lives in the world
do not holler for more blood like football fans
Somewhere, Lord,
there must be a stable center,
a star above a mountain,
an energy of peace

that will return and settle accounts,
and seize this soft fascism by its talons
and drop it in a deep deep sea
—unless the Star of Peace has already crumbled
and is the sawdust helplessness
inside me
This soft fascism
has seized me by its talons
I need a shield
but I have no hands to hold a shield
Everything clatters to the ground
I cannot even cover my face
It is shame
that covers me
Lord, I only want a canvas thick
enough to shelter me
from the monsoon winds ahead
I only want to stay in bed—
yet, Lord, do not let courage
abandoned this address
Hate inside
and Fear outside
Lord, when again
will it not be night?
This soft fascism
is running as fast as oxytocin
through the world's IV
From these unnatural contractions
what birth, what new deformity?
Everybody braces
for the next blow
of terror
Everybody practises and stays
in the posture of this fear
Our world constricts:
Soft fascism is here.

POSTCARDS FROM GOD

Imtiaz Dharker

Whim

How did it begin?

Where did my whim start
its journey into this
monstrous, magical thing?

I think I travelled
not outward, but within,
and came back
dragging bits of wreckage
from my dreams:

the ragged cloud, the twisted tree,
a concept of eternity,
a man.

Strange,
to have thought up this thing
in its asymmetry,
no longer an abstraction,
quite complete

from collar-bone to rib to hip,
A length of arm, a fingertip.

What was I thinking of
when I made this?

Naming the Angels

And Adam, when the names
of all the angels flowed
sweet as a prayer upon your tongue,
into a flurry, whisper-wing,
what skies split wide and glowed,
what bells were rung
ice-sharp upon the air?

A hush: each one held his breath
before the word enfolded him, strung
up, suspended there
like beads upon your voice;
and each one bowed,
perhaps to you, perhaps under the great
load of this new knowledge,
the real beginning of the road
from flight to fall.
All of them stung
into separateness.

Alone, within
the pride of being named –
the first sin.

Namesake

Adam, your namesake lives
in Dharavi, ten years old. He
has never faced the angels, survives
with pigs that root
outside the door,
gets up at four,
follows his mother to the hotel
where he helps her cut
the meat and vegetables, washes
it all well, watches

the cooking pots over the stove
and waits, his eyelids drooping,
while behind the wall she sells herself
as often as she can before
they have to hurry home.

He very rarely runs
shrieking with other rain-
splashed children
down the sky-paved lane.

He never turns to look at you.
He has no memory
of the Garden, paradise water
or the Tree.
But if he did, Adam, he
would not think to blame you
or even me
for the wrath that has been visited,
inexplicably, on him.

Reflected in sheets of water
at his back
stand the avenging angels
he will never see.

Adam from New Zealand

Adam is a journalist,
newly arrived in India
at twenty-six, eager to seek
and understand,
and to record it all first-hand.
So on his way into Bombay
he has decided he must see
the real India in Dharavi.
He wants a guided tour,
to be fitted in his schedule
between the film studio

and a visit to the Chor Bazaar.

He doesn't understand
why I refuse to take him,
like all the others, lugging
cameras and microphones,
sunguns, recorders, dictaphones.

How can I serve up Zarina
or her brother Adam
to their random cameras?
They will smile shyly.
The aperture will open
to swallow up their souls.

Their mother will send out
for Thums Up, or
from the stall at the corner of the lane,
glasses of hot, sweet tea.
She will put on a brave face,
but everyone in Dharavi will know
the world has come with cameras
to make a side-show
of her poverty.

And will you come back,
in ten years' time,
with your unidirectional mikes
and your portapacks
to make a record of Zarina's wedding,
or a video of Adam's bride?

Adam, your namesake lives in Dharavi.
But I will keep him out of reach
of your greedy camera.

He is too precious for you to see.

Guardians

Strange how the guardians
of our morals
have jellyfish mouths
and jamun eyes.

Funny how your fingers
slither into juicy things
where they don't belong;

how the pot-belly
sits with your holy abstinence.

Odd how, in those frequent mirrors,
your haloes don't show up,
and your media-buttered goodness
turns gargoyle.

Dealing with the devil

Arshad said his uncle from Bradford
switched off the TV set one day
right in front of the children's faces
in the middle of Ice T,
dragged it out, smashed the screen
and carted the corpse away
to the dump,

leaving them sitting there,
the world cast out, all chatter exorcised,
Arif, Zubeida, open-mouthed Nasreen,
their faces left quite bare
as if they had been pulled off.

One devil had been dealt with.
You have to start somewhere,
Arshad's uncle said.

6 December 1992

This morning I woke
and found my eyelids
turned to glass.
Through closed lids
I saw the whole world
changed to glass.
Glass door, glass lock,
glass gods in makeshift shrines.

When I blink,
glass eyelashes crack.

Outside,
blood runs in transparent veins,
fragile bodies walk the streets.
Through glass clothes
it is clear:

Some are circumcised, some not,
but circumcised or not,
they are all glass.

Glass leaders laugh
and the whole world can see
right through their faces
into their black tongues.

And through the crystal night
the bodies begin to burn.

The right word

Outside the door,
lurking in the shadows,
is a terrorist.

Is that the wrong description?
Outside that door,

taking shelter in the shadows,
is a freedom fighter.

I haven't got this right.
Outside, waiting in the shadows,
is a hostile militant.

Are words no more
than waving, wavering flags?
Outside your door,
watchful in the shadows,
is a guerrilla warrior.

God help me.
Outside, defying every shadow,
stands a martyr.
I saw his face.

No words can help me now.
Just outside the door,
lost in shadows,
is a child who looks like mine.

One word for you.
Outside my door,
his hand too steady,
his eyes too hard
is a boy who looks like your son, too.

I open the door.
Come in, I say.
Come in and eat with us.

The child steps in
and carefully, at my door,
takes off his shoes.

REVIEWS

DISGRACEFUL FANATICS? *By Hassan Mohamdallie*
ELECTRIFIED STATE *by M A Qavi*
WOUNDED VERSE *by Claire Chambers*

DISGRACEFUL FANATICS?

Hassan Mahamdallie

I was standing with a friend on the subway platform late one evening travelling back from some much needed halal food at a Senegalese restaurant in Harlem, New York. I glanced up at an advertisement hoarding above me. A photo of one of the twin towers on fire was juxtaposed with a quotation from the Qur'an: 'Soon We shall cast terror into the hearts of the Unbelievers' with the explanation: 'This is a paid advertisement sponsored by the AMERICAN FREEDOM DEFENSE INITIATIVE', along with the serious-sounding web address TruthAboutQuran.Org.

After I recovered my initial shock and annoyance, I got my mobile phone out to take a snap of the advert. As evidence that I had actually seen such a thing. And then for a moment I looked around to see that no-one was watching. Why did I do that? Why did I check myself? In truth, I wanted to reach up and tear the advert off the wall. But I didn't. I didn't want to get arrested. I thanked God I live in London and not New York and haven't (up to now) had to put up with that particular kind of hateful provocation.

Disgraced by Ayad Akhtar, Bloomsbury Methuen Drama, London, 2013
American Dervish by Ayad Akhtar, Phoenix, London, 2012
The War Within written by Ayad Akhtar, Joseph Castelo and Tom Glynn, directed by Joseph Castelo, released 2005

I was reminded of this awful moment at the start of Ayad Akhtar's play *Disgraced*. The protagonist Amir Kapoor (real name Amir Abdullah) goes over with his wife Emily a racial slight he suffered at the hands of a waiter during dinner the previous night:

Amir: I mean the guy was a dick.
Emily: He wasn't just a dick. He was a dick to you. And I could tell why.
Amir: Honey, it's not the first time –
Emily: A man, a waiter, looking at you.

Amir: Looking at us.

Emily: Not seeing you. Not seeing who you really are. Not until you started to deal with him.

Amir seems to brush off the incident 'The guy's a racist. So what?' but then two weeks later he is still talking about it. 'Some waiter is a dick to me in a restaurant...'

It is an accumulation of those small acts of humiliation, those casual slights that strike at a person's psyche. The greater the absurdity and irrationality the more they hit home and succeed in wounding you. It takes a mental effort to lift oneself out of the hurt, to rise above it, to shake it off and go on with life. Otherwise the danger is that one sinks into bitterness, depression and paranoia. We adopt all kinds of defensive strategies to avoid being exposed to insult and hatred, along with mental mechanisms to nullify the degrading effects.

Amir Kapoor decides to be pre-emptive by putting his Pakistani Muslim identity almost completely behind him. He conceals all that he sees as hindering assimilation into the American dream – his home culture, the religious framework he was brought up in, even his Muslim surname. His carefully engineered identity, and presumably his talent and drive, have helped him to build a career as a high-flying New York corporate lawyer. The strategy seems to have paid off – he is on the brink of becoming a partner in his prestigious law firm and talented artist Emily is on the eve of her first major exhibition of artwork inspired by Islamic art. Amir and Emily enjoy a spacious Upper East Side apartment and act out the role of a wealthy and socially attractive power-couple.

Yet a series of events open and expose the fault-lines in his constructed identity, drag him down to a deep and dark place of personal and public ruin, humiliation and disgrace. *Disgraced* is structured as a fleet-of-foot three-act Shakespearean tragedy, and has strong echoes of *Othello*. Ayad Akhtar has explained how an afternoon's staged reading of Shakespeare's play about the Moor fired his creativity. 'I started to imagine an American, of Muslim origin, whose identity was fissured at the root, a man haunted by contradictions'.

Akhtar explained that Amir Kapoor has 'separated from the old world ways of his Muslim childhood, has adopted every inflection and attitude required to remake himself into the brilliant American success story that he is. A corporate lawyer living in Carnegie Hill on the Upper East Side. In a splendid apartment. With a beautiful and brilliant American wife. And yet, the price of his wilful rupture from the past remains partly unpaid, for in post-9/11 America, anti-Muslim prejudice will not allow the still glowing ember of his childhood to be snuffed out.

One is reminded of the lyrics to New York band Talking Heads' song *Once In A Lifetime*:

You may find yourself behind the wheel of a large automobile
You may find yourself in a beautiful house with a beautiful wife
You may ask yourself, well, how did I get here?
…You may ask yourself, what is that beautiful house?
You may ask yourself, where does that highway lead to?
You may ask yourself, am I right, am I wrong?
You may say to yourself, my god, what have I done?
Letting the days go by, let the water hold me down
Letting the days go by, water flowing underground
Into the blue again, after the money's gone
Once in a lifetime…'

I met Ayad Akhtar during rehearsals for the London premiere of *Disgraced* which enjoyed full houses and an extended run at the Bush Theatre in west London. The Bush's artistic director, Madani Younis, had already sent the script to me. And as soon as Akhtar arrived in London we arranged to talk. We met in Shoreditch, in the East End, in my youth a total no-go area and fascist National Front stronghold, today a complex mix of ethnic diversity and trendy artists. It's important sometimes to remind oneself that things can, and do, change for the better.

Akhtar chooses his words very carefully. He has just been awarded the Pulitzer Prize for Drama for *Disgraced*, is in the media spotlight and has had to run a gamut of interviews, many of which deliberately confuse Akhtar the man with Amir Kapoor the theatrical invention. Does Ayad Akhtar believe in God? Does 'the marriage in the play resemble his own failed stab at matrimony?'

Perhaps understandably, he is not keen to explain what they play is about, or to make judgements on the characters – that is up to the audience. 'I see Amir's trajectory as an act of creative destruction', he says. 'But it is not my job to sit in judgement as to whether it's okay for my characters to do things. But I think there is a good reason for the audience to ask that – to mull over the implications of his choices'. But he is eager to articulate his view of the world that informs what he chooses to write about. Like all of us he is both a product of his time and place and impatient to escape from its confines. Like all of us, he struggles to imagine how a world beyond this war- on-terror epoch might be.

Akhtar has mined the post-9/11 landscape and exposed the ways in which it has impacted on American life. He co-wrote and starred in the film *The War Within*. The central character, Hassan, is a Pakistani suicide-bomber who takes refuge in the house of a childhood friend in New Jersey while planning to blow up Grand Central Station. The film was followed by a very successful debut novel *American Dervish*, a rites of passage story about a young boy Hayat and his life-defining relationship with a female relative who comes to stay at his Midwest family home. *Disgraced* premiered in Chicago before finding wide acclaim at New York's Lincoln Center and next year he plans to mount another play *The Who & The What*, in which the central character clashes with her conservative family over the position of women in Islam.

He explains the American Muslim immigrant experience through the lens of his view of the position of Britain's Muslims.

British Muslim identity appears to me to be somewhat less confused, because there is a colonial past and a larger community and historical narrative people can situate themselves in. So they understand why they're here, what they're doing here, why this culture may not accept them, or the ways in which they can find acceptance. They've had more time to work through all of those nuances. I'm not saying there's no problem here – it's just a different set of givens. In America, there's such a higher premium on homogeneity and fitting in and just accepting and adopting the American way of being as the answer to all those socially existential questions. The problem for American Muslims is that they are not really being allowed to do that by society.

What strategies do individuals or groups employ when faced with these societal and 'existential' barriers? In *Disgraced* Amir conjures up an identity that combines capitalist pursuits with apostasy. His nephew Hussein rides on the slipstream of ubiquitous American youth culture – taking the name Abe Jenson and dressing in t-shirt, hoodie, skinny jeans and trainers:

Abe: You know how much easier things are for me since I changed my name? It's in the Qur'an. It says you can hide your religion if you have to.
Amir: I'm not talking about the Qur'an. I'm talking about you being called Abe

Jenson. Just lay off it with me and your folks at least.

Abe: It's gotta be one thing or another. I can't be all mixed up.

The mechanics of self-destruction are what drives both *The War Within* and *Disgraced*. Hassan has decided to be a suicide bomber, Amir performs his own 'spectacular' act of detonation when he admits during an increasingly fractious dinner party with Jewish New York art dealer Isaac and his African-American wife Jory that he had a taboo emotional response to 9/11:

Amir: And so, even if you're one of those lapsed Muslims sipping an after-dinner scotch alongside your beautiful white American wife – and watching the news and seeing folk in the Middle East dying for values you were taught were purer – and stricter – and truer...you can't help but feel just a little a bit of pride.

Isaac: Pride?

Amir: Yes. Pride.

Isaac: Did you feel pride on September 11th?

Amir (with hesitation) If I'm honest, yes.

Emily: You don't really mean that, Amir.

Amir: I was horrified by it, okay? Absolutely horrified.

Jory: Pride about what? About the Towers coming down? About people getting killed?

Amir: That we were finally winning.

Jory: We?

Amir: Yeah...I guess I forgot...which we I was.

The final disintegration of Amir's existence occurs later on in the evening when, upon discovering that his wife Emily has had a fling with Isaac, he beats her.

How did it all go so horribly wrong for Amir (and Emily)? For Akhtar, *Disgraced* is in part concerned with the extent to which we are all imprisoned in the war on terror binaries – East versus West, Good Muslim versus Bad Muslim. At the start of the play we find Emily painting a portrait of her husband in the style of a famous Valazquez work *Portrait of Juan de Pareja*. It is explained that De Pareja was a Moorish slave/assistant of Valazquez. At the very end of the play we see Amir staring at the finished portrait his ex-wife has left him. Stage directions: *He takes a searching long look. Lights Out.*

Akhtar says:

One of the things the play is about, inside my mind, is how Muslims exist inside the representation that the West has of them. The play begins with a Western artist [Emily] painting a Muslim subject [Amir], and the play ends with that Muslim subject observing that image. In between those two things is the entire world of the play. The play is suggesting, or might be suggesting, that Modern Muslim identity is still entirely wrapped up in what the West thinks of the Muslim *ummah*. It's a cul-de-sac. There's no way out of the question, and so the final image of the play is Amir 'accounting' for that image, because that's what I think we have to do as Muslims. We have got to figure out, not how to counteract that image, but how to understand it and then move on'. It's not enough to deconstruct 'their idea of us'.

Akhtar's conviction is that the Muslim intellectual community has failed to equip Muslims in the West with a roadmap out of that cul-de-sac. We are thus locked into this false portrayal of ourselves provided by 'the West' and doomed, thus far, to merely reacting to it. For Akhtar figures such as Edward Said have 'walked us to the door, but we have got to go out into the world'. It seems to me that Akhtar's creative project is an attempt, at least, to 'go out into the world'.

To a Muslim audience it can seem as though Akhtar is throwing all the Muslim stereotypes back at us – Amir is the non-believing, scotch drinking, self-hating, woman-beating, intrinsically violent sub-continental. This view of the character, and on the play as a whole, is perhaps reinforced by the way in which the play accelerates to its end. There is no slow burn, there are no soliloquies by which we have privileged access to the internal life of the character, there is very little backstory. *Disgraced* is a tightly written, well-crafted piece of dramatic writing that with breakneck velocity drags you to its climax and denouement. The speed is unsettling, deliberately so. And of course there is that lingering embarrassment; that fear that producing such a powerful character on the stage will play into the negative narratives that seek to circumscribe us. My contention is that, firstly Amir is not a negative stereotype, but more importantly, that we have to risk 'the message' being misread by some, wilfully or otherwise, if that is the price to pay for putting 'dangerous ideas' onto the stage. Surely that is the point of theatre.

However, it does seem to me that although the play touches on universal themes such as love, hate, subterfuge and truthfulness, it speaks most directly to a non-Muslim audience. For example, narrative strands in both

Disgraced and *American Dervish* seem to be fashioned in such a way as to educate or inform a non-Muslim audience about essential aspects of Islam and Muslim history, culture and thought.

Disgraced is designed, at least in part, to confront a non-Muslim audience with stereotypes of Islam and Muslims they may hold in a similar way that an Alan Ayckbourn play is crafted to play back to a middle class audience all their worst petty prejudices and hypocrisies, but magnified to absurdity. In *Disgraced* you are asked to be attracted to Amir, even if you don't like him, to share his hostility to literalist interpretations of Islam and the worst aspects of Pakistani culture, only to find yourself wrong-footed when you realise you have been seduced into being complicit in his disgrace. In fact – you may be the cause of his disgrace. Whether you identify yourself as this particular 'you' is another matter of course.

The clearest 'political' statement in *Disgraced* is placed in the mouth of Abe/Hussain at the end of the play (who by this time has abandoned his Western disguise):

Abe: The Prophet wouldn't be trying to be like one of them. He didn't conquer the world by copying other people. He made the world copy him…That's what they've done. They've conquered the world. We're gonna get it back. That's our destiny. It's in the Qur'an….For three hundred years they've been taking our land, drawing new borders, replacing our laws, making us want to be like them. Look like them. Marry their women.
They disgraced us.
They disgraced us.
And then they pretend they don't understand the rage we've got.

Of the pivotal moment of Amir's disgrace Akhtar told me: 'I want the audience at that point to have agreed enough with Amir, that they think he is right, and *they* have found themselves in this paradoxical situation where they, the non-Muslim audience, realises that *they* have conquered the world, and that *they*, the ones that have agreed with Amir, have disgraced him, and that *they* are at the root as to why this has happened to him'. He continues: 'giving the title of the play to Abe at the end of the play, is not a particularly Western-friendly gesture on my part, because I'm not undermining what he says – if anything, if anything, the author appears to be saying "*the kid is right!*"'.

What are we to make of Abe/Hussein's uncompromising and angry speech? We know that he is in trouble. He and a friend have been pulled in for interrogation by the FBI after they are reported for letting slip in a coffee bar, to a non-Muslim, a sliver of what they really think:

Abe: We were in Starbucks. Just drinking coffee. Tariq starts talking to this barista who's on a break. I can tell she's not into him. He's not getting the message…She starts talking about our *kufi* hats and are we Muslims. And then she asks us how we feel about Al-Qaeda. So Tariq tells her. Americans are the ones who created Al-Qaeda.

…So she got snippy. And Tariq got pissed. He told her this country deserved what it got and what it was going to get.

The playwright seems to be indicating to us that the anger Abe/Hussein feels is not only explicable but understandable and legitimate. That doesn't mean we should jump to the lazy conclusion he is on the road to becoming a suicide bomber, but it does mean that henceforth he will be viewed by the authorities as having suspicious, if not fanatical, tendencies.

Perhaps we should think more about fanaticism. The Marxist writer Alberto Toscano has written extensively on the historical use of the term, against the prevailing notion that the mere uttering of the word 'fanatic' signals the end of discussion and a place well beyond the boundaries of all rational thought. In his 2006 essay 'Fanaticism: A brief history of the concept', Toscano observes that when fanaticism is introduced in debates it 'seems to lean more towards cultural and psychological causes than political, strategic, and material ones. Fanaticism often appears as an invariable that transcends historical events, or even, in an Orientalist and racist vein, a characteristic of fantastical entities such as "the Arab mind"'.

Toscano traces back the term to its historical root in Europe's Reformation. Martin Luther used the term 'fanatic' to demonise the preacher Thomas Müntzer, who sought to mobilise the German peasantry against expropriation of their lands and labour. Luther, calling for the extermination of the rebellious peasantry 'like dogs', 'saw in the "fanaticism" of the peasants, above all in the case of the fanatic *par excellence*, the preacher Müntzer, an assault against social order as such. It is here, at the dawn of the discourse on fanaticism, that the oppositional and biased character of the term shows itself most clearly'.

Toscano examines various theories on the nature of the fanatic advanced by philosophers such as Kant and Hegel until he arrives at the young Hegelian Arnold Ruge, who in 1842 published a text entitled 'Hegel's Philosophy

of Right and the Politics of Our Times'. For Ruge fanaticism could be understood as a particular reaction to a denial of social equality. For the fanatic,
religion manifests itself as desire for liberation, with fanaticism representing
an 'intensified religion', or 'a passion for liberation that is born from a prior
failure, from a blockage of the routes to emancipation'. For Ruge, fanaticism
is a product of 'the failure to incorporate the passion for liberation into the
mechanisms of the State'.

Toscano goes onto observe that in the twentieth century fanaticism is
widely seen as the cause, as opposed to the effect, of social evils. The Cold
War, according to the West, was the fault of a fanatical (and oriental) creed,
Communism, pitted against the liberal rationalism and Enlightenment intellectual scepticism of the 'free world'. Today the West is at war with what it
regards as another fanatical oriental creed – Islam/Islamism. As Toscano
notes:

such a vision of fanaticism not only forgets that sceptics and liberals are perfectly
capable of causing enormous harm, or indeed evil (especially when legitimated by
a "just war", which wars against "fanatics" are by definition), and that not all reactionaries can be classified as "fanatics", but it also ignores the lesson of Ruge: a
"history without fanaticism" can only be the result of a politics of real emancipation
and not of an abstract battle of ideas.

We have thus to rethink fanaticism, Toscano concludes, as 'a precise historical, political, and psychological concept for the present and not simply
as a talisman for exorcising or eliminating absolute enemies'. As the case of
Luther and the rebel peasants shows, 'the designation of one's enemies as
"fanatics" is often the sinister prelude to treating them "like dogs", or like
"unlawful combatants"'.

But are there spaces where we can actually rethink fanaticism? Is the com-
bustible material of fanaticism – rage – a legitimate focus for public discourse? Can Muslims, particularly in the West, talk about these things freely,
without hesitation or self-censorship?

I asked Akhtar to reflect on the legitimate nature of discourse on rage. He
points out that the Qur'an reveals 'a divine voice that threatens and casti-
gates humanity. It's relentless. It just goes on and on and on, and lots of
people read the Qur'an who are not Muslim and say, "well it's very angry"
and dismiss it. Well yeah it is. But look at humanity, look at what we are
doing to the planet – we can't even come to an agreement about global

warming. That is the kind of stubbornness that the Qur'an is addressing at a fundamental level. There is no spiritual text that does it as aggressively and as thoroughly'.

However, Akhtar explains that he is not seeking to advocate a literal reading of the text. He points to the Quraysh, the dominant tribe of Mecca, to which the Prophet Muhammad belonged, and which became the bitterest enemy of Muslims. The Qur'an sometimes addresses them directly. The problem emerges, Akhtar says, 'when you start to see the Quraysh as the Quraysh. The Quraysh are not the Quraysh – they are the larger human species, and when the Qur'an is read very literally, it might be safe to say that we lose all the possibilities of wisdom that we can derive from it'.

For Akhtar the nub of the matter is whether we can have truthful conversations about the Qur'an, or about the realities of our world post 9/11 without being closed down:

But you know what, my attitude is, I'm going to have that conversation. I don't care. Okay, I'm going to go about it in an intelligent way, or try to, but I'm going to have the conversation. What artist worth their salt has ever allowed the prevailing discourse to define what they think?

Revisit the tragic flaw that brings down Amir. It's not, as one might first conclude, living a lie that destroys him; it is his compulsion to tell the truth when asked that proves to be his ruination. As an American press review of *Disgraced* observes, during the course of the play:

Racial tensions are exposed, religious prejudices are aired, and the liberal principles these people supposedly live by are totally trashed. Among this enlightened company, Amir is the only one with the courage to admit his true feelings about racial politics – and he's doomed by his own honesty.

Towards the end of our conversation I asked Akhtar whether he has ever censored himself. He replied half in jest: 'I've never had to self-censor up to now because I never thought anyone would take me seriously'. It will be interesting to see, post Pulitzer Prize, when he is taken seriously, whether he will temper his own rage.

ELECTRIFIED STATE

M A Qavi

I have been trying to get to Gaza for the last few years. I have no problem in getting into the West Bank part of Palestine. When I tell Israeli immigration at Ben Gurion airport the purpose of my visit is 'to pray' they hasten to cut the bureaucratic knots short to let me speed my way to Al Quds. Gaza is a different matter, sealed as it is since 2006 by an electrified and barbed wire fence. The only other point of entry into Gaza is from the Egyptian side of Rafah border. Last September I thought I had cracked it. A summer university for international participants was planned in Gaza for which I had enrolled and made necessary travel arrangements. Two weeks before departure the newly elected administration in Cairo withdrew its permission for us to travel through Sinai to Rafah on security grounds and the whole project fell through. But Dervla Murphy, the Irish 'semi-toothless, slightly stooped, old white-haired woman' as she describes herself, was luckier. She made the journey in the immediate aftermath of the Arab Spring when things in Cairo were unsettled and traversing the bureaucratic maze of permits for travel to Gaza was relatively easier. She spent one month in the open air prison that Gaza has become since 2006, exploring the alleys and narrow lanes of refugee camps and the segregated beaches of Mediterranean coast. *A Month by the Sea* is an eye witness, and eye opening, account of what she saw and experienced during her sojourn.

A Month by the Sea by Dervla Murphy, Eland, London, 2013

But first what do we know of Gaza?

Gaza with its natural deep water harbour and strategic location on the road to Egypt and Africa is an ancient city that has been continuously inhabited for as long as, if not longer than, Damascus and Jerusalem. Its splendour and historic place in the Hebrew mythology were well captured by Cecil B de Mille in his 1949 film 'Samson and Delilah'. Delilah, in the guise of shapely

Hedy Lamarr, succeeds in seducing Victor Mature's swarthy Samson into revealing the secret of his awesome strength, but betrays him. Samson destroys her tribe in revenge by bringing down the Temple in Gaza over the heads of carousing men and women celebrating a festival. In 635, Gaza was conquered by the Arabs and was, for centuries, a cosmopolitan city. Under the Mamluks and Ottomans it prospered as a seat of learning and scholarship; the noted jurist Imam Shafi (769-820), who established the eponymous school of theology, was born in Gaza.

On 27th December 2008, Israel unleashed the terror of operation Cast Lead on the heads of defenceless, unarmed Gazans in a spectacle the world watched in real time on its TV and computer screens. Murphy was in West Bank at the time, living in the refugee camp Balata, a bastion of resistance to Zionist Occupation. I have known the camp since my first visit in 2002 when it was being brutally punished for its role in the Second Intifada. Between November 2008 and December 2010, Murphy spent three months in Israel and five months in West Bank. This gave her the opportunity to cast a critical eye over the tensions between Fatah and Hamas, since Hamas' unexpected 2006 victory in the Palestinian Legislative Council elections was an obstacle to Palestinian unity. She went well prepared, light of baggage but heavy on the contemporary history of the region. She describes how the Muslim Brotherhood set up a string of Islamic Social Institutions [ISI] in the 1950s, when Egypt administered the area, to help Gaza's disadvantaged; and how Israel, after conquering the territory in 1967, continued to commend and facilitate their work well into the 1980s, by which time Sheikh Ahmad Yassin had become the overall leader of all ISIs operating in the Strip. These ISIs were the crucible from which Hamas emerged, a fortnight after the start of the First Intifada in December 1987, to pose an existential threat to Fatah's control of the PLO.

Murphy's life choices produce some fascinating encounters in Gaza. She never married but has a grown up daughter and granddaughters and lives by herself in county Waterford, Ireland. Time and again this causes an outpouring of heartfelt sympathy from her female interlocutors at her misfortune in not having a proper family. A young female teacher of English that she encounters with her lover in a gloomy room of a café accuses her of being 'naked' for not covering her hair because, she informs Dervla, 'the Holy Qur'an orders every woman to keep every one of her hairs covered'. This, after the two lovers, both with arranged marriages over the horizon, had informed her that they were planning to elope! She hears of instances of 'honour killing' to restore family honour (thirty-two such murders reported in the occupied territories in 2010) and is cheered when she finds the al-Rahma Association in Gaza, set up in 1993 by a brother of Mahmoud Al-Zahar, the Hamas foreign minister, to care for 'infants of unknown parentage'. The average intake at al-Rahma, she informs us, is of one parentless newborn a month. She navigates with amusement through the double standards and faux religiosity that is family life in Gaza.

Like all colonial powers, Israel requires a network of informers and collaborators among the Palestinians to sustain its occupation. In the occupied territories the informers have helped Israel identify candidates for elimination by what is euphemistically known as 'targeted killing'. The list of senior Hamas leaders in Gaza thus taken out by Israel since 2002 is long, and includes a number of prominent resistance leaders such as Sheikh Yassin. There is now an added threat from within posed by the burgeoning Salafi movement whose adherents, small in numbers but ferocious in their determination to turn the clock back, act outside the law. The Salafis do not consider the Hamas leadership good enough Muslims, or tough enough, to lead the struggle against Occupation. Dervla the 'semi-toothless' octogenarian finds herself on more than one occasion under intimidation in public places by young men with long beards who take exception to her uncovered grey hair. She notices and reports on how the Salafis are forcing Hamas into adopting increasingly restrictive policies in the public sphere. The cold-blooded killing of peace activist Vittorio Arrigoni in Gaza at their hands, weeks before Murphy's sojourn, is a grim reminder of the darkness at the heart of Salafism.

It is in Dervla's detached description of the dynamics of various families she gets to know in Gaza that the book really comes alive. The most beautiful woman she saw in Gaza was a mother of nine whose seventeen-year-old second son was shot dead by the Israelis just three weeks before she went to see the family. Living in a 'two roomed, earthen-floored concrete shack', with no windows, in a camp lacking basic amenities, she marvels at the fortitude of striking Tahany in raising such a well-behaved and loving family with so 'few shekels' — an observation I, too, have made often in my travels in West Bank. In the travails of Nasser, who lost his wife and a child in the thrice shelled home on land his family struggled over two generations to buy

and build, she sees 'courage, obstinacy and a calm sort of pride'. The Palestinians call it *Samoud* – a quality the Israelis have not found an answer to yet.

But not all women in Gaza are covered from head to toe. Murphy encounters the old Mrs Halaweh, a native of Gaza, on the beach. Halaweh, who
comes from a family of old money, spontaneously invites Murphy to her
home. Over coffee she tells her of her rage at her granddaughter's insistence
on wearing the *thobe* in public and not wanting to be free. 'I'm faithful to
Islam!' declares Halaweh. 'Every Friday I go to the mosque, I keep the Ramadan fast – but I'll never wear the hijab and *thobe*!' And there is Fikr Shaltoot,
born in a refugee camp and schooled by UNRWA before graduating from an
American university, who came back to be with her own people but on her
own terms – that she will not cover her head and will drive her own car.

The Israeli leadership never misses an opportunity to tell the world how
moral, disciplined and well behaved their 'citizen army' is. The reality for
Palestinians is different. The night-time raids conducted in the Occupied
Territories usually follow an established pattern. They come after the IDF has
vandalised several homes, breaking televisions, computers, fridges, 'ripping
upholstery, smashing kitchenware, scattering food all over floors before uri-
nating on it'. Abdel, whose relations had been victims of such a raid in Rafah,
says 'the IDF is a very sick institution' but he does not blame the soldiers.
'We shouldn't blame individual kids', he says, 'they're taken out of the
school-room, processed in a dehumanising machine, injected with fear and
loathing of Palestinians. I hear people say, in another way they're victims'. It
is people like Abdel who bring out the humanity of Gaza.

Dervla Murphy's account of her month in the open air cage of Gaza is a
grim reminder of how tenuous the earthly comforts we take for granted in
our supposedly well ordered societies can be in a different setting. She has an
eye for detail and writes exquisitely about the places and the people she
encounters from a wide spectrum of Gazan society. Her narrative of entering
Gaza, a Kafkaesque vision of bureaucratic nightmare she went through,
speaks volumes of her Irish grit. *A Month by the Sea* is required reading for
anyone interested in peace and Palestine, and a testimony that abuse of
authority and arrogance of office are endemic in states where the rule of law
is perverted at the highest level.

WOUNDED VERSE

Claire Chambers

John Siddique is a British author who was born in 1964 in Rochdale, Lancashire to an Irish Catholic mother and a Muslim father originally from Jullundur (a city which after Partition was renamed Jalandhar and came to be situated in the Indian Punjab). His first collection *The Prize* (2005) was nominated for the Forward Prize and contains 'Variola', a poem that describes his father's traumatic journey to Pakistan during the violent Partition of the subcontinent in 1947, during which his three sisters died of smallpox. This story is echoed and developed in Siddique's prose piece, 'Six Snapshots of Partition', written for the online issue of *Granta 112: Pakistan*. His children's book *Don't Wear it on your Head, Don't Stick it Down your Pants*, was shortlisted for 2007's CLPE Poetry Award. Siddique's second adult collection, *Poems from a Northern Soul*, was also published in 2007. His next book, *Recital: An Almanac* (2009), contains the most important and sensitive poetic response to the 2005 London bombings yet to be written: this sequence, 'Inside', constitutes an urban series at the centre of a largely rural collection, and offers a nuanced, even-handed response to 7/7.

Full Blood by John Siddique, Salt, Cromer, Norfolk, 2011

In his most recent collection *Full Blood* (2011), John Siddique turns his attention to love, a subject which, as he rightly notes, all his poems to date have been about, 'even when they turn out to have bombs in them, or politics, or light switches'. The poems contain acute observations about such topics as race and racism, urban degeneration, and death. However, readers may be most seduced by *Full Blood's* interplay of tenderness and erotica, although the frankness of several poems in the collection's second section, 'Reclaiming the Body', is not for the faint-hearted.

The collection begins with a Prologue, which contains 'Every Atom', the perfect poem to replace Khalil Gibran's 'The Prophet on Marriage' as a wedding reading for our times. Celebratory but never trite, it makes sense that this poem, with its evocation of physical juxtapositions, has been turned into a dance piece by the Northern School of Contemporary Dance. The dance piece, along with the fact that Blackpool residents knitted a huge version of his poem 'Why' for the Wordpool literature festival in 2010, indicates that Siddique has greater impact and connects with readers more directly than many more overtly 'highbrow', elitist contemporary British poets. Siddique is also a tireless performer, blogger, and marketer of his poems, so it is perhaps unsurprising that *Full Blood* reached number 1 in Amazon's contemporary poetry chart in October 2011.

After the Prologue, there follow four parts to the collection: the first, 'Via Negativa', recalls the Christian philosophy that God is formless, so it is restrictive to describe Him through language, and preferable to discuss instead what He is not. The *via negativa*, or 'negative theology', is similar to the Islamic concept of *lahoot salbi*, popular with the Mutazali or rationalist school of philosophy and theology as well as Shia Islam; and it also overlaps productively with meditation (a practice Siddique himself adopts), in which the subject makes his or her mind blank in order to achieve self-transcendence. The first poem in the section, 'Thirst', resonates with this kind of negative theology:

Imagine thirst without knowing water.
And you ask me what freedom means.
Imagine love without love.
Some things are unthinkable,
until one day the unthinkable is here.
Imagine thirst without knowing water.
Some things we assume just are as they are,
no action is taken to make or sustain them.
Imagine love without love.
It is fear that eats the heart: fear and
endless talk, and not risking a step.
Imagine thirst without knowing water.
Fold away your beautiful thoughts.
Talk away curiosity, chatter away truth.
Imagine love without love.
Imagine believing in the whispers,
the screams and the gossip. Dancing to a tune
with no song to sing inside you.
Imagine love without love.

This poem about freedom is also extremely timely, given the volume's publication in 2011, the year of revolutions ('one day the unthinkable is here'). In the ensuing five-poem sequence '*The Knife*', Siddique discusses racism in northern England, juxtaposing half-remembered puppy love with Andrea ('or was it Julie') with the need to escape from jackbooted Rochdale FC supporters. 'Read your books,' Siddique apostrophises himself, and by extension his introverted, misfit readership, 'go from house to house, live/within sanctuaries, the streets are theirs'.

After the achingly personal and carnal 'Reclaiming the Body' comes the quasi-religious 'Tree of Life' section, which has overtones from all three Abrahamic religions, as well as Hinduism and Buddhism. Here, Siddique plays with the myth of Lilith, the female aspect of God, which is found in Judaism and Christianity, possibly dating even further back to *Gilgamesh*, the epic from third-millennium BCE Mesopotamia. Siddique posits the idea that Lilith is excised from the Bible by religious scholars, who un-write her name, stealing God's wife from him and 'make him lonely'. In the central seven-poem sequence, Siddique suggests that human life centres on the quest to discover the secret of the sacred masculine and feminine. The form of these poems is also innovative, as Siddique takes the traditional villanelle form and blends it with blank verse, creating a modern, unrhymed villanelle. Without the strictness of rhyme, the reinvented form allows greater scope for story-telling, and the three-line stanzas of the villanelle creates the quality of an incantation to reflect the ritualistic nature of the seven poems. This is most apparent in the triumphant final poem in the sequence, 'Trial Seven – Love and the Body', with its chant-like iteration 'and all there is, is love and the body/[…] and this moment and this moment'.

The final part, 'Xibulba' takes its name from the Mayan underworld, and includes poems such as 'Lustre', a Keatsian reflection on a pot from the Manchester Art Galleries exhibition, and 'Why' about life as a second-generation migrant in Britain and the myth of return. The volume as a whole contains complex references, which serve to remake both European and Eastern literary traditions and evoke textured human experience: mortality, tenderness, war, peace, and alternative modes of living. Technically virtuosic yet direct and sensual, this is a collection I keep returning to.

ET CETERA

TEN SPECIES OF
ANGRY MUSLIM MEN

You are sitting comfortably in an assembly of Muslim men. Women are, as usual, segregated and safely secluded in a different room – as far as possible. Conversation is flowing with endless cups of *chai* as you begin to listen carefully to this fairly representative sample of Muslim masculinities. What are you going to hear? The discussion would inevitably focus on Islam with, as in any human gathering, a host of different views and positions. But there will be a certain variety, Little Big Men Little Overblown, who will be jostling each other to claim that they are the only true representative of God on earth. So here is a list of the type of Muslim men you may encounter in a typical gathering anywhere on the planet.

1. Preacher Man

Harbouring an unhealthy obsession with 'infidels' and all things *kafir*, products of grimy unbelievers, the excruciating agony of the hellfire dominates the fire and brimstone televangelist preacher's every thought. In an effort to save souls he rails against the decay and degradation of Western society and can often be found regaling simple fellows of the joys and superiority of a certain kind of Islam, while attacking other faiths and denouncing women. His every sentence is punctuated with quotations from the Qur'an and the traditions of the Prophet. Although physically a mess, he is also quite imprudent. He will not rest until Shari'a is implemented on the planet, for which incidentally he needs to become a citizen of the US or Europe with attendant social housing and state benefits.

2. Rocky, the Fighter

Rocky, the Fighter (henceforth known as a Salafi) constitutes a subset of Preacher Man. He imbibes all of the latter's (un)qualities with the addition that he would dearly like us all to return to the purity of an imagined formative period of Islam, exemplified by the first generation of Muslims, the Salaf. The Salaf, we are told, were clones of the Prophet, copying how he dressed, ate, slept, and so on. Today's Salafis go to great lengths at such imitation and are savvy users of technology. Laser-scanners can ensure beard-lengths are accurate to the nano-metre, and music, sorry, MP3 players can recite the Qur'an on a continuous loop. Strangely, the Prophet's other virtues (compassion and kindness, for example), are absent from the Salafi playbook. The Salafi male's main habitat is likely to be a Saudi-sponsored mosque, where Salafis of the senior species can be identified by the numbers of wars they have fought in. There is also a lesser form of Salafi who wakes up all set to fight the jihad, but, upon landing at Kabul airport, misses the creature comforts of home so much that he becomes an aid worker-cum piety policeman, chasing after the sisters with the intention of 'educating' them as to appropriate Islamic behaviour such as the correct length of skirt.

3. Tambourine Man

Islam's 'happy clappy' tradition has roots in a north Indian town called Bareilly in the nineteenth century and its followers are known by their enemies as Barelvis. Tambourine Men need no excuse for a song, or a dance at the mosque. If you're lucky you might even witness spontaneous performances of the Harlem shake as worshippers jive in rapture to devotional music. Tambourine Man's copy of the Qur'an is to be found on a high shelf in his home and wrapped in a silk, gold scarf. It is kissed before and after recitation. He also has a fondness for graveyards and a Goth-like reverence for all things death-related. The demise of a near and dear, twice-removed cousin-in-law requires him to drop everything that instant and travel 250 miles across the country to express his condolence (*afsos*, as he calls it) to the bereaved. If you, too, can weep uncontrollably at the mere mention of the Prophet's name then do consider membership of this large and expanding club.

4. The Orthodox Man

As Newton pointed out, for every action there is an equal and opposite reaction. In the case of the Barelvis, it comes in the form of Deobandis, the followers of the Deoband seminary in Uttar Pradesh, India. In some circles, he is also known as Wahhabi; either way, he is an ultra-conservative orthodox man who hates women, secularism, and Salman Rushdie. But most of all he hates the Barelvis, and lives in constant feigned horror at the activities of his Barelvi neighbours. He promotes campaigns such as 'No to Graveyard Worship' and his favourite term of abuse is to call something *shirk* (idolatry) or *biddah* (innovation). But he is not against all innovations – he is happy to divorce his wife via a text, use television for *dawa* (literally 'inviting to all that is good', but in his case good is not a moral but an instrumental concept) and issue truly dumb on-line fatwas. The highlight of his calendar is the anniversary of the Prophet's death, not to celebrate it but to make a big point of NOT celebrating it. He has a prurient interest in the personal lives of others and wants to dictate everything from personal hygiene habits to the rules of the marital bedroom. Anything remotely fun is strictly forbidden and having a sense of humour is a sure-fire way to be consigned to the depths of Hell. He would prefer that women stay at home. In fact he would prefer if women did not exist at all but life is not perfect and that is Allah's will.

5. The Puritan

We have our Puritans, and none more so than the *tablighis*, the Jehovah's Witnesses of the Muslim world. An off-shoot of the Deobandi school, the movement was started in 1926 in India to invite people to 'the way of Muhammad'. If you are a Muslim, sooner or later you will find a *tablighi* knocking on your door to ask if you are familiar with the basics of Islam and know how to pray properly. *Tablighis* are obsessed with the minutia of rituals: is your beard the correct length, how far you must wash your elbow during ablution, which direction you should face during sex – that sort of thing. Prayers must be performed at the appointed time, regardless of where you might be or what else you might be doing. Driving on a motorway? Then pray on the hard-shoulder. Playing an important international cricket match? No matter. Mecca cannot wait. The *tablighi's* idea of a spiritual retreat involves abandoning his family for months at a time to do God's work. This all-male affair involves going from mosque to mosque, to eat, pray, and invite Muslim men to do the same. It is, in effect, an extended alcohol-free stag-do. One of the six *tablighi* principles includes 'honouring other Muslims' – but this does not include women, presumably because they do not have beards.

6. The Exceptionalist

Islam is a broad church, encompassing many sects and nationalities. That is in effect a licence for males of any nationality to assume that their Islam is superior to any other. The Exceptionalist Arab never fails to remind you that he speaks 'the language of the Qur'an', has an innate and superior understanding of the Sacred Text, and his Islam is superior to all others. Urdu-speaking males from Pakistan will insist that theirs is the language of Heaven. It's the same when it comes to clothing, food, and national cultures. The Shalwar Kameez, according to its wearers, is more 'Islamic' than the *jalabiyya* of the Arab world – and both are infinitely preferable to anything emanating from the Western world, except men's shoes, which seem to have transcended both religion and nationality.

7. Movement Man

Movement Man exists solely for the purpose of achieving a utopian Islamic state under Shari'a. Islamic movements include the Jamaat-e-Islami of Pakistan, the Muslim Brotherhood of Egypt and possibly Turkey's Justice and Development party, too. Movement Man believes in slogans such as 'the Qur'an is our constitution' and 'Islam is the Answer' even though he has no idea what question 'Islam' is in fact responding to. Feminists, secularists, nationalists, modernists and all other ists (except Islamists) are abhorred equally. Governments led by men from Islamic movements tend towards a kind of totalitarianism *à la* Iran, with its infallible Supreme Leader and an Impeccably Pious 'Council of Guardians' at the helm. Mercifully, not many Muslims want to vote for the Movement Man.

8. The Zealous Convert

'Convert', 'revert', or, simply 'New Muslims' – more and more men seem to want to adopt Islam by choice. Scientists have been unable to work out a reason or formula, except that converts are as likely to be rich bankers as they are likely to be guests at Her Majesty's Pleasure (possibly both). Male converts do have one thing in common though: a healthy scepticism of their brothers and sisters who take the lazy road to 'choosing' belief because it runs in the family. A male convert's first goal after conversion is often to find a nice, uncomplicated, passive and obedient Muslim wife. But he soon discovers that such a person exists only in Orientalist fantasies. His second objective is to convert more men to the cause, including lazy 'born' Muslims. He feels he is a far better Muslim than them, indeed he is more Muslim than the Muslims themselves, and hence in a natural position to be a leader.

9. The Conspiracy Theorist

By means of intuition and with the aid of esoteric knowledge, our Conspiracy Theorist Muslim man has access to truth at a level far beyond the merely factual. So, for example, where others see hapless and incompetent politicians failing to run national and global affairs, the Conspiracy Theorist sees the work of phantoms menacing and controlling the world. His most prized possession is a well-thumbed copy of *The Protocols of the Elders of Zion*. Beyond that he cannot get enough of Internet searches for The Bilderberg Group and the Illuminati. In the world of the Conspiracy Theorist, there is no such thing as responsibility: everything is always someone else's fault.

10. The Pious Package Holiday-maker

He regularly forgoes family holidays in order to top up his savings in the piety bank to go for pilgrimage (*hajj*), or lesser pilgrimage (*umrah*), to Mecca. Or rather, the pilgrimage is a holiday trip where the highlight is the family bucket meal at the KFC in Mecca. He is thrilled with the construction of five-star facilities in the Holy City and thinks that the Clock Tower in Mecca is the epitome of style and taste. After all, we have to move with the times and pilgrims, like other consumers, need a little luxury when performing their religious duty. His twenty-something daughter who would have baulked at a hole in the toilet floor can now be persuaded to join him and his wife next year. Some years, he will perform hajj or *umrah* on behalf of a deceased relative or a member of a family unable to afford the trip. But it never occurs to him to lend them a financial hand to make the trip themselves.

ON CHASTITY

Jenny Taylor

Since the Second World War, the post-Christian West has tried to solve the old sexual 'double standard' by erasing all the bad vibes surrounding it. The answer, where men got their kicks and women got hurt, was to teach women to have sex like men - without conscience. All that mattered was to avoid pregnancy, and practise appropriate 'protection'. Children were taught – apparently – not to have sex until they felt ready for it, which being children, sounds like 'Whatever'. Despite some slender research from the US to the contrary, the old Christian categories of chastity before marriage, and children within it, and of course the consensus about what marriage actually is, broke down. Religion was responsible for shame, went the thinking, so religion must go. 'Civilisation, built on religious self-discipline, demands sacrifices in sexual behaviour that are harmful, especially to women,' wrote the father of that pseudoscience, psychotherapy, Sigmund Freud – and all the people said 'Amen'.

Now all that's left is sex. Sexualisation without hedges. The glorious open uplands of 'confluent love'– a phrase Anthony Giddens, the intellectual father of Tony Blair's 'third way', coined to describe the 'transformation of intimacy' into self-autonomous-relations-of-equally-negotiable-satisfactions – have been ours for the roaming. 'Until death do us part' was replaced with 'until further notice'. But now sexualisation and globalisation have met above a kebab shop in Oxford – and the weather's closing in.

Schools, the media and even parents helped further to dismantle the stigma of premarital sex in Britain. The mother of the clergywoman I met told her that unless she had sex, she would never get a husband. The boy at the back of the Newcastle classroom was not being flippant when he put up his hand and asked: 'Miss, with all these condom machines in the toilets, are we supposed to have sex?' As parents colluded in subverting the norms of English female sexuality — once a by-word for propriety and modesty (think of Jane Austen and you get the point) — TV celebrities and grooming gangs assumed it was open season. At the same time as modernity eroded guilt over sex in 'broken' Britain, it not only brought to UK shores a number of men and their backwards Imams with historic attitudes of domination, but permitted a culture of licence for such attitudes to thrive in what we thought was 'progress'.

How did we get into this mess?

Sigmund Freud is without doubt the ghost in this once humming machine. The British philosopher Roger Scruton, in his updated survey *Sexual Desire* republished in 2002, writes that Freud's 'science of sex' (which he puts in inverted commas) 'led to a greater revision in our moral attitudes than has accompanied any social upheaval or religious crusade' — Freud still provides the general background to much of this country's received wisdom about sex and mental health, even though his work has been viewed with considerable scepticism, and is widely regarded not only as unscientific but even as mildly deranged. Scruton calls it 'myth' — a plausible way of explaining things - but since it is myth that describes itself as science, it therefore resists scrutiny by objective criteria. Words and ideas like 'sex drive', 'libido', 'sublimation', 'neurosis', 'sexual repression', 'the ego', are all common parlance, part of the coinage of our understanding of ourselves — and all owe their origins to Freud. Our strong belief that sex is good for you per se; that our greatest joy comes from the 'convulsing of our physical constitution' (confusing orgasm with ecstasy); that the Victorians repressed their sexuality and were therefore hypocrites; that sex is a prime motivator and even the core of our personality, are Freudian reductions. That we are essentially animals, subject to unconscious, sexual and aggressive forces deep in the mind that we can do little to control by our own volition, are Freud. That there are those who do control them but who are therefore considered to be distorted, evasive or mentally ill, is Freud. It is difficult if not impossible to defend ourselves against opinion that poses as fact. The foundation of the 'facts' of sex — or sexology as it is also called — is often little better than well-targeted guess-work, collapsed into and inspired by anti-religious spite. Says Scruton: Freud 'was neither an accurate observer nor a plausible theorist'.

Freud turned on its head hundreds of years of received wisdom, perhaps not well-practised but potent nonetheless. The result of his deconstructing of the traditional religious taboos protecting women from otherwise rampant and unchecked virility — he was especially concerned that women should have sexual experience before marriage to avoid hysteria at the shock of it all — are everywhere to see. TV and film have returned sexuality to its merely animal state, shorn of transcendent or social value or any investment in character formation. Virginity — or the losing of it — has become a spectator sport. MTV filmed young couples before and after their first sex for a series called *Virgin Diaries* with appropriate comments from Mum cut in. Catherine von Ruhland, who writes for the post-evangelical *Third Way* magazine, paid an 'escort' to rid her of her virginity — for a Channel 4 documentary. She has established something of a career out of castigating the Church of England for failing to find her a life-long mate.

One young informant in the US tells Ariel Levy in the highly acclaimed *Female Chauvinist Pigs* that 'Sex is something you do to fit in.' This is a world where simulating sex for baying crowds of men on shows like 'Girls Gone Wild' and going to lap dancing clubs — as patrons — is seen as a short cut to cool. Ariel Levy says the joke's on the women if they think this is progress. She makes the case that the rise of 'raunch' does not represent how far women have come - it proves only how far women have left to go.

The breakdown in traditions of both guilt and shame fuelled by the media, ease of travel, international finance and the rest, is universal and omnipresent. The Moroccan Muslim feminist, Fatima Mernissi, in typically trenchant fashion, says rapid social transformation, migration and westernisation have a profound effect on sex roles. Deviant sexual behaviours are 'anxiety-reducing mechanisms in a world of shifting, volatile sexual identity'. Indeed, it is all too obvious to Mernissi that sex is the locus of an Islamically-driven attempt to regain control of something, anything, as western distortions impact all the conservative Muslims hold dear.

For Nazih Ayubi, Professor of Political Science at the University of California, the connection is clear. 'With the move from village to city, the individual is abruptly confronted with the... alienating impact of a modernisation drive that is in many of its aspects little more than an enforced process of Westernisation', he says. 'Such agonies' he goes on, 'become most alarming to the individual when their impact encroaches upon him within his own family — for the family is, after all, the last vestige of security and identity for him.' This, he says, is the very last arena to be invaded by secularist European-inspired laws and it is also the first line of attack for any demand for the establishment of a so-called 'Islamic order'.

Under the pressure of globalisation, Mernissi explains, a sexually repressed man has only one 'Islamic' solution and that is early marriage, but in today's conditions this is not easy to come by. Ayubi adds that some Islamists are so out of touch with reality that they still speak — in the present tense — of the man's right to have intercourse with his female slaves. The Syrian Islamist Sa'id Hawwa is a subscriber to this fantasy: 'What would a man whose lust has been aroused do? He has no option of course except to marry or possess a female slave (*ama*)'. After all, God will forgive her.

It is here that what's rotten in British parenting hits the proverbial fan. The groomers — for lack of a better word — whose own culture hedges female sexuality about with fear and even death, meet a society that teaches that wantonness is wisdom. Wilhelm Reich, prolific author, inventor of the 'orgasmotron' and father of so-called 'free love' who died in 1957, was enormously influential on this point. His most infamous book *Listen Little Man* gave particular attention to the 'sexual rights' of children and adolescents. He wrote — in capital letters: 'YES, WE WANT OUR SONS AND DAUGHTERS TO BE OPENLY HAPPY IN THEIR LOVE INSTEAD OF ENGAGING IN IT CLANDESTINELY, IN DARK ALLEYS AND ON DARK BACKSTAIRS'. Antony Giddens, who also advised Tony Blair on families, interpreted Reich thus: 'Children are to be given the right to engage in sexual play with others and to masturbate; they are also to be protected from the domination of their parents. Adolescents are to have the opportunity to fulfil their sexual needs in an unbridled way, in order that they might be the agents of future social change.'

This hippy sensibility that dreamed of utopia and for many became an on-going manifesto, ended for Reich in a federal penitentiary. Reich's brand of madness was infectious and deadly. History shows again and again that male sexuality is constrained only by women. Yet here was the arch pervert insanely describing a future when:

Your adolescent daughter's happiness in love will delight instead of enraging you; when you will only shake your head at the times when one punished little children for touching their love organs; when human faces on the street will express freedom, animation and joy and no longer sadness and misery; when people no longer will walk on this earth with retracted and rigid pelvises and deadened sexual organs.

The trouble with the la-la-land this thinking is marching us to becomes obvious when police are trying to investigate sexual exploitation. For it is only parents who can help spot the tell-tale signs in their errant offspring, according to the Coalition for the Removal of Pimping now known as PACE — Parents against Child Exploitation. 'The true scope of in-country grooming and trafficking is currently hard to gauge. Piecing together parents' stories is the only way of gaining a clear picture of what is happening in the UK' says Christine Miles author of a book on pimping *Stop! She's my Daughter!*' But unfortunately parents have been too busy 'protecting the loves of their adolescent sons and daughters' in Reich's chilling words, to protect their lives. Seventeen towns and cities in Britain have seen cases of street grooming networks, a Pakistani-Kashmiri variant on white paedophile networks, according to *The Times* (6 June 2013). Fifty-four such gangs are being investigated by police across the country. Further celebrity convictions for child sex and sexual harassment are in the pipeline. Freud gave his great-grandchildren a one-way ticket to court. What we are witnessing now is a tsunami of repressed pain. Children don't stay children. Exploited teeny-boppers are exacting an awful revenge on the tawdry old groovers who thought they had got away with it. The establishment's blind eye to Jimmy Savile, a BBC television presenter and celebrity, whose libido was so protean it made its object just about anything sentient, is a harrowing reminder of the potential vulnerability of all girls in all male company, and the social nature of sex. Legislation cannot stop the devious or deviant. Only more rigorous social consensus can do that. In Savile's case it was too late by the time the alarm sounded for he was dead — but the alarm rings urgently enough still.

Recovering a norm of continence in Britain is perhaps a forlorn hope but what choice is there? The alternative will be increasingly furtive sexual predatoriness, the degrading of our expectations of each other, and even worse sexist, racist and religious stereotyping. What is civilisation if not the ability to write love sonnets to each other? But that requires loveliness. We must recover a sex ethic that is noble, beautiful, and even a little chilly, or at the very least teach female children that sex outside marriage is stupid and dangerous. 'The double standard implies that chastity is primarily a woman's domain', laments Elizabeth Abbott in her exhaustive *A History of Celibacy*.

Well then, if it's ok for men to have sex where they can get it, then it has to be once again dinned into silly girls' heads that they're targets. Their inherent rights to freedom without fear — which was my birthright with two parents both virgins when they married — will otherwise have gone forever, and the male need to ejaculate will once again rule.

But here's where a nobler ideal of love may just be discernible once again. A recent survey in America showed that students long for a return to romance, and old-fashioned dating. 'Hookup culture' — defined as brief, alcohol-fuelled sexual intimacy, with no strings attached — is ceasing to satisfy, according to Donna de Freitas. The veneer of the 'anything goes' attitude to sex belies the reality, with a full 40 per cent of respondents within a 2,500 survey on campuses saying that hooking up made them feel anything from angry, sad, frustrated and regretful to alienated from their peers and even abused. Groups of students are organising a response to this 'tyranny' with Anscombe Societies (after the Catholic philosopher G.E.M. Anscombe) and Love and Fidelity Networks springing up nationwide in the last five years. Says de Freitas: 'Across the board, students reported a longing for less hookup culture, more meaningful sex, and the desire for old-fashioned dates, where a person could spend hours "just talking" with a potential partner, getting to know that person — emotionally, spirituality and physically.' She notes though that many young women and men felt ashamed of wanting romance and attachment from sex, since they believed they should be 'beyond such desires': the ghost of Reich rattling his chains.

Romance comes from the French *roman* meaning story: meeting, falling in love, courting, engagement, marriage being once considered a journey with a destination. How about it? In Christian courtly tradition, love was not a mutual convulsion that ends with a fag, but an opportunity for the male to prove his devotion, his valour, his continence. A literary invention of the medieval troubadours, who were themselves influenced by Muslim culture in Spain, it lasted as an ideal for hundreds of years. Courtly love acknowledges human sexual longing but incorporates it into a great passion guided not by carnality but by the highest moral and aesthetic values. It was defined in the twelfth century as the inherently painful, ceaseless meditation on the beauty of one's beloved, whom one glimpses from time to time but cannot possess. Obsessive, endured by constant contemplation of the beloved, it was inherently pure. And it gave rise to the secret feudal societies such as the

Knights Templar, excommunicated knights who swore oaths of poverty, obedience and chastity and dedicated themselves to the most sexually immacu-
late of all, the Virgin Mary.

Sexual attraction fuelled courtly love, but never dominated it. It titillated,
gushed, chased, enraptured. Most emerged from its clutches with their virtue intact. It generated a literature so vast that one survey begins 'One thousand people could have shaped this section in one thousand different ways,
without duplicating each other's selections'. Amazingly, it was a tradition that
survived right up to the 1950s. One can even detect it in old Bollywood
films of Dilip Kumar and Guru Datt.

The mid-1800s marked a high-water mark in edifying literature with the
morally righteous woman often at its heart, beset by drunkards and violent
libertines. *The Sacrifice of Catherine Ballard* published in 1894 is just one of
many that provide searing insights into the brutality of gender relations in the
Victorian period, that women themselves fought to overcome: here is a tale of
colonialism, debt, a marriage of convenience and slavery gelling topical issues
of race, sex and human dignity in a single Christian perspective. Stories, magazines and tracts constituted the vast bulk of women's reading, exhorting her
to a pure, virtuous and productive life. Mass-circulation 'improving magazines'
of the 1860s told of heroes and heroines overcoming insuperable odds —
poverty, crime, drunken husbands — all allegories of social redistribution and
social reconciliation, providing an insight into the moral drama of an unequal
society. Even up to the 1920s, the discourse of virtue survived with the *Girls'
Own Paper* including weekly 'Prayers of Unfolding Womanhood', 'The Verse
Book of a Homely Woman', and a story on 'The Barrier to Intimacy: the Joy
that Followed a Broken Engagement'. Femininity had been pietised, and piety
had been feminised — all because men were incapable of controlling their
nether regions, and had to have it done for them.

What ended with the Pill in 1963 was not chastity itself but the narrative
of chastity. For stories guide action. We inhabit some narrative or other, and
historians and theologians are increasingly focussing on 'speech act' theory
and narrative function. Identities are constructed within a repertoire of stories, memories, experiences which derive from available social, public and
cultural narratives.

These narratives were virtue-laden. And they were derived from the Gos-
pel. The celibate life was celebrated. 'At the resurrection people will neither

marry nor be given in marriage; they will be like the angels in heaven' says Jesus, himself unmarried. The married woman devoted herself to her home and family: the 'angel of the house'. The unmarried, re-virginised, single person was allowed to devote herself to Christ's Kingdom and His work, as a sign — a palpable locus of infinitude.

In the 1860s, talented Western women emerged from the shadows of enforced domesticity not by throwing their sexuality to the winds, but by reclaiming and keeping it. It was ever thus. A less sex-mad reading of history reveals a huge variety of movements and individuals who used their bodies against sex in order to achieve ends both spiritual and political. Again and again social reform across cultures began with sexual 'purity' movements: from Lysistrata's ultimatum in Aristophanes' comedy where the endless Peloponnesian War between Athens and Sparta is ended by a sexual strike by the combatants' wives: a fictional coup that summons up fantastical scenarios for ending the interminable Middle East and Afghan stalemates. The Vestal Virgins were the only women in Rome allowed to vote — and guaranteed by their exalted sacrifice the honour of the empire — for hundreds of years. Fast forward through a thousand years of monasticism that laid the foundation of the European economy, to the Wild West — which was tamed not by gun-slingers and lone rangers but by the founders of the Male Purity Movement, dating from the 1830s when infamous womanising, tobacco-spitting Davy Crockett and thousands of losers like him were cutting up the new country. Books like Sylvester Graham's *Lectures to Young Men on Chastity* or S B Woodward's *Hints for the Young* preached temperance, vegetarianism, moral reform and chastity before marriage. Alcohol and rich, spiced foods over-stimulated and led to eroticism, masturbation, moral decay and the dissolution of society. Loss of paternal control over their sons was eroding and with it, the attendant lessons in discipline, manhood, and morality as they poured into New England's new cities and threatened the future. 'The chaos, formlessness, and surging changes in this new America horrified these men', writes Abbott. Apprenticeships, the traditional job-training system, were disappearing. Unskilled, unattached, owning nothing and with nothing to lose, young men seemed like a threatening and dissolute urban mob. The Male Purity Movement changed all this - and was the only concerted chastity campaign ever to focus exclusively on bachelors. Chaste women deserved the chaste males the reformers were attempting to create. The suffrage movement grew out of this narrative — a narrative of feminine redemption through the struggle for jobs and votes that was sustained to a remarkable degree for the next forty years until the Great War.

Jane Austen's (1775–1817) rejection of a marriage proposal gives the lie to the common view that chastity is vaguely synonymous with asexuality. A quick trawl of the web following the BBC dramatisation 'Miss Austen Regrets' revealed almost universal surprise that Jane was not simply a cold fish uninterested in relationships. It was, after all, her core material; Mr Darcy a byword for male 'hotness' constrained, and even two whole centuries later, the eponymous hero of Bridget Jones's infamous diaries. Austen's biographer Claire Tomalin writes: 'As the years went by she knew that she didn't want to become a "poor animal", like her sisters-in-law and nieces, bearing yearly babies. Her books were her babies'.

Florence Nightingale (1820–1910), called, she believed, by God, for some as yet unspecified service, according to her diary, transformed nursing into an honourable, caring profession, by refusing to marry. She turned down her suitor of nine years, a man she admitted she 'adored' because she could 'not satisfy [her] nature by spending life with him in making society and arranging domestic things'. God, she believed, had marked her out to be one of the single women, whom He 'organised . . . accordingly for their vocation'. On her thirtieth birthday she prayed for this vocation to be revealed, and slowly, it became clear: she would devote her life to nursing. But this was the profession of slatterns, drunks, prostitutes, and criminals. Abbott describes hospitals in Florence's day as 'cesspools of filth, degradation, abuse, and death'. Only the most destitute and desperate would go to an institution where the floors were slimy with vomit, feces, and blood, where patients were jammed together in filthy, linenless beds, and surgeons routinely seduced the degenerate nurses. Until quite recently in Pakistan, nursing was not considered a suitable occupation for a Muslim girl, so non-Muslims were trained instead. I once met a very pregnant Pakistani beauty on an aeroplane, flying to Karachi from the Gulf just so she could have her baby at Multan Christian Women's Hospital. I passed out watching a (single) woman doctor from the Lake District perform a (successful) caesarean operation there on a poor village girl she had first given her own blood to, since the family had refused.

Nightingale remained strictly celibate. Her fervour meant she could deal openly with the important male officials of the day without a whiff of scandal. In Turkey during the Crimean War, the 'Lady of the Lamp' transformed the death rate at hellish Scutari Hospital from 42 per cent to 2.2 per cent. She went on to write the world's first training manual for the nursing profession, ennobling a low-life occupation. Her testimony could read as a rallying cry for oppressed women everywhere: 'keep clear of... the jargon, namely, about the 'rights of women' which urges women to do all that men do, merely because men do it... and the jargon which urges women to do nothing that men do, merely because they are women.... Surely woman should bring the best she has, whatever that is, to the work of God's world, without attending to either of these cries'.

Celibacy guaranteed a woman freedom because it guaranteed respect. This was at a time when to be single often meant having to be a prostitute through destitution and lack of access to work. The Contagious Diseases Acts of the 1860s meant you could be legally plucked off the streets by government warders, in Britain and India, examined internally for venereal diseases and locked up in special 'lock hospitals' until cured. After Nightingale, a single woman's chastity was more likely to be assumed. Women's contribution to public life, from nursing to campaigning for the vote, depended on a presumption of sexual continence.

For Mahatma Gandhi (1869–1948) sexual continence was not the only viable birth control in a continent teeming with wanted boys and unwanted girls, but it also had a far nobler purpose. For it was the only way, he believed, to attain the state of selflessness necessary for the realisation of truth. To him, unchaste men were weak, incapable of leading. 'He whose mind is given to animal passions is not capable of any great effort', he declared. The preservation of semen, careful fasting and vegetarian diet, clean companions and prayer would lead to the attainment of the goal. 'Victory will be ours in the end if we non-cooperate with the mind in its evil wanderings.' For Gandhi, *brahmacharya* or intense self-control leading to enlightenment, was actually an eccentric mix of Hindu Tantricism and Christian self-denial for the pursuit of altruistic goals which he learned about from a vicar in England where he trained as a lawyer. (He called his ashram Tolstoy in honour of that great soul's own experiments with celibacy, described in *The Kreutzer Sonata*). He strengthened his ascetic muscles as it were by lying unflinching with a succession of nubile young girls whom he refused to touch. While castigating him for this 'emotional abuse' and hinting at mere 'old-goatism', author Elizabeth Abbott marvels at his effort:

The strength it injected into Gandhi's psyche and the enormous prestige it brought him among his countrymen are its most wondrous dimensions. His coupling of an elaborate philosophy of militant nonviolence with *brahmacharya* also affirmed the power of a celibate lifestyle in the creative process — in this case, the birth of a political movement.

Today we are in dire need of models like Gandhi, Nightingale and Austen to demonstrate the true value of womanhood. The liberated woman is discouraged from being chaste or feminine, but merely 'sexually self-efficacious' and able to practise 'protection behaviour'. Sexual self-efficacy is the grim goal of Californian feminists. US academics define it as 'being able to voice and enact one's own desires, interests and needs... central to our conceptualisation of sexual health.' Instead of exhorting women to please men for future happiness, or deny them for the sake of moral character and the well-being of wider society, intellectuals have decoupled sex from outcomes of any kind.

But that's where the worm may eventually turn, for desire itself is dependent on denial. No is the sexiest word in the English language. Dogs don't desire, write couplets and grow saintly with longing. They copulate and run off to chase a stick. No need for social constraints there. But 'No' is arguably the only word that will save our multi-cultural future from the predatory and restless loins of the world's men. Girls — your time has come.

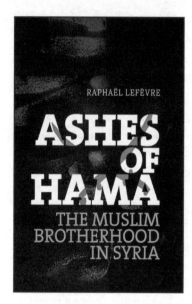

ASHES OF HAMA

The Muslim Brotherhood in Syria

RAPHAËL LEFÈVRE

When the convulsions of the Arab Spring first became manifest in Syria in March 2011, the Ba'athist regime was quick to blame the protests on the 'Syrian Muslim Brotherhood' and its 'al-Qaeda affiliates.' But who are these Islamists so determined to rule a post-Assad Syria?

ISBN: 9781849042857
£30.00 / Hardback / 288pp

Little has been published on militant Islam in Syria since Hafez Assad's regime destroyed the Islamist movement in its stronghold of Hama in February 1982. This book bridges that gap by providing readers with the first comprehensive account of the Syrian Muslim Brotherhood's history to date.

In this groundbreaking account of Syria's most prominent, yet highly secretive, Islamist organisation, the author draws on previously untapped sources: the memoirs of former Syrian jihadists; British and American archives; and also a series of wide-ranging interviews with the Syrian Muslim Brotherhood's historical leaders as well as those who battled against them—many speaking on the record for the first time. Ashes of Hama uncovers the major aspects of the Islamist struggle: from the Brotherhood's radicalisation and its 'jihad' against the Ba'athist regime and subsequent exile, to a spectacular comeback at the forefront of the Syrian revolution in 2011—a remarkable turnaround for an Islamist movement which all analysts had pronounced dead amid the ruins of Hama in 1982.

'No book could be more timely than Lefèvre's on the Muslim Brotherhood. Anyone wishing to understand Syria must understand the long and bitter history of the Muslim Brotherhood's struggle with the Assad regime.' — Joshua M. Landis, Director, Center for Middle East Studies, University of Oklahoma, and author of Syria Comment

WWW.HURSTPUBLISHERS.COM/BOOK/ASHES-OF-HAMA

41 GREAT RUSSELL ST, LONDON WC1B
WWW.HURSTPUBLISHERS.COM
WWW.FBOOK.COM/HURSTPUBLISHER
020 7255 2201

CITATIONS

Introduction: The Shadows of Muslim Men
by Ziauddin Sardar

The stories from *The Guardian* of 6 July 2013 can be found on its site: www.theguardian.com

Sheikh Al-Qaradawi's quotation, broadcast on his Al-Jazeera show 'Shariah and Life ' can be found here:
http://wikiislam.net/wiki/Al-Qaradawi_-_Waging_War_Against_Allah_-_Qur%27an_5:33_-_Refers_To_Apostasy

Sheikh Wahba az-Zuhaili quotations are from Anne Sofie Roald, *Women in Islam: The Western Experience* (Routledge, London, 2001), p.147; the quotations from Syed Qutb's *Social Justice in Islam* (Octagon Books, New York, 1970) are from pp.49-50; and Ziauddin Sardar's quotation from *Islamic Futures: The Shape of Ideas to Come* (Mansell, London, 1985) is from p.102.

'The leaders are from Quraysh' hadith is from al-Hakim's *Al-Mustadrak alaa al-Sahihain*; and the 'Story of Umm Zar' from *Sahih Muslim* (number 4481); it is also found in other collections.

Other books mentioned are Stephen Collins, *The Gigantic Beard That Was Evil* (Jonathan Cape, London, 2013); B van Hoven and K Horschelmann, *Spaces of Masculinities* (Routledge, London, 2005).

On Islamic masculinity see Lahoucine Ouzgane, editor, *Islamic Masculinities* (Zed Books, London, 2006) and Amanullah De Sondy, *The Crisis of Islamic Masculinities* (Bloomsbury Academic, London, 2013).

On hegemonic masculinity, see R W Connell, *Masculinities* (Polity Press, Cambridge, 2005); R Longhurst, 'Geography and gender, masculinities, male identity and men' *Progress in Human Geography* 24(3) 439-444 2000; M Berger et al, editors, *Constructing Masculinity* (Routledge, London, 1995).

The Problem of Men by Merryl Wyn Davies

Diane Abbot's speech at Demos is available at: http://www.demos.co.uk/ files/DianeAbbottspeech16May2013.pdf and 'Fractured Families: Why Stability Matters', the report by the Centre for Social Justice, UK, is available from: http://www.centreforsocialjustice.org.uk/UserStorage/pdf/Pdf%20 reports/CSJ_Fractured_Families_Report_WEB_13.06.13.pdf

See also: Merryl Wyn Davies, *Knowing One Another: Shaping an Islamic Anthropology* (Mansell, London, 1998) and Merryl Wyn Davies and Piero *Introducing Anthropology: A Graphic Guide* (Icon Books, London, 2002), now available in a new edition as a pocket book.

Muslim Masculinities by Abdennur Prado

The quotations by Lahoucine Ouzgane are from the 'Introduction' to his edited volume *Islamic Masculinities* (Zed Books, London, 2006), pp.1 and 22, respectively; the Al-Ghazali quotation is from *The Alchemy of Happiness* (ME Sharpe, New York, 1991); ibn Arabi quotations are from Sachiko Murata, *The Tao of Islam: A Sourcebook on Gender Relationships in Islamic Thought* (State University of New York Press, Albany, 1992), p.266; and Gema Martín Muñoz is from *Patriarcado e islam* (Quadrens de la Mediterrània, 2007) pp.40–41.

On the Taliban, see Durre S. Ahmed in Lahoucine Ouzgane, editor, *Islamic Masculinities* (Zed Books, London, 2006), pp.25–28. See also: Sheikh Nefzawi, *The Perfume Garden* (Harper Collins, London, 1968); Fatim Mernissi, *Beyond the Veil* (Indiana University Press, Bloomington, 1987); Abdelwahab Bouhdiba, *La sexualité en Islam* (Edition Puf, Paris, 1975); Annemarie Schimmel, *My Soul Is a Woman: The Feminine in Islam* (Continuum, London, 2003); and Sadiyya Shaikh, *Sufi Narratives of Intimacy: Ibn 'Arabî, Gender, and Sexuality* (University of North Carolina Press, Chapel Hill, 2012).

Out of this dead-end by Ziba Mir-Hosseini

The quotation from ibn Qayyim al-Jawziyya is from *I'laam ul Muwaqqi'een 'an Rabb il 'Aalameen* (Beirut: Dar al-Fekr el-Arabi, 1955), vol.3, p.1; and ibn Rushd is from his *The Distinguished Jurist's Primer*, vol.2, translated by Imran Ahsan Khan Nyazee (Reading: Garnet Publishing, 1996), p.63; as quotationd in Yossef Rapoport, *Marriage, Money and Divorce in Medieval Islamic Society* (Cambridge: Cambridge University Press, 2005), p.52.

Ahmad Shamloo, 'In This Dead End' can be found at: http://shamlu.com/trama.htm.

'Divorce Iranian Style', a 78-minute documentary first broadcast by Channel 4 in August 1999 in its 'True Stories' series, is available at http://www.secondrundvd.com/release_disr.php

Both *Wanted* and the *Framework for Action* were published by Sisters in Islam, Kuala Lumpur, in February 2009 at a conference in Kuala Lumpur for the launch of Musawah, attended by over 250 participants from 47 countries. They can be downloaded from; www.musawah.org

Other works mentioned in this essay include Ziba Mir-Hosseini, *Marriage on Trial: A Comparative Study of Islamic Family Law in Iran and Morocco* (London, I. B. Tauris, 1993: second edition with new Preface, 2000); *Islam and Gender: The Religious Debate in Contemporary Iran* (Princeton University Press, 1999; London, I. B. Tauris 2000). See also 'Muslim Family Laws, Justice and Equality: New Ideas, New Prospects', in Ziba Mir-Hosseini, Lena Larsen, Christian Moe and Kari Vogt (eds) *Gender Equality in Muslim Family Law: Justice and Ethics in Islamic Legal Tradition* (London: I B Tauris, 2013), pp. 7–34.

The Omnipresent Male Scholar by Kecia Ali

The quotation is from Muhammad Qasim Zaman, *Modern Islamic Thought in a Radical Age: Religious Authority and Internal Criticism* (Cambridge University Press, 2012) is from p.35.

The phrase 'custodians of change' is from his *The Ulama in Contemporary Islam: Custodians of Change* (Princeton University Press, 2002).

The quotations from Sherman A. Jackson are from *Islam and the BlackAmerican: Looking Toward the Third Resurrection* (Oxford University Press, 2005), p.20; and *Islam and the Problem of Black Suffering* (Oxford University Press, 2009), p.166 n.2 and p.168, n.2); and Nasr Hamid Abu Zayd, *Reformation of Islamic Thought: A Critical Historical Analysis* (Amsterdam University Press, 2006), p.90.

Also discussed is Tariq Ramadan, *Radical Reform: Islamic Ethics, and Liberation* (New York: Oxford University Press, 2008); Marnia Lazreg's remark on Ramadan appears in her *Questioning the Veil: Open Letters to Muslim Women* (Princeton University Press, 2009), p. 115.

The quotation from John Esposito, *The Future of Islam* (Oxford University Press, 2009), p.94; and for Mohamed Keshavjee's list, see 'Dispute Resolution,' in Amyn B. Sajoo, ed., *A Companion to Muslim Ethics* (IB Tauris, London, 2010) pp.151–66.

Important studies on late-nineteenth- and early-twentieth-century Egypt include, Leila Ahmed, *Women and Gender in Islam: Historical Roots of a Modern Debate* (Yale University Press, New Haven, CT., 1992), Beth Baron, *The Women's Awakening in Egypt, Culture, Society and the Press* (Yale University Press, New Haven, CT., 1994); Margot Badran, *Feminists, Islam and Nation: Gender and the Making of Modern Egypt* (Princeton University Press, 1994); and Hanan Kholoussy, *For Better, For Worse: The Marriage Crisis that Made Modern Egpyt* (Stanford University Press, 2010).

Samira Haj, *Reconfiguring Islamic Tradition: Reform, Rationality, and Modernity* (Stanford University Press, 2010) undertakes similar analysis to Zaman in comparing Egypt's Muhammad Abduh with the Arabian ibn 'Abd al-Wahhab. Amina Wadud's books are *The Qur'an and Woman: Rereading the Sacred Text from a Woman's Perspective* (Oxford University Press, 1999) and *Inside the Gender Jihad: Women's Reform in Islam* (OneWorld, Oxford, 2006). Asma Barlas's essay on Wadud, 'Amina Wadud's hermeneutics of the Qur'an: women rereading sacred texts,' is in Suha Taji-Farouki, ed., *Modern Muslim Intellectuals and the Qur'an* (Oxford University Press, 2004), pp.97–123.

Barlas' own monograph is *Believing Women in Islam: Unreading Patriarchal Interpretations of the Qur'an* (University of Texas Press, Austin, 2002).

On Wadud, see also the e-book *A Jihad for Justice: Honoring the Life and Work of Amina Wadud*, Kecia Ali, Juliane Hammer, and Laury Silvers, eds, available from: http://www.bu.edu/religion/files/2010/03/A-Jihad-for-Justice-for-Amina-Wadud-2012-1.pdf).

For extensive engagement with women's Qur'anic interpretation, see Aysha A. Hidayatullah, *Feminist Edges of the Qur'an* (Oxford University Press, forthcoming, 2014).

On the prayer as well as the broader issue of American Muslim women's authority, see Juliane Hammer, *American Muslim Women, Religious Authority, and Activism: More than a Prayer* (University of Texas Press, Austin, 2012), and the works in her extensive bibliography.

The quotation from Ingrid Mattson comes from her talk 'Can a Woman Be an Imam: Debating Form and Function in Muslim Women's Leadership,' http://www.onbeing.org/program/new-voice-islam/feature/can-woman-be-imam-debating-form-and-function-muslim-womens.

The full text of Riffat Hassan's 'Members, one of another' can be found at http://www.religiousconsultation.org/hassan.htm

Judith Plaskow's 'The Right Question is Theological,' appears in Judith Plaskow, ed. *Donna Berman, The Coming of Lilith: Essays on Feminism, Judaism, and Sexual Ethics, 1972-2003* (Beacon Press, Boston, 2005), pp.56–64. Both Laury Silvers' essay 'In the Book We Have Left Out Nothing: The Ethical Problem of the Existence of Verse 4:34 in the Qur'an,' *Comparative Islamic Studies* 2:2, 2006 and Sa'diyya Shaikh's monograph *Sufi Narratives of Intimacy: Ibn 'Arabi, Gender, and Sexuality* (University of North Carolina Press, Chapel Hill, 2012) draw critically on thirteenth-century Andalusian mystic ibn al-'Arabi to address issues of sexuality, violence, and gender hierarchy.

OtherThan Men by Asma Afsaruddin

For a detailed account of the contribution of women in early Islam see Asma Afsaruddin, 'Education, Piety, and Religious Leadership in the Late Middle Ages: ReinstatingWomen in the Master Narrative' in *Knowledge and Education in Classical Islam,* Sebastian Guenther, ed. (Brill, Leiden, forthcoming); 'Early Women Exemplars and the Construction of Gendered Space: (Re-)Defining Feminine Moral Excellence' in *Harem Histories: Envisioning Places and Living Spaces,* Marilyn Booth, ed. (Duke University Press, Durham, 2010) pp. 23–48; and *The First Muslims: History and Memory* (OneWorld, Oxford, 2008).

See also: Asma Sayeed, *Women and the Transmission of Knowledge in Islam* (Cambridge University Press, 2013) Mohammad Akram Nadwi, Al-Muhaddithat: *The Women Scholars of Islam* (Interface Publications, Oxford, 2013, second revised edition); Leila Ahmad, *Women and Gender in Islam: Historical Roots of a Modern Debate* (Yale University Press, New Haven, 1993); and Fatima Mernissi, *TheVeil and the Male Elite* (Perseus Books, Jackson,TN, 1993).

Beyond the Crooked Rib by Saleck Mohamed Val

The quotations from al-Tabari and ibn Khathir are from *Jami` Al-bayan `an Ta'walay Al-Qur'an* (Markaz Hagar Li Al-BuhuthWa Al-dirasatAl-arabiyaWa Al-Islamiya, Cairo, 2001) volume 1, p.356; and *Tafsir Al-Qur'an Al-Azim* (Dar Al-Fiqr, Beirut, 2002) volume 2, p.206. The quotation from Al-Shinqiti is fromAd'wa Al-bayan *Fi I'dahi Al-Qur'an Bi Al-Qur'an* (Dar Alam Al-Fawaid, Riyadh, 1995), vol. 1, p.186; and from Chouki El Hamel, 'The Transmission of Islamic Knowledge in the Moorish Society from the Rise of the Almoravids to the 19th Century', *Journal of Religion in Africa* vol.29, pp. 62–67 1999.

The quotations from Aicha Abd Rahman are from *Al-tafsir Al-Bayani Li Al-Qur'an Al-Karim* (Dar Al-Ma'arif, Cairo, 1967) p. 18 and *Maqal fi al-Insan: DirasaQur'aniyya* ((Dar Al-Ma'arif, Cairo, 1969) p33.

The citations from Al-Azhari scholars: ZainabAl-Ghazali, *Nadharat Fi Kitabillah* (Dar Al-Shuruq, Cairo, 1994) vol.1 p.37–38; Fawkiyah Sherbini, *Taysir Al-Tafsir* (Maktabat Al-Iman Li-atiba'aWa Al-NashrWa-al-Tawzi, Cairo, 2008) volume 1 p. 27 and pp.548–9; and Kariman Hamzah, *Allu'luWa Al-Marjan Fi Tafsir Al-Qur'an* (Maktabat Al-Shuruq Al-Dawliyah, Cairo, 2010) vol.1, p.334. The Asharq Al-Awsat article, 'Al-Azhar Hails First Female Interpretation of the Quran', published on 25 January 2009, is available from: http://www.asharq-e.com/print.asp?artid=id15494

See also: Mohamed Amin, 'A Study of Bint Al-Shati's Exegesis', PhD thesis, McGill University, Montreal, 1992; and Nuruddin Farah, *From A Crooked Rib* (Penguin, London, 2003).

The Groomers by Shamim Miah

The reports mentioned in this article include S. Berelowitz et al, 'I thought I was the only one. The only one in the world: The Office of the Children's Commissioner's Inquiry into Child Sexual Exploitation in Gangs and Groups' (Office of the Children's Commissioner, Oldham, 2012); and 'Basically... porn is Everywhere' (Office of the Children's Commissioner, Oldham, 2013).

See also Tony Mitchell, ed., *Global Noise: Rap and Hip-hop Outside America* (Wesleyan University Press, Middletown, Connecticut, 2001); and Murray Foreman and Anthony Neal, *That's the Joint: The Hip-hop Studies Reader* (Routledge, London, 2004).

Sheikh Taj Din Al-Hilali's comments can be found at: http://news.bbc.co.uk/1/hi/world/asia-pacific/6086374.stm and the Metropolitan Police Service and the National Society for the Prevention of Cruelty to Children report of Jimmy Sevile's case can be found at:
http://www.theguardian.com/news/datablog/2013/jan/11/jimmy-savile-abuse-cases-detailed-data

Qutb: Poet and Islamist Tanjil Rashid

There are numerous, widely available editions of Sayyid Qutb's *Milestones*, which was originally published in 1964; a translation of *In the Shade of the Qur'an* by Adil Salahi and Ashur Shamis is also widely available; some of his writings are collected in *The Sayyid Qutb Reader,* Albert J Bergesen, ed. (Routledge, London, 2008).

The Complete Poetical Works of Sayyid Qutb is yet to be translated in English, but a pirated version of the 2012 Cairo publication is available, search for it online!

Other works mentioned in this essay include: John Calvert's *Sayyid Qutb and the Origins of Radical Islamism* (Hurst, London, 2010), which is the best-known scholarly account of Qutb's life; Adnan Musallam, *From Secularism to Jihad: Sayyid Qutb and the Foundations of Radical Islamism* (Praeger, London, 2005); Ibrahim Abu-Rabi's *Intellectual Origins of Islamic Resurgence in the Modern Arab World* (SUNY, New York, 1996); and Muhammad Siddiq, *Arab Culture and the Novel: Gender, Identity and Agency in Egyptian Fiction* (Routledge, London, 2007), which examines Qutb within the Egyptian literary context. Michael Gove's *Celsius 7/7* (Weidenfeld & Nicholson, London, 2006), is worth reading for its hysterical chapter on Qutb.

Both Martin Amis's essay collection *The Second Plane* (Jonathan Cape, London, 2008) and Lawrence Wright's *The Looming Tower* (Knopf, New York, 2006) contain imaginative studies of Qutb's life and ideas. Wright's book is a genuinely judicious investigation into the background to 9/11, thoroughly steeped in the sources while remaining a gripping narrative account. *The Second Plane* is only notable for its lack of either of these qualities.

Harun Yahya's Fast Food by Stefano Bigliardi

The quotation from Ziauddin Sardar is from 'Weird Science' *New Statesman* 22 August 2008; available at: http://www.newstatesman.com/books/2008/08/quran-muslim-scientific; the quotation from Rana Dajani is from 'Evolution and Islam's Quantum Question' in Zygon, *Journal of Religion and Science* 47:2

2012, pp. 343–353. The books mentioned are Ziauddin Sardar's *Explorations in Islamic Science* (Mansell, London, 1989) and Nidhal Guessoum's *Islam's Quantum Question. Reconciling Muslim Tradition and Modern Science* (I B Tauris, London, 2011).

I met and interviewed Adnan Oktar and some of his closest collaborators in the night between 12–13 February 2011 in Istanbul; I am grateful for their friendly if somewhat extravagant reception.

All data regarding Yahya's production can be obtained from http://www. harunyahya.com/ accessed in July 2012. Martin Riexinger scholarly reconstructs the dissemination of 'Islamic creationism' on the Internet ('Propagating Islamic Creationism on the Internet', Masaryk University *Journal of Law and Technology*, Vol. 2, No. 2, 2008, available at: http://www.digitalislam.eu/ article.do?articleId=1980).

Nathan Schneider has interviewed Harun Yahya and given an interpretation of his thought in 'Evolving Allah. Can One Man Succeed in Stirring Up the Muslim World Against Darwin?' in *Search*, March–April 2009; available at: http:// www.docstoc.com/docs/42950056/EVOLVING-ALLAH).

Halil Arda has produced a thorough investigation of Harun Yahya's legal indictments and of his sect's structure and activities in 'Sex, Flies and Videotape: the Secret Lives of Harun Yahya' 2009, *New Humanist*, 124, (5); available at: http://newhumanist.org.uk/2131/sex-flies-and-videotape-the-secret-lives-of-harun-yahya).

A brief account of Harun Yahya's ideas and activities in the more general context of the history of Creationism can be found in Ronald L. Numbers, *The Creationists: From Scientific Creationism to Intelligent Design* (Harvard University Press, 2006) pp. 421–427.

The Aesthetic of Promise by Marjorie Allthorpe-Guyton

The catalogue of the Iraqi Pavilion at Venice Biennale, *Welcome to Iraq: The Pavilion of Iraq at the 55th International Art Exhibition La Biennale Di Venezia* by

Tamara Chalabi and Jonathan Watkins is published by the Ruya Foundation for Contemporary Culture in Iraq and Ikon Gallery, Birmingham, 2013. *The Unexpected Guest: Art, writing and thinking on hospitality,* Sally Tallant and Paul Domela, eds (London: Art/Books, 2012).

The quotation from Jonathan Watkins is from *Ibraaz* 30 May 2013; and of Hassan Janabi from *The Wall Street Journal* 29 March 2011. Sir Terence Clark's lecture 'Iraq People and Places' can be viewed on YouTube: http://www.youtube.com/watch?v=eyi-uneNkVc

See also: Tamara Chalabi, *The Shi'is of Jabal 'Amil and the New Lebanon 1918-1943* (London: Palgrave Macmillan, 2006); and Neil MacGregor, *A History of the World in 100 Objects* (London: Penguin, 2012). Details of Venice Biennale can be found at: http://www.labiennale.org/en/art/exhibition/55iae/

Disgraceful Fanatics? by Hassan Mahamdallie

Alberto Toscano's essay, published on 7 December 2006 in the internet magazine, *Eurozine*, can be downloaded from: http://www.eurozine.com/articles/2006-12-07-toscano-en.html#

For a more detailed analysis, see his *Fanaticism: On the Uses of An Idea* (Verso, London, 2010)

Last Word on Chastity by Jenny Taylor

The quotations are from Roger Scruton, *Sexual Desire* (Continuum, London, 2002) pp.180 and 196; Fatima Mernissi, 'Muslim Women and Fundamentalism', *Middle East Report* 153, July–August 1988; Nazih Ayubi, *Political Islam: Religion and Politics in the Arab World* (Routledge, London, 1991) p.41; Wilhelm Reich, *Listen, Little Man!* (Farrar, Straus & Giroux, New York, 1974; original 1948), p.95; Anthony Giddens, *Transformation of Intimacy* (Polity, Oxford, 1992) pp.105 and 163; Elizabeth Abbott, *A History of Celibacy* (Lutterworth Press, London, 2001) p.363; Monica Baly, ed., *As Miss Nightingale Said . . . Florence Nightingale Through Her Sayings – a Victorian Perspective* (London: Scutari Press, 1991); Elspeth Huxley, *Florence Nightingale* (London: Weidenfeld and

Nicolson, 1975) p.190; Judith Brown, 1989 *Gandhi: Prisoner of Hope* (New Haven: Yale University Press, 1989), p.86; and the Claire Tomalin quotation is from *Radio Times* 26 April–2 May 2008, p.14.

The American survey is presented in Donna de Freitas, *Sex and the Soul: struggling sexuality, spirituality, romance, and religion on America's college campuses* (Oxford: Oxford University Press, 2013); the quotation is from her article in *The Tablet* 23 February 2013, p.11.

The definition of sexual self-efficacy comes from 'To be Seen and Not Heard: Femininity Ideology and Adolescent Girls' Sexual Health' in *Archives of Sexual Behaviour*, 35 (2) April 2006, pp.131–144, the official publication of the International Academy of Sex Research.

CONTRIBUTORS

Alev Adil is the Head of the Department of Communication and Creative Arts at University of Greenwich, London ● **Asma Afsruddin**, Professor of Islamic Studies and Chair of the Department of Near Eastern Languages and Civilizations at Indiana University, Bloomington, is the author of *The First Muslims: History and Memory* and *Striving in the Path of God: Jihad and Martyrdom in Islamic Thought* ● **Kecia Ali**, Associate Professor of Religion at Boston University, is the author of *Sexual Ethics in Islam* ● **Marjorie Allthorpe-Guyton** is President of the International Association of Art Critics (AICA), British Section ● **Stefano Bigliardi** is Post-Doctoral Researcher at the Centre for Middle Eastern Studies, Lund University ● **Claire Chambers**, Senior Lecturer in Postcolonial Literature, Leeds Metropolitan University, is the author of *British Muslim Fictions* ● **Merryl Wyn Davies** is co-director of the Muslim Institute, London ● **Imtiaz Dharker**, a Scottish Pakistani poet, artist and documentary maker, is a Fellow of the Royal Society of Literature. Her collections of poems include *Purdah*, *Postcards from god*, *I speak for the devil* and *The terrorist at my table* ● **Mark Gonzales** is an internationally renowned performance poet ● **Tam Hussain** is a writer and journalist who contributes to a host of British and Middle Eastern papers ● **Leyla Jagiella** is a cultural anthropologist ● **Mohja Kahf** is an internationally acclaimed poet and writer ● **Hassan Mahamdallie**, co-director of the Muslim Institute, specialises in arts and diversity ● **Shamim Miah** is Senior Lecturer in Sociology, University of Huddersfield, and a youth worker based in Oldham ● **Ziba Mir-Hosseini**, a legal anthropologist, is a founding member of the Musawah Global Movement for Equality and Justice in the Muslim Family; her latest publication is the co-edited *Gender and Equality in Muslim Family Law* ● **Abdennur Prado** is the Director of International Congress on Islamic Feminism based in Spain ● **M A Qavi** is a life-long peace activist ● **Tanjil Rashid**, whose film *Puja Nights* recently premiered at the BFI, is a Commissioning Editor at Pod Academy, a platform for free podcasts on academic research ● **Jenny Taylor** is founder and CEO of Lapido Media, which promotes religious literacy in world affairs. She is the author of *A Wild Constraint: the Case for Chastity* ● **Saleck Mohamed Val** teaches Gender Issues in Islam at the Department of Islamic Studies, Sidi Mohamed Ben Abdullah University, Fez.